BETWEEN
JIHAD AND SALAAM

BETWEEN
JIHAD AND SALAAM

PROFILES IN ISLAM

Joyce M. Davis

St. Martin's Griffin

BETWEEN *JIHAD* AND *SALAAM*
Copyright © Joyce Davis, 1997, 1999. All rights reserved. Printed in the
United States of America. No part of this book may be used or reproduced in
any manner whatsoever without written permission except in the case of brief
quotations embodied in critical articles or reviews. For information, address
St. Martin's Press, 175 Fifth Avenue, New York, N.Y. 10010.

ISBN 0-312-21781-1 (paper)
ISBN 0-312-16587-0 (cloth)

Library of Congress Cataloging-in-Publication Data

Davis, Joyce, 1953-
    Between *Jihad* and *Salaam* : profiles in Islam / by Joyce Davis.
    p. cm.
    "Revised version, April 1996."
    ISBN 0-312-16587-0   ISBN 0-312-21781-1
    1. Muslims--Biography. I. Title.
BP70.D32 1997
332'.1'0917671--DC21   96-48928
                                                                 CIP

Design by Acme Art, Inc.

First cloth edition: July 1997
First Griffin paperback: March 1999
10 9 8 7 6 5 4 3 2 1

CONTENTS

Acknowledgments

I am indebted to the United States Institute of Peace, which allowed me the time and resources to complete this work. I am especially grateful to Allison McGandy, who helped me compile the research and transcribe many of the interviews in this book. I must also thank Hiyam Afram, my Arabic teacher, who often helped me say the right things at the right time to the right people. And I owe a profound debt to Nigel Quinney, who served as my initial editor and encourager.

Above all, I must thank my husband and sounding board, Russell W. Goodman, for his patience, guidance and loving support during the years it took to see this work to completion.

Introduction

IT WAS JUNE 10, 1996, and Binyamin Netanyahu was making his first tour of Washington, D.C., as prime minister of Israel. Standing at the podium of the Willard Hotel's ballroom, Netanyahu was as confident and energized as a prized cock just unleashed from his pen.

The room was filled mostly with Arab journalists and diplomats, many of whom feared the worst from Israel's new government. In response to increasing attacks from Iranian-supported Hezbollah guerrillas in southern Lebanon (and in the run-up to national elections), Israel's former prime minister and peace advocate Shimon Peres had launched intensive bombing raids that had targeted even Beirut. Arab anger boiled as CNN broadcast pictures of the charred remains of women and children, killed when Israel bombed a United Nations refugee camp. One particularly chilling magazine photograph showed a crying man cradling the blackened, lifeless body of a baby, with her bloody head blown apart. Netanyahu had promised to be even tougher with his enemies, and the people who greeted him with diplomatic applause were looking for a clue as to just what more horrors might await.

Netanyahu offered the predictable spiel of peace with security and regional cooperation, but at the end of his speech he said something unpredictable. And he seemed to say it with sincerity.

"I do not view Islam as the enemy of the West or the enemy of Israel," he said. "Islam is one of the world's great religions. We have no quarrel with Islam; we have no enmity with Islam. We have a problem with a militant few who want to twist Islam into a perverted ideology of violence and aggression. They not only threaten us; they threaten just about everyone sitting here—perhaps without any qualification."

Although Netanyahu did not win friends that afternoon, those words impressed many of the Arab elite in the room. They knew too well that militants who misused Islam were a threat not only to Israel and to the West but to their states as well. And Netanyahu had drawn a distinction that often eluded American leaders. He saw clearly that a religious creed so similar to both Judaism and Christianity was not the enemy. Its perversion was.

In the West, Islam has long been viewed as a threat to its civilization and values. In fact, since the rise of the Ayatollah Khomeini in Iran and the taking of American hostages in Tehran in 1979, Islam has come to represent an ideology as dangerous as communism. And the media publicity surrounding groups in the United States such as Louis Farrakhan's Nation of Islam only contributes to the perception of Muslims as radical and anti-American. Yet the Nation of Islam represents only a fraction of the Muslims in the United States, and its followers often ignore or are ignorant of the basic teachings of Islam— among them, the equality of all races and deep respect for both Christianity and Judaism.

It is unfortunately a fact that for many in the United States, the word "Muslim" is synonymous with angry mobs screaming about the Great Satan, with suicidal bombers like the one who in 1983 drove an explosives-laden truck into a U.S. Marine barracks in Beirut and killed 241 American soldiers, or with the underground guerrillas who in 1985 snatched journalist Terry Anderson from the streets of Lebanon and added him to their list of Western hostages. It is puzzling but true that the religion whose name is built on the root word *salaam,* or "peace," also has been used as a justification for murder and terror.

The Western world has had a turbulent history with Islam, and it is fair to say that both sides have been guilty of aggression. During the Middle Ages, Muslim people called Moors by Europeans conquered Spain and other parts of southern Europe, bringing with them a rich civilization that surpassed that of Western Europe at that time. In the eleventh century Western armies launched the Crusades with the goal of recapturing Jerusalem for Christianity. And the Ottoman conquest of Constantinople in 1453 represented a major loss for the West and a major victory for Islamic civilization. In modern history, the peoples of the West have sought to protect if not improve their standards of living, often through colonizing Muslim lands and exploiting their natural and human resources.

I began serious study of Islamic movements several years ago in preparation for a series of stories on Muslim women aired by National Public Radio (NPR). As editor for the Middle East and Africa for NPR, I knew how important Islam had become in the politics of many countries in the region as well as in the cultural identity of people still traumatized by their subjection to Western colonialism. And since the failure of Egypt's Gamal Nasser to unite the Arab people under the political banner of Pan-Arabism, defeat the Western-supported state of Israel and rekindle the fires of a once-glorious Islamic civilization, there remained one untested philosophy—Islam. Where Pan-Arabism had failed, there was hope that Islam as a political force would succeed.

I embarked on the travels that produced these interviews to get a personal glimpse of the kind of people influencing the development of Islamic thought. I wanted to know something of their personalities, their character, emotions and intellect. I wanted to see them in their natural environs and to talk to people who lived and worked with them. I wanted to know their feelings toward the West. And I asked for their suggestions on how to improve the relationship between the West and the Islamic world.

Except for my first trip for NPR, I traveled alone, a Western woman plunging into the undeniably male-dominated sanctums of Islam. I met and talked to far more people than are featured in this book, people from diverse races, ages, classes and cultures. Most of the people whom I interviewed were eager to talk about their religion and were easily accessible. Some, such as the spokesman for two militant groups in Egypt, were less so. Meeting Muntassir al-Zayat took extensive preparations and trustworthy contacts. I was not granted an interview with the leader of Egypt's notorious Al-Gamaa al-Islamiyah who was in exile in Switzerland, although I flew there hoping for one.

Some of the interviews were very formal and were conducted in offices, although I generally preferred more relaxed settings whenever possible. Most of the people spoke good English, but in some cases I used the services of a translator. Whenever I interviewed any of the men in this book, I always covered myself, generally with the Pakistani "shalwar khameez," a long tunic with billowy pants and a matching shawl that I draped across my head, in the style of Benazir Bhutto. Like

Ms. Bhutto, I always wore makeup, which didn't seem to upset anyone, not even the most hard-line Islamists.

Most of the people I interviewed would be labeled fundamentalists. But in fact, the term has no meaning in the Islamic world and has been used in the West as a synonym for radical or militant. I have opted to use the term "Islamist" when referring to Muslim scholars or intellectuals who are socially or political active, usually in organizations advocating reform of society or government. I have chosen to use the term "Islamic militant" when referring to those who advocate armed struggle to bring about reform and who usually advocate establishment of a strict Islamic state, if not the unity of the entire Islamic world. But as the profiles in this book will show, not only are Muslims united in their religion, they are divided by it, as well.

More than one billion people in the world call themselves Muslim. They make up most of the population in the Middle East, North Africa and much of Southeast Asia. In North Africa and the Middle East, Islamic political parties have been gaining popularity as people grow more and more frustrated with stagnant economic and political systems. Much of this region is still underdeveloped, and many of its people still suffer under the weight of despotism or one-party rule. Many of these countries have been struggling to overcome the effects of centuries of colonialism, and many of their people are searching for a sense of identity, self-esteem and a solution to their economic problems.

It is not surprising that when people are weighed down by problems, they turn to religion. This has been true for suffering peoples throughout history, even in the United States, which reveres a separation of church and state. In recent American history, the civil rights movement grew from the black church, from the unified expressions of suffering that grew into the unified rejection of that suffering. Black Americans looked to their religion for emotional and spiritual sustenance, and they looked to their religious leaders to help them gain political, social and economic power. Just as the black church led a revolution in the United States, the mosques have been doing the same in many parts of the Muslim world. Many Muslims are looking to their religious leaders—people the West castigate as fundamentalists—to help them build what they hope will be just and moral societies and, in some cases, to overthrow tyrannical regimes. There is one key difference, however. The movement that grew from the black churches of the United States had a doctrine of non-violence. In contrast, some of the movements that were ignited in mosques are based on the doctrine of *jihad,* or "holy war."

This is one of the key differences between Islam and Christianity. My father, a Baptist minister, and the Catholic nuns who educated me, taught me that Christians are to "turn the other cheek," to befriend their enemies and to allow God to exact justice. It is a sign of the weakness of my faith that I have always found this particular teaching of Christianity illogical and potentially suicidal. The Muslim teaching seems far more practical. In the Qur'an (Surah 2:190-191), Muslims are told:

> Fight in the way of Allah against those who fight against you, but begin not hostilities. Lo! Allah loveth not aggressors.

> And slay them wherever ye find them, and drive them out of the places whence they drove you out, for persecution is worse than slaughter. . . .

Muslims are clearly enjoined from aggression, but throughout the Qur'an they are permitted, even encouraged, to defend themselves and those who are persecuted. However, it must be pointed out that *jihad* has an even deeper meaning than external struggle for many Muslims. It also means the inner struggle against evil, the struggle for the self-discipline needed to follow the teachings of Islam.

The Islamic activists' reminder of the importance of both inner and outer *jihad* is attractive to many Muslims, especially to those who believe they are oppressed by corrupt societies and governments that can be reformed only through intense struggle.

For the affluent and educated, Islamic political parties advocate a system that offers them a voice in government and a path to end the corrupt, one-party (or one-man) states that dominate the region. Islam gives them an intellectual and moral creed rooted in their own culture and civilization. But like any political or religious movement, the Islamic political and social movements around the world also are vulnerable to elitism, corruption and dogmatism.

Among the poor, Islamists have established personal networks of support through social services, from free medical care to education. Islamic organizations set up schools to teach adults to read the Qur'an and to educate children who otherwise would be as illiterate as their parents. But the radical groups also use such services to nurture bitterness and to indoctrinate vulnerable young minds with ideologies of anger and revenge.

Fahmy Howeidi, a journalist whom I interviewed in Cairo, blamed repressive regimes so prevalent in the Middle East for pushing young people into militant organizations. He noted that in Egypt the government is stifling the political representation of moderate religious groups such as the Muslim Brotherhood, forcing young people into the enclaves of underground extremists.

Many Arab regimes are unable to draw the kind of distinction that Netanyahu so clearly delineated and that Islamist writers such as Howeidi advocated. In Egypt, even moderate Islamic groups such as the renowned Muslim Brotherhood, are banned from forming political parties. The Brotherhood was founded in Egypt by Hassan al-Banna in the 1920s on a platform of social and political activism, based on his understanding of Islam's teachings. Its doctrines and example of political activism spread throughout the Islamic world; chapters of the Muslim Brotherhood currently exist in many capitals, whether as part of the Islamic establishment, or underground. Today, it generally is considered to be a moderate group led by men long past their prime but who still are devoted to reforming their societies and governments. If once they had been prone to violence in the name of Allah, the aging process long ago forced the group's senior members to abandon that path in favor of working inside the system for a political voice. Many Egyptians believe that the Muslim Brotherhood is the only group that could pose a serious challenge to Hosni Mubarak's ruling National Democratic Party. But Mubarak's government staunchly opposes its participation in politics. And there are those who suspect the Brotherhood in Egypt and elsewhere of supporting, if only in spirit, the more radical groups trying to overthrow the government through campaigns of terror.

Although "Islam is the solution" rings like a bell of liberty throughout much of the Muslim world, it is a threatening toll in the West, because even those Islamic movements that are peaceful denounce what they see as their leaders' dependence on Western powers. And most of the movements call for changes in their governments and leaders, some of whom are allies of the United States.

Islamic groups are threatening the status quo throughout the Middle East, in some countries with the ballot and in others through violence. When I conducted most of the interviews included in this book, peace talks between Israel and the Palestine Liberation Organization (PLO) had just begun. Most of the people associated with the Islamic organizations were vehemently opposed to peace with the state of Israel, contending that Israel had stolen Arab land through force and collusion with Western powers. And many were decidedly opposed to what they saw as the continued domination of the West in all aspects of their lives.

Many of the Islamic leaders I interviewed were hostile toward the West because of the effects of colonialism on the development of their societies. They were angry at the onslaught of Western culture through television, movies and music. They considered Western mores and culture immoral, and they feared Western influence would undermine the religious values of their own societies. Many devout Muslims, whether politically active or not, were disdainful of people in their own societies who mimicked Western fashion and culture. And they were embittered with their own leaders, whom they accused of being little more than puppets of Western powers.

Anger toward the West was evident, although sometimes restrained, in almost every interview I conducted and in all save one included in this book. Only Said al-Ashmawy, the former chief justice of the Egyptian Supreme Court, expressed no such anger toward the West and, in fact, seemed to appreciate Western music, art and literature. As a self-described "liberal Muslim," Ashmawy was the exception in my interviews, however. Most Islamic scholars I met, and especially the youths I interviewed, blamed the West for the state of their world today.

Many Islamic leaders maintain links to each other through conferences and writings in religious publications. Yet during the time I conducted my interviews, there was no one strong, united Islamic movement, although the Sudan's Hassan al-Turabi was working to strengthen his Popular Arab and Islamic Conference. Mostly I found a myriad of organizations with different ideas of how to achieve their goal of a just, Islamic society. Al-Gamaa al-Islamiyah felt compelled to launch a guerrilla war against the one-party–dominated state of Egypt, even if it meant killing tourists. Yet Rachid al-Ghannouchi's EnNahda (Renaissance) Party eschewed violence and had not harassed the Tunisian government with a terrorist campaign.

Even the goals of Islamic movements are often different. Al-Gamaa al-Islamiyah in Egypt wanted an Islamic state, while Ghannouchi asserted that his EnNahda Party's first priority was establishing democracy. Some groups rejected the word "democracy" as a Western term, preferring to use terminology peculiar to Islam. They spoke of *Shurah,* an Islamic system of consultative government in which people discuss an issue with the aim of reaching a consensus. Others embraced the concept of Western democracy without qualms, but with the reservation, as Ghannouchi explained, that it should not be devoid of moral "spirit."

It is fair to say most Islamists as well as most devout Muslims want to see the moral principles of Islam influence their governments and their societies. But most of the people I encountered in my exploration into the heart of Islam did not advocate reaching their goals by force, although some expressed empathy for those who took that path. Most people said they favored a representative form of government similar but not identical to Western democracies. And most said they would accept the possibility that their groups could be voted out of power as they were struggling for the right to be voted into it. Skeptics believe that such vows are a ruse. As they see it, religious fanatics, once in power, will never relinquish it peacefully.

The one major divide between secularists in the West and most of the Islamists I interviewed was the question of separation of religion from politics. Most Islamists, and many but not all Muslims, believe there can be no separation between their religion, society and the governments that rule them. It is important to bear in mind, however, that while the United States may have been established on the principle of separation of church and state, that certainly has not been the case in many Western countries. Throughout the Western world, there are religiously based parties and countries, such as Switzerland, Ireland and England, that consider themselves Christian states whose laws are based on the moral principles of Christianity. There also are growing voices in the United States for expanding the role of religion, specifically the Christian religion, in government and society. The Christian movement in the United States, dubbed the Moral Majority or Christian right, is strikingly similar to the peaceful Islamic movements in the Muslim world. Both are concerned with what they perceive as unchecked immorality in society; both believe that their governments have become corrupt and are helping to promote immorality; both believe that their religious values are the solution to the moral decay of their societies; and both are fighting for political power.

The United States is a diverse nation of many different religions, including many different versions of Christianity. It would be disastrously divisive to establish one religion as the foundation for government. But Muslims are the overwhelming majority in many of the nations where Islamic movements are gaining popularity. In most states, Islam is already the state religion.

It should be pointed out that not all Muslims want to live in a Muslim state and many certainly would not want to live in the kind of state that seems to be taking shape in Afghanistan under the victorious student militia known as the Taliban. I conducted several interviews with members of the Islami Jamiat-i-Tulaba in Pakistan, who were supporting, even on the battlefield, their brothers in Afghanistan. I visited their headquarters and spoke with their president, Mohammad Abas Qasin, and his secretary general, Amer Jamat. The young men were disciplined and severe, hostile to what they considered to be the immoral influences of Western culture and committed to the strictest interpretation of Islamic law. But the repression unleashed by the Taliban as they took control of Kabul prompted even Iran's government to describe it as extreme. After the public hanging of Afghanistan's former president, the Taliban began exerting full control, much of it directed at women. They forbade women to go to their jobs, demanded and enforced complete veiling and forced many to flee the country altogether. The actions of the Taliban were exactly what so many in the West fear and have come to expect from those who brandish the name of Islam.

Yet, across the oceans, outside of the Middle East, there is a far different view of Islam. In Indonesia, where Muslims make up more than 90 percent of the population, the people have decided not to establish an Islamic state. And I was told by a leader of the Muhammadiyah, the country's preeminent Islamic charitable organization, that his group has decided to stay out of politics while putting Islamic teachings into practice through charitable and educational work.

Even those groups around the world that are actively seeking an Islamic state disagree on its definition. Few envision a state as totalitarian as that which many fear is forming in Afghanistan. And it is important to note that there are several schools of Islamic law, in addition to differences between Islam's two main branches, Shia and Sunni Islam. Sunnis make up the majority of Muslims in the world today, and both Shias and Sunnis believe in one God and accept Muhammad as his prophet. They disagree over the lines of succession after Muhammad's death. Shias believe the Prophet's cousin and son-in-law was the rightful heir to leadership of the faithful. The majority Sunnis decided the leadership should pass to Abu Bakr, the first person outside of Muhammad's household to become a believer in his teachings. Sunnis and Shias remain divided, often violently, on that point to this day.

I have always fumbled for an answer to one question constantly put to me by Americans who know little about Islam: "What is an Islamic state?" I fumble because the answer is so complex. There is no one answer. Iran, with its majority Shias, believes it is an Islamic state led rightfully by Allah's appointed teachers. Saudi Arabia, which is predominantly Sunni, believes it is an Islamic state led by a monarch. None of the people I interviewed saw these states as the Islamic ideal. Al-Ashmawy believes that Egypt is an Islamic state because it contains a majority of Muslims and its laws are based on values enshrined in the Qur'an. Yet most of the other people I interviewed would vehemently disagree with calling Egypt an Islamic state. There can be no one definition of an Islamic state because its definition is subject to interpretation of God's will as revealed in the Qur'an and the example of the Prophet. Any system of laws seeks to impose order on society, to promote justice and equality among people and to address their needs. The same can be said of Islamic law. Any system of laws must be analyzed and debated to ensure it is appropriate for society. The same could be true of the laws that would govern an Islamic state. Some of my subjects, particularly Sheikh al-Qaradawi of Qatar, Khurshid Ahmad of Pakistan and Hassan al-Turabi of Sudan, discussed some aspects of what they believed to be required by Islamic law. But as with Christianity and Judaism, the word of God is subject to interpretation, and the most educated, reasonable and open-minded scholars can study the same scripture and offer different opinions.

Some scholars believe that Islamic law allows polygamy; others do not. Some would prefer simply to look the other way if a Muslim takes a drink now and then; others would hunt him down and have him whipped. This is why it is important to examine the personalities and characters of the people behind Islamic movements. In real life, a law is as good or as bad as the one who enforces it. And these interviews show that in the Islamic world, there are good and bad leaders molding the minds of millions of people.

Many of the people featured in this book are well known and respected in the Islamic world, although they are unknown in the West. Practicing Muslims throughout the world, especially Islamic scholars, know of the work of Khurshid Ahmad, Ghannouchi, al-Qaradawi and Anwar Ibrahim, one of Malaysia's leading politicians.

Millions of Muslim women have gained inspiration from women such as Bint al-Shati, who for decades has promoted female equality by citing the Qur'an, the Muslim holy book, and the *Hadith*, the authoritative reports of the words and deeds of the Prophet Muhammad.

Each of these people possesses religious principles and moral leadership that many Western readers will find admirable. But each also expresses sentiments that some may find alarming.

Most of the people profiled in this book are considered moderates in the Muslim world, in that they do not promote violence and they are active in political, social or educational affairs in their countries. Still, it must be emphasized that "moderate" is a relative term and that people the West consider radical are considered moderate to many Muslims. Hassan al-Turabi, for example, is often described in the Western media as the greatest threat to world peace since the Ayatollah Khomeini. Yet many of the religious scholars I met described him as a man of great intellect and moderation, one who, they insisted, is working for the good of his country as well as the Islamic world at large. Sudanese opponents of the regime he supported said he was not to be trusted and was leading the country into chaos.

There are some common threads running through the interviews. Many of the Islamists I interviewed had actively opposed the policies of their governments and had been imprisoned by current or former rulers who felt they represented a threat to their power. Except Abida Hussain, Pakistan's former Ambassador the United States, who is a Shia, all of the people featured in this book are Sunni Muslims.

What is clear from these profiles and interviews is that there is a debate raging in Islam—one that not only will shape the lives of more than one billion Muslims in the Middle East and Asia but also will inevitably affect the political life of the Western world. This debate not only challenges traditional interpretations of Islamic teachings but seeks to release Islam from the shackles of cultures that are still struggling to adapt to the modern world. It seeks to answer questions about the role of women in Islamic societies, about the role of religion in the state and about how the people should be represented in such a state. The people of the Islamic world are searching for answers about their relations to other countries, particularly to those that once were their oppressors. They are searching for answers about how to maintain their strong religious values without persecuting people who hold different beliefs.

Many of the people I interviewed are at the forefront of this debate. Some of their movements are legally active, both politically and socially, in their countries. Others have been forced into the shadows of the underground. Some of the leaders are living in exile, while others are close to the holders of power in their countries. Most believed it would be only a matter of time before Islamic movements gain power throughout the Middle East and North Africa, whether by ballot or bloody revolution backed by the people.

It is impossible not to draw two major conclusions from my research, travel and interviews. The first is that all Islamic leaders cannot be lumped into one category. They are different people with different beliefs and different goals. Some of them, as in Jordan, are working within the political system and are considered strong supporters of stability and the status quo. Some are allied with weak political parties, as in Pakistan, but they are optimistic about improving their clout through the political process. Others, such as those allied with the breakaway groups of the Islamic Salvation Front in Algeria, are convinced the only path to their goal is *jihad* and they have embarked on that course.

Most of the people I interviewed were well educated, often in Western universities, and had lived in the West. Most were sophisticated, principled people who believed in dialogue to resolve differences. They represented that quiet majority in Islam that is rarely heard in the West because there is nothing sensational enough about their message to capture the attention of the Western press. Many called for an inner, not an outer, *jihad.* They believed a Muslim's first priority should be inner control and outer piety. And they believed in tolerance for other religions. They told me that they see Christians and Jews as their brothers in the worship of one God, and many were active in groups promoting interfaith dialogue.

Yet in my interviews I did not ignore those who have resorted to violence, because they too are part of the story, however small their numbers. They are represented by Muntassir al-Zayat, who, shortly after I interviewed him, was rounded up in the mass arrests conducted by the Egyptian authorities and was imprisoned for several months. And they are represented by Anwar Haddam, of Algeria's Islamic Salvation Front, who has confessed that he believes the only way to bring about justice in Algeria is through violence against the government. That violence has claimed the lives of many innocent victims, including Christian nuns, journalists, oil field workers and average Algerians trapped in what amounts to civil war.

Another conclusion can be drawn from my research, one that I consider profound. There seems to be a relationship between the incidence of religiously motivated violence against the state and the participation of Islamic groups in the political process. It is evident that in those countries where there is at least the semblance of a democratic system in which Islamists are allowed to participate, there are far fewer incidents of religiously motivated violence than in those countries where religious parties are banned.

There were two major disappointments in my quest. Iran did not grant me a visa during my limited research time, so I could not interview Iranian scholars. And I was not allowed to bring taping equipment into Saudi Arabia, whose far from democratic regime the

United States counts as an ally. I was unable to record what turned out to be an enlightening interview with Fatima Naseef, a professor at King Abdul Aziz University and a renowned Islamic scholar. I had heard that her lectures had begun drawing so many women that she was forced to cancel some of them. Over tea in her home in Jeddah, she told me of the work she was doing to educate Saudi women about the true teachings of the Qur'an with regard to women, and she chastised me as a member of the Western press for painting an inaccurate picture of the Muslim world.

Although her interview is not included in this book, the information, books and tapes she provided gave me a sound basis for my subsequent research. Naseef and many other Muslim women whose interviews I could not include told me that Middle Eastern culture is often confused with Islam, and Islam's teachings actually raised the status of women.

Sharifa Al-Khateeb, leader of a Muslim women's organization in the United States, taught me that Muhammad had railed against the practice, common during his day, of burying infant girls alive. She insisted that Islam had granted women the right to own property and to work long before such rights were granted to women in the West. The Qur'an, she noted, prohibits women from being forced into marriage. And she told me the story of Khadijah, the Prophet's first wife, a successful and rich businesswoman who actually asked the Prophet to marry her.

Muslim women directed me to the Qur'an and the Surah entitled "Al-Nisah," or "The Woman." That Surah discusses the rights of women, and throughout the Qur'an Surahs instruct men to treat their wives with gentleness and respect. But the Qur'an also says women are entitled to less inheritance (Surah 4:11). Islamic scholars say women are denied equal inheritance since they are always the financial responsibility of their nearest male relative. Especially in marriage, they note, a woman's private money is her own and is never to be demanded by her husband to support the family. The Qur'an makes the testimony of a man equal to that of two women (2:282). Some Muslim women, including Wisal al-Mahdi of Sudan, whom I interview in this book, told me that they believed this Surah is appropriate because many, although admittedly not all, women are emotional, less experienced in business and public life and, therefore, would not make reliable witnesses. One of the most extreme interpretations of Islamic doctrine was offered by an American Jewish convert to Islam, whose interview I have not included. She told me quite emphatically that women should not freely associate with men or work outside the home. And whenever they go out, they should cover from head to foot, including their faces. That is how she lives—in what is called strict *purdah.*

Other women offered another explanation for the controversial Surahs that seem to sanction female inequality. Concerning the worth of a woman's testimony, they said that at the time the Qur'an was written, women were less educated, were unaccustomed to public life and therefore were not dependable witnesses in legal and business proceedings. One of the men interviewed in this book, Said Al-Ashmawy, contended that such Surahs should no longer be considered valid, since times had changed. For this and other such ideas, hard-liners had labeled Al-Ashmawy a heretic and his life was in danger.

As for myself, neither Islam nor my own religion, Christianity, seem to grant women full equality with men, certainly not the kind of equality feminists would demand. As the Qur'an places men "a degree above" women (Surah 3:228), the Bible (Ephesians 5:22) states, "For the husband is the head of the wife, even as Christ is the head of the Church. . . ."

Many of us in the West may look at the teachings of Islam as impossible to fathom and alien to some of our basic values. Yet an open mind may show that the religions we respect as fundamentally Western also have doctrines that require what amounts to blind faith and simple acceptance of what we believe to be God's word. Such is also the case in Islam.

Islam today represents a wide spectrum of theological and philo-sophical beliefs that span the gamut between *jihad* and *salaam.*

This book will not answer every question about Islam and its leaders, and it probably will raise more than a few. It is designed to help us understand the intellectual vitality that is now igniting the Muslim world and to help us see Muslims as human beings. In the final analysis, we cannot help but conclude that some of the people we once feared are worthy of our trust, while others, undeniably, are not.

ONE

HASSAN AL-TURABI

POPULAR ARAB AND ISLAMIC CONFERENCE, SUDAN

PROFILE

THERE WERE FEW CARS along the wide paved road from the Khartoum airport into town. The gleaming October sun, sweeping across rows of palm trees and parched flowers, gave this gateway to black Africa the air of a dilapidated tropical resort, much like Merida or Tangier. But it wasn't long before the gray concrete blended with the dust of the city, curving along the Blue Nile and past the faded white columns of colonial buildings. I imagined that once British officers in khaki shorts walked along this quai to their social clubs or dinner parties. But this day, it was the sole domain of brown-skinned men in long white robes and willowy women draped in fabrics as sheer and colorful as the wings of a butterfly.

I had traveled to what in 1992 was the world's youngest Islamic state primarily to learn about how it treated its women. Islamists all over the world pointed to Sudan as an example of an Islamic state where women had won equal civil rights and where Hassan al-Turabi, one of the world's most renowned Islamic leaders, had actively crusaded on their behalf. In the West, that was the reputation of neither Sudan, a country embroiled in a gruesome civil war, nor of

Turabi, described by his opponents as a new-age ayatollah, as dangerous as the one who had sent Iran on a collision course with the West.
Although Colonel Omar al-Bashir declared himself president of Sudan,
many believed that Turabi actually held the reins of power, crowning
the regime with a semblance of religious legitimacy.

Compared to Cairo, where I had just left, Khartoum was an oasis.
It seemed less like a Third World city than a quiet, sprawling village of
low concrete houses and tin stalls. The streets, although hot and dusty,
were remarkably clean. The Sudanese woman who was to be my
official escort during my stay in the country proudly pointed out the
Friendship Hotel, which just might be Khartoum's tallest and most
modern building.

When I first met Dahlia at the airport, I was ecstatic that the
Sudanese Friendship Club, which was serving as my quasi host, had
found me what appeared to be an efficient, Western-educated guide.
Her English was impeccably American, even though she said she had
studied British English in Khartoum. She could have been mistaken
for an African American, although she said she had never even been to
the United States. And she was a popular television anchor, though she
wore no makeup and wore conservative Islamic dress—a scarf, long
sleeves and skirt.

The government had assigned Dahlia to watch my every move.
Two guards accompanied us wherever we went. I was a virtual
prisoner. Even the phones didn't work in my room or anywhere in the
hotel—or so they said. Dahlia, and sometimes the security guards, sat
in on almost every interview I conducted. Finally, out of desperation
and a growing sense of alarm, I secretly summoned the U.S. Embassy
to win some freedom.

One morning during breakfast at the Hilton Hotel, I was jolted by
the sweet, welcome sound of loud, self-confident Americans. I waited
until Dahlia left the table to go to the rest room. Then I walked over to
them, slipped one of them my business card, told them I was a virtual
prisoner and asked them to contact the embassy. At first they were
reluctant. They were in Sudan on secret business, they said, and the
last person they wanted to see was an American journalist. But that
evening a contingent of five American diplomats swooped down on
the Hilton to rescue me from Dahlia and the guards. My compatriots

scurried me into a waiting van that took me deep inside a residential area of Khartoum. There I looked over name after name and case after case of people who said they had been arrested without charge, beaten or tortured, all because they opposed the government. The young woman whose house we were in mentioned somewhat casually that the last journalist who saw this information, an Egyptian woman, had been arrested and questioned for several days before being thrown out of the country. She was lucky she hadn't been accused of spying, considering the animosity between Egypt and Sudan. But relations also were tense between Sudan and the United States. My sense of dread increased to the point of paranoia and I longed to be on a plane out of Khartoum. At least I was thankful the American embassy knew of my whereabouts and that I could not simply disappear into a Sudanese jail. Or could I?

When I interviewed Turabi, I decided to confront him about the allegations of arrests without charge and about my constant surveillance. The guards were there, and so was Madame Dahlia. The guards waited near the door, but the rest of us were seated around a large conference table in a room of the headquarters of the Popular Arab and Islamic Conference. Turabi founded the organization shortly after Operation Desert Storm. A little way into the interview, after the atmosphere had warmed a bit, I dropped what I thought would be a bombshell.

"With all due respect," I said politely, "I have to tell you that I am beginning to feel like a prisoner under the constant scrutiny of guards and minders. Is this your idea of an Islamic utopia where journalists have to be constantly watched?"

Without the slightest sign of defensiveness and with what almost was condescending patience, Turabi soberly explained why governments must be cautious in times of war. And he proceeded to give me a lecture about the actions of Western governments during World War II and during the conflict in the Persian Gulf. Turabi did his Ph.D. dissertation at the Sorbonne on Western emergency law. He said that he believed governments had a right to restrict individual civil liberties during states of emergencies such as civil wars, and for the good of the society as a whole. After initially denying that any Sudanese had been detained without charge for opposition to the government, Turabi justified what he called "preventive detention" as a reasonable way to safeguard the stability of the state and to protect society.

In his eloquent, if slightly accented British English, Hassan al-Turabi was able to make the most radical ideas sound reasonable and rational. I was impressed at how calm and self-assured he remained throughout my questioning. He laughed easily and also seemed to be an attentive listener. He presented his argument with the organized clarity of an experienced lawyer. In fact, when Turabi visited the United States in the spring of 1992 and spoke to the Africa subcommittee holding hearings on Islamic movements, he was so articulate and charming that Representative Howard Wolpe of Michigan, widely considered an expert on Africa, demanded to set the record straight.

Wolpe declared, "There is an enormous tragedy in the Sudan that is very largely of the making of those people that are in control of the government that this gentleman represents. I am, frankly, very troubled that people who do not have enough background about the Sudan in our own country might take at face value the testimony of this gentleman."

The civil war in southern Sudan, which killed hundreds of thousands of people, was the Sudanese government's biggest atrocity and the biggest flaw in Turabi's posture of piety and religious authority. He supported the government, even if he did not control it. And in my presence, he did not speak out against the tactics it was employing in the southern region to put down the rebellion.

A report by David R. Smock of the United States Institute of Peace estimated that, in the decade after 1983, the war cost the lives of an estimated 1.3 million people in the southern region, either directly or indirectly. And the level of brutality compelled human rights groups such as Amnesty International to raise alarms. In a 1993 report, Amnesty International said: "All parties to the conflict [in Sudan] have been ruthless in their assaults on civilians. There has been nothing accidental about these attacks, they are not the by-products of war. The targeting of the rural population has been a deliberate military tactic used by government forces seeking to regain control of areas held by the armed opposition Sudan People's Liberation Army (SPLA) and by all factions of the SPLA in the increasingly bitter conflict between different wings of the rebel movement."[1]

The peoples of northern and southern Sudan have long been divided, often violently. The most recent flare-up can be traced back to the regime of Jaffar al-Numeiry, when in 1983 he decided to enact Islamic law throughout the country. Hundreds of thousands of Sudanese died as a result of the fighting between soldiers from the North and South. Yet the rift that developed in 1991 in the SPLA also was responsible for a great deal of suffering in southern Sudan, and hundreds of thousands died from the infighting between the southern factions. Amnesty International found in its 1993 report: "Each war is a war without prisoners. Few SPLA combatants captured in battle are held by the government. The evidence available indicates that they are routinely extrajudicially executed, either on the battlefield or after torture and interrogation. The SPLA holds few government soldiers; government troops captured in combat appear to be killed there and then." [2] Khartoum also was accused of blocking humanitarian relief to the South to try to starve the rebels as well as the southerners who supported them. Turabi neither justified the government actions nor condemned them. As he put it, the war had to be better "managed."

Turabi said he supported economic development of the South and improvement of educational opportunities there. And he said he was willing to work out a system of laws and government that would provide the non-Muslim southern region more autonomy and exemption from many, but not all, aspects of Islamic law. Islamic civil law did not apply in the South, Turabi told me, but no one would be exempt from the criminal law: the punishment for drinking is beating; the penalty for serious crimes such as armed robbery is maiming; and murder brings the death penalty if the victim's family demands it.

But the war in the South was only one of the issues that compelled the United States and other Western nations to try to isolate Sudan. The other was terrorism. Sudan was suspected of harboring Islamic militants and had once provided safe haven to Sheikh Osama bin Laden, the man accused of masterminding the August 1998 bombings of the American embassies in Tanzania and Kenya. The United States lashed out at bin Laden and sent cruise missiles into his suspected hideout in the mountains of Afghanistan, it also bombed a factory in Khartoum. The Clinton Administration said that the factory was capable of producing chemical weapons for bin Laden's terror organi-

zation. Turabi said that the factory was actually used to make medi-
cines, and he accused the United States of treachery and brutality.

The United States wanted to send a message that even countries that
provide safe haven for terrorists would be subject to superpower wrath.
But severing ties with people such as bin Laden was in direct opposition
to what Turabi was trying to achieve at his Popular Arab and Islamic
Conference. From Turabi's perspective, Muslims of all stripes needed a
place where they could come together to discuss issues of importance to
their world. And from his perspective, the only way to influence
radicals, for better or for worse, was by maintaining a dialogue with
them. He believed he could not hope to unite the Arab and Islamic
world if he excluded Islamic militants from Khartoum. But it should be
noted that Turabi did not join the ranks of Islamists around the world
who vehemently opposed the Palestinian-Israeli peace accords.

In December 1992 Turabi hosted what was billed as an Islamic
conference, attracting scholars from Iran, Yemen, Algeria and Afghan-
istan as well as other parts of the Islamic world. The previous year
Iranian president Ali Rafsanjani had trekked to Khartoum to reinforce
ties between Iran and Sudan. Turabi said he had personally worked to
mediate differences between the Palestine Liberation Organization
(PLO) and HAMAS as well as between warring factions in Afghanistan.
In doing so, Turabi hoped to further his goal of creating a worldwide
Islamic union. Such a union, he envisioned, would solve crises such as
Saddam's invasion of Kuwait without calling for American missiles.

When I visited, Turabi's Popular Arab and Islamic Conference was
housed in a sprawling modern building in Khartoum that looked very
much a center of Islamic authority. White-robed, bearded men roamed the
hallways, while others clustered in corners of a large central hall, en-
grossed in conversation. There were those who seemed to have no
particular mission other than simply to while away the time, listening to
the ruminations of the devout. As I was finally ushered in to greet Turabi,
I wondered if the man before me was an impostor. He was strikingly
different from when we last met in the spring of 1992 in Washington, D.C.

His visit to Washington came about a year before relations
between the United States and Sudan had deteriorated to the point that
Sudan was placed on the U.S. list of countries supporting terrorism. It
was then that Turabi addressed the House Subcommittee on Africa and

stirred Representative Wolpe's wrath. And it was then that I met Turabi for the first time, in a suite in the Watergate Hotel.

But when I arrived at the Watergate, the woman at the front desk had no record of a Hassan al-Turabi. No one by that name had checked into the hotel. She had never even heard of the man. It wasn't long before a dark, bearded man quietly approached me in the lobby and I found myself being discreetly escorted down the Watergate's plush corridors and into a room on the second floor. As it would turn out, Turabi needed such special security precautions. Although at that time he had no official role in the government of Sudan, he was very much a symbol of it, as he was of a new wave of Islamists advocating social and political reform based on Islamic law. With the war in southern Sudan, with Egypt accusing Sudan of supporting terrorism in the Nile valley, and with Israeli leaders warning that Islam was a threat to world stability, Turabi knew there were many who would prefer him dead. What he didn't know was that within weeks, one of them would come very close to killing him.

But on that chilly spring morning, Turabi was the picture of health. The small, beaming man who greeted me inside the Watergate suite hardly looked the part of a fearful ayatollah. Dressed in a dark, dapper suit, Turabi looked more like a Western entrepreneur than a religious radical. His sparse gray beard, one sign of a devout Muslim man, seemed designed more to flatter his deep brown skin than to promote piety. In fact, his whole demeanor radiated energy and good humor. And far from shrieking like a deranged fanatic, Turabi spoke eloquent English punctuated frequently with laughter that served to reduce tension, while underscoring the passion of his beliefs. His voice had a rich, radio-announcer quality and he greeted each question with an openness that I did not expect.

It was the same voice in Khartoum, but a different look. The well-tailored suit was gone. Instead, Turabi was dressed in the traditional style of Sudanese men, his head covered in a giant white turban and his small frame draped in a long white *jallibiyah*. This time Turabi looked the part. But he also looked weaker. He was noticeably thinner and somewhat drawn in the face. During our conversation, Turabi confided that he had almost died from an assassination attempt. After he left Washington, he had flown to Canada. And at the airport in Ottawa, a Sudanese who was an expert in karate attacked him. Human rights organizations said the man who attacked Turabi had been tortured in Sudanese jails and that he held Turabi personally responsible. Turabi spent months in a Canadian hospital and doctors told his wife he would probably die there. If by some miracle he survived, they warned, he would certainly suffer severe brain damage.

But Turabi proved them wrong. Not only did he eventually make a full recovery, both mentally and physically, but he would go on to increase his influence in the Islamic world, using Khartoum as a base. In the fall of 1993, former president Jimmy Carter traveled to Khartoum and met with Turabi as well as Colonel Omar al-Bashir, the country's military ruler. Carter believed Turabi to have by far the superior intellect, if not the real power in Sudan. In fact, it seemed much of Turabi's life had been dedicated to politics and power in Sudan.

Turabi was born in 1938 in Wad al-Turabi, a village in central Sudan, named after his great-grandfather, also a religious man. Eventually Turabi made his way to the city to study law at Khartoum University, where he later became dean of the Faculty of Law.

His career of political activism began in the 1960s when he led protests against the government of General Ibrahim Abboud and founded the Islamic Charter Front, a coalition of several Islamic groups. Abboud's regime lasted from 1958 to 1964, and upon his overthrow Turabi helped bring about the reestablishment of the Sudan's parliamentary system.

In 1969, Colonel Jaffar al-Numeiry seized power, and Turabi was imprisoned for almost eight years for allegedly working against the state. According to Turabi, it was during this time in prison that he became an avid reader and began writing about his theories of Islam and politics. After his release from prison in 1977, as part of the government's attempt at political reconciliation, Turabi once again involved himself in politics, but not as part of an Islamic party. They were outlawed. Turabi joined the Sudanese Socialist Union, the only legal party, and in November 1981 he became attorney general in the Numeiry regime. Numeiry was deposed in a military coup in April 1985, but by then Turabi was no longer in government and had become actively opposed to it.

After Numeiry was toppled, Turabi founded the National Islamic Front (NIF), a coalition of Islamic parties that was dominated by the

Muslim Brotherhood. Turabi had been secretary general of the Muslim Brotherhood since 1964. As a result of democratic elections for the National Assembly in 1986, the NIF was among the top three political parties. Sadiq al-Mahdi, the brother of Turabi's wife, was elected prime minister. And Turabi was named minister of foreign affairs.

It seems that Sadiq al-Mahdi and Turabi became friends while studying in Europe, and Turabi arranged to marry Wisal al-Mahdi. Wisal and Sadiq al-Mahdi's great-grandfather was the heralded Mahdi who founded the Ansar Islamic movement. And it was this Mahdi who led his army to throw the British out of Khartoum in the late 1800s. Sadiq al-Mahdi inherited the leadership of the Ansar. He served as leader of the movement's Umma party and as prime minister of Sudan until his government was overthrown by Omar al-Bashir in 1989. Bashir even imprisoned Turabi for several months before the men apparently reached a working agreement.

When I visited with him in Khartoum, Turabi had no official role in Sudan's government—identifying himself only as a spiritual advisor. But it was clear that he was very much involved in Sudanese political affairs; only a few years later, he was elected speaker of the parliament. His paramount dream remained strengthening and uniting Muslims around the world. To that end, his home often served as a meeting place for Islamists from throughout the world.

Many nights, Turabi's large living room became a kind of Islamic salon. The night I was his wife's dinner guest, Turabi received his own guests from a long sofa pushed against a wall that faced a large tapestry with swirling Arabic script, a verse from the Qur'an. Groups of men, some in Arab robes, some in Western suits, huddled in animated debate. A long buffet was against another wall and was covered with dishes of roasted beef, lamb, rice and rows of honey-coated desserts. Turabi seemed to enjoy serving as host, and he made a point of popping into the *harem*, or women's part of the house, from time to time, personally making sure his wife was attending to her Western guests.

After graduating from the University of Khartoum, Turabi spent many years in Europe, studying at the Sorbonne in Paris and at London University. He prided himself on being a rational, well-educated man, well steeped in Western thought and culture. And he conceded that Western philosophy helped shape his own philosophy of Islamic reform.

Turabi insisted that the Khartoum government wanted to establish a society based on democracy and the moral principles espoused by Islam. Such a society would outlaw alcohol and drugs. Adultery would be a punishable offense for both men and women. The economic system would incorporate the best of capitalism without what he saw as its apathy toward the poor and the oppressed.

Turabi believed the government was trying to make the country fiscally responsible and independent of foreign interests. The government was in the midst of privatizing many industries, and food production, at least in the North, he said, was increasing.

What I saw in Sudan disagreed with Turabi's bright outlook. Even my minder, Dahlia, complained bitterly about the price of food and how she was unable to buy even fruit for her infant daughter. Many of the youths I spoke to worried about finding work. Human rights agencies had documented case after case in which government opponents routinely were rounded up and detained for weeks in "ghost houses," where there were reports of torture. The times I managed to break away from Dahlia (once with the help of the U.S. embassy and once when I simply bolted and sent my captors on a wild hunt through Khartoum University), I easily found people who corroborated such stories. One woman, a Western expatriate, told me her Sudanese husband had been imprisoned for weeks on several occasions, without being told why he was arrested. Another young woman said her mother had been detained and beaten and had since fled the country.

But I also spoke to other women, many who supported the government, who also told me of some good things that were happening in Sudan. The government was actively supporting efforts to stop female circumcision, they told me. It had outlawed the practice, but that was only a small part of the battle. Since it was commonly believed that cutting the external sex organs prevented promiscuity, people had to be convinced that the practice did more harm than its reported good. The government supported grass-roots efforts targeted at mothers and midwives offering proof of the severe physical and emotional harm caused by circumcision.

I interviewed women at Afhad College for Women in Omdurman, on the outskirts of Khartoum, who were passionate in their campaign to wipe out FC, as they called it. They said many religious leaders had joined them to convince women that the practice had no basis in Islam. Sudanese women had long ago won the right to vote and to run for public office. Women who said they were among those who took to the streets in the 1960s to demand such rights credited their gains to the Islamic movement in the country (although they came long before Bashir's Islamic government). And many of the women I spoke to also credited their gains to the support of religious leaders such as Hassan al-Turabi. As of 1993, there were an estimated 25 women in the Sudanese parliament, and Ihsan al-Ghabshawie, then a member, told me that the parliament had passed a law setting aside at least 10 percent of elected positions for women.

When I was there, young women were beginning to outnumber men at Khartoum University, specializing in such demanding fields as engineering and medicine. Turabi expressed many views on women that had put him at odds with more conservative Islamists. His wife (he had only one) was among those working to improve the status of women in the country and throughout the Islamic world by pushing legislation and encouraging education.

But Sadiq al-Mahdi, whom I also interviewed, said the current Islamic regime had nothing to do with granting civil rights to Sudanese women. In fact, he said, many were worried that their rights might be revoked. Al-Mahdi did not trust the Bashir government. Other people I interviewed noted that women who once were able to earn a meager living selling tea or trinkets on the streets were now harassed and intimidated by self-styled morality enforcers. Some women complained that the atmosphere was becoming more hostile for women in public, especially if unaccompanied by a male escort.

When I spoke to him, Turabi claimed to be bewildered by his critics, those in Sudan as well as abroad. He believed Western leaders were guilty of religious prejudice and were out to destroy Islam and its leaders.

Many of the dozens of Islamists I interviewed for this book described Turabi as a moderate and as an intellectual. They said he had the authority among Islamic leaders to serve as a bridge between Islam and the West and that his Western education made him able to communicate Islamic ideals effectively to a Western ear.

Yet Turabi lacked one key ingredient to serve as an effective go-between: he lacked the trust of Western leaders. They saw him as one of the Islamic world's most dangerous figures, and his eloquence and intelligence only made him more insidious. Turabi would be a formidable enemy for the West, if he chose that path. And the U.S. bombing of Khartoum in 1998 may well have provoked him toward a more violent philosophy. I believe he is too smart (some would say too devout) ever to choose it willingly. But if Turabi should ever be moved to summon the faithful to *jihad*, be warned. More than a few would heed his call.

INTERVIEW WITH HASSAN AL-TURABI

OCTOBER 1992, KHARTOUM, SUDAN

JD: Would you tell us a little bit about the organization you represent here in Sudan?

HT: This organization? This is the Popular Arab and Islamic Conference. It's an organization rather than a single conference. It was a get-together of all Arab and Muslim public opinion after the Gulf War. All over the world there was a consensus of public opinion and we thought that the official international organization like the Arab League or the Conference of Islamic States is not truly representative of them all . . .* And it convenes not only Muslims, but also Arabs, even Christians. Not only Islamic attitudes, but also even nationalist attitudes.

JD: I thought there was another organization, the Popular Front?

HT: Oh, yes. When there were political parties here, I was the secretary general of the Popular Islamic Front in the Sudan. And that Front

---

* While I have tried to remain faithful to the interviewee's comments throughout, in some cases it has been necessary to streamline their answers for clarity. Ellipses have been used to mark such editorial deletions.

represented the latest development in the Islamic movement in the Sudan. It started very early as the liberation movement. Those were the independence days. It was called later the Muslim Brotherhood. All over the Arab world, the Muslim Brotherhood was the brand name of Islamic movements. Later on, it became the Islamic Charter Front. Later, it became the Popular Islamic Front. Unlike the earlier organization, it was a popular organization which brought together men and women for the first time. It brought together north and south, elite and people, just ordinary people, for the first time.

JD: Are you still associated with the Islamic Front?

HT: The Islamic Front doesn't work anymore. Islam has been turned now into a current rather than an organized, institutionalized party.

JD: Do you serve as an advisor to the government?

HT: No. Not official advisor.

JD: Not official? But yet, at least everything that I've read says you're certainly one of the authorities in this country and that you have a great influence on the government. Is that true?

HT: Oh, I don't have a direct influence on the government as a government. But for the last 40 years I was in the Islamic movement all over the world, not only in the Sudan. So, anyone who plays a public role in life would probably attend to what I say here and there. That much, at that intellectual level, yes. But I'm not an advisor of any government institution and I'm not a member of the government at all.

JD: So it's because Sudan is now an Islamic state and because you are an Islamic thinker, in that way you have some influence.

HT: That's right.

JD: We understand there are several movements in Islam, ranging from [what] we know of in Saudi Arabia or in Iran, that seem to have a more restricted role for women, to other theories that allow women to pursue their lives as they see fit within certain contexts of duties to families, duties to children. Would you tell me where you fit in?

HT: Yes. Yes. Well, like all religious communities, you can have traditional religious establishments, something analogous to a church in Christian society. And that's particularly so about Saudi Arabia and about Iran, unfortunately. Both of them are Muslim communities where the *ulama,* the scholars, the mullahs, as they are called, are very important. They almost have a monopoly over Islam and they are very conservative in their attitudes, very, very old book. They are not conscious of developments, and they never renew religious spirit and religious thought from time to time. That's true about Saudi Arabia and about Iran, except that in Saudi Arabia, there is a [regression from] Islam toward secularism. But the government doesn't openly confess it, but, in fact, the law is moving away from religion. Economics, money is moving away from religion in order not to control the money, because the princes want the money for themselves. If they adopt the *Sharia* (Islamic law), the *Sharia* will control them . . . And in their international relations they have associations which are not very consistent with Islamic logic. Whereas Iran has made a movement forward. But the movement forward in Iran has not been a full Islamic movement because they have not institutionalized Islam in the economy, in the judiciary, in education, in public life, but only as a political slogan.

In the rest of the Muslim world, there are Islamic movements. What we call Islamic movements the West calls fundamentalist movements. They are actually movements of renewal, mostly led by elites. They are movements which revive the religious spirit. They renew Islamic institutions and Islamic thoughts. It's quite true that they go back to original Islam to criticize the historical legacy that has reduced Islam to something very conservative. Most of the [repression] of women in particular is only an example of many other forms of religious life which are not necessarily true to Islam itself, but they are done in the name of religion, so to speak.

These Islamic movements, whatever their names are, are very similar . . . And they are now becoming very popular because in the whole of the

Muslim world, like in the rest of the world at large, there's hardly any nationalism anymore. There were days of nationalism after independence. There were days of Western liberalism. There were days of socialism, very popular days of socialism. All of this now has disappeared. There is such an empty world that Islam has become the only dominant theme now. The leadership is mostly elites, and they want to renew. They are very critical of the history, so to speak. And they are very independent of the West or East or whatever, [independent of] any subservience to any international pattern besides Islam. And here in the Sudan, for example, they are the only movement which worked for the liberation of women. No other movement ever did anything about women.

JD: When I spoke to you in April, I basically challenged you and I said that from the perspective that we saw, Islam was oppressive to women. I said that because of institutions such as polygamy, because of restrictions on divorce, it seemed to me to confine women, to prevent them from really fulfilling their full potential. You answered and you said no, Islam was actually a liberator. I'd like you to just tell me some specifics about what Islam here has done for women in this country, since the revolution.

HT: Well, since the revolution, they were represented in a big scale in the parliament of today. There were never that many members of parliament. It's the first time to expand their functions. They were allowed to join even the Popular Defense Forces. Definitely the military was completely outside women's access. They were a few, not doctors, but a few hospital servants in the military hospitals, but nothing else. But they are now members of the Popular Defense Forces. They are military forces, I mean. This is the first time that women were told that they can enjoy any function. Women were not allowed to go to the mosques because custom was against their public appearance. Women were always advised to stay at home, confined to the *harem* area in the home. But now they are left to go out and join. As far as education is concerned, that has taken place some time ago, but now it has been accelerated. They have an equal right as men to all, access to all education, higher education. And as far as salaries are concerned, they have absolutely complete equality.

JD: If you had to envision the ideal Islamic state, which I would assume you are trying to help achieve here in the Sudan, how would you see women fitting into that Islamic ideal?

HT: Well, according to the Qur'an itself, the Qur'an itself pronounces that men and women both have to help each other in public life. Public life does not mean politics only. Even if it comes to defense, both of them, I mean, the Qur'anic text itself says both of them are responsible. I mean in the model of the Prophet himself, they are present in public life, present in social life, they are present even in military life to some extent, except to some extent they have to recognize their female condition. I mean, they are not bound to play the same role. It's not always a duty, but it's a right for her to be everywhere. It's a religious obligation for her to contribute. But she may have excuses, which men don't enjoy.

JD: What would be a woman's excuse for not contributing to her society?

HT: She may not be able to go to serve in the military like a man would serve. She may be pregnant, for example. She is not bound to appear to public prayer on Friday, if she has to attend to her children, but she may, she may do that. It's definitely something that she will get rewarded for. But she's not bound. A man is bound to do it. So she gets a few excuses, not prohibitions, not bars.

JD: There are some things that you think Islam has a right to demand by law, such as, I would take, not killing another person. What things are the actual demands of Islam as opposed to recommendations of Islam?

HT: In the family? Well, once they are married, it is known by law, the male is bound to maintain the family and not the female. Even if she is rich, she can give away her money or divert her wealth away. But the husband is bound by law and he can be taken to court. Because of that, he is the only one who has the right to declare a divorce himself. A woman because she would get some compensation from it, she can't divorce, except by referring to the courts. She would have to go to the courts and ask for a divorce. She will get a divorce because the court will consider if that is a reasonable divorce, she will get the compensation. If it is not a reasonable divorce, she will get her divorce without the compensation.

JD: Does a man have to go to court to divorce under Islam?

HT: No.

JD: He just divorces?

HT: He just divorces.

JD: But a woman has to go to court?

HT: Yes, because a man would suffer for a divorce. That's the reason why he's given the right because he knows he'll have to bear the consequences. But the woman can always get the fruits of such an act; therefore, she'll have to go to the courts and apply for such a divorce. She'll get it anyway, but the court will evaluate how reasonable it is. If it is not very reasonable, she will not get the compensation after the divorce.

JD: I see, so she will get the divorce, she just might not be entitled to any financial support.

HT: She'll just walk away, without any support. That's it.

JD: In your ideal Islamic state, would Islamic dress be demanded?

HT: Not by law, but by moral instruction. Of course, complete obscenity of men or women, the law can take care of that. But normal obscene and proper dress, or whatever, I mean, is just moral instruction.

JD: Sudan is a society that has different religions. I've talked to many Muslim women who see no problem with Islamic dress. It's perfectly fine with them. What if I were to come and live in the Sudan, and I'm a Christian?

HT: No, they won't interfere.

JD: There would not be any forcing?

HT: Oh, no, Islam, of course, preserves the freedom of non-Muslims completely in their private life. Not only their dress but their family law is completely private. Completely private.

JD: Would you talk a little bit about that? You told me that *Sharia* law was applied to Muslims, for example, but would not be applied, for example, in the South, where there are Christians.

HT: Well, *Sharia* law in [civil] law. I mean, marriage, inheritance and so on is applied only to Muslims, right across the Sudan. Non-Muslims, I mean, will have other laws applied to them. Their own church law, for example. Their own customary law, like in the South. Some of them have no churches. There are just primitive leaders with customs, whatever they are, twenty wives, thirty wives, they can have whatever they like. But the rest of Islamic law, I mean, criminal Islamic law, we apply only in the majority populated areas of Sudan. In northern Sudan, whether they are Muslims or non-Muslims, they will have to abide by that criminal law.

JD: And so this criminal law would involve things like what happens to you if you steal, what happens to you if you kill someone, the main things we know of as criminal law.

HT: Well, yes. If you kill someone, there isn't really much difference. The customary law of the South has always been like that. If you kill someone, you can either get a pardon from his relatives or, if they insist, you can get an execution.

JD: So, Islamic law allows for a family to pardon?

HT: Oh, yes, absolutely. A man will get free without paying any money or even having to serve any prison sentence at all.

JD: And yet I do understand that Islamic law would, if you steal, cut off your hand.

HT: Well, it's not just any ordinary stealing. It's a capital theft, a very high amount. The evidence has to be two witnesses, not just ordinary evidence. If it's ordinary evidence, they will give you another punishment. And then the amount has to be that high and there is no excuse for the theft itself. That's why it has been applied for over a year here and I think there is only one case, or two cases, actually qualified to meet those conditions. And the most important thing is liquor.

JD: Liquor? Oh, okay, tell me about liquor?

HT: Well, in the South, for example, liquor is free [easily obtainable].

JD: Is it?

HT: Absolutely.

JD:. But in the North it isn't?

HT: No, it's not. A man would be whipped for consuming liquor.

JD: A man would be whipped for consuming liquor? Would a woman be whipped?

HT: Oh yes, yes. I mean, we don't discriminate in criminal responsibility between men and women. Except, of course the judge would always [try] to be nice.

JD: If she were pregnant, for example . . .

HT: Yes, they won't whip her too much, anyway.

[LAUGHTER]

JD: But this part of it does sound really severe to me, you know. Consuming a little liquor, a woman could be whipped.

HT: Well, if you take liquor as a system, just consider it as a system in a country, there would be a lot of alcoholism. Many people will die. Many people will be run over by motor vehicles driven by drunken drivers. Many people will be victims of crimes by drunken people. They are fighting with each other. In the whole society, it's something horrible. But in a society like ours, liquor is not there. It's not a habit and there are very few people who are taken to the courts for it because it has been completely eradicated.

JD: And drugs, of course, is also a very serious offense.

HT: There are very few people who are taken [arrested], actually. Most people never consume liquor at all. It is not around for you to be tempted to consume it little or much. But look at any European country, if you can see all the damage of liquor, it's something very horrible. And I think I'll definitely punish a few people to stop all that damage falling upon society. There is no doubt, this is very reasonable, I'd say. Very reasonable.

JD: Can we talk a little about your views on polygamy? I have heard various interpretations of this, from people who are devout Muslims and who read a lot, study a lot about the Qur'an and the *hadiths* [the recorded sayings and deeds of the Prophet Muhammad]. I've heard some say it's permitted. And I've heard some say it's not encouraged and is actually discouraged.

HT: You're absolutely right. I mean, the Qur'an allows it ultimately, up to four. But it discourages it and it warns people against embarking upon it if they can't do it. I mean, observe perfect justice. And they can cope with supporting two wives or three wives. Of course, it depends on the contract with the first wife. If she can provide against this and she can say that if you marry again I'll go away, she can go away. The idea is that if for one reason or another . . . although he's married to X he would want to give birth to few children, but she can't for any reason . . . he's allowed to do that. But he has to be very fair and very equal. And he's discouraged from doing this because normally it's very difficult to maintain equality and justice.

JD: Can we talk a little about the marriage contract? I understand that is a way that a woman can try to protect herself from the possibility that if she doesn't want to live with a second wife, etcetera . . .

HT: Yes.

JD: But in practicality, how much freedom do women have with their marriage contracts? Are there more pressures on them just to hurry up and get married and don't worry about a marriage contract?

HT: Well, I mean, well, strictly speaking, the marriage contract can be very complicated. Most people don't really involve that much in a marriage contract. Most marriage contracts are very simple. Of course, legally, a marriage contract can contain any conditions, except those conditions which are against the fundamentals of Islamic marriage itself. Of course a marriage contract, like an ordinary commercial contract, cannot go against the state law, for example. A man cannot in a marriage contract dictate upon his wife to support him. She may be a very rich woman, I mean, or whatever she is, a manager of a company or the heir of a very rich person, but he cannot put in his contract with her that all the family expenses are drawn from the woman. No, you can't do that.

JD: What is Islam's position on abortion?

HT: It's much more liberal than some Christian views on abortion. In the very late stages of development, it's not legitimate, but in the early stages, it's not really a very serious offense. If there is any risk to the woman, definitely abortion is [allowed] right up to the end. We don't want it to become subject to just any whims. But [the mother's] health has absolute priority. But now, of course, some view it seriously because of the influence of the West, actually.

JD: So the West is having an influence on Islam. Is there any good influence? Or is it all bad?

HT: Even if it's a bad influence, it's good. Because it's an experiment. I don't have to run through the same experiment. For example, you have established democracy. We are always looking for a consultative system. But what form of consultation? We have an attitude to elections which is against your attitude. No one is allowed to make publicity for himself or to offer himself as a candidate. An independent institution should suggest possible candidates for an office. There should be an independent institution, an election commission. It should try to interview as many people as it can and then offer five or six or whatever. And then they should interview them and introduce them to the public. They should not allow them to use money. Otherwise the rich candidate can always win an election over a poor candidate.

But in the West, I don't know why they refuse to notice discrimination. Elections are very bad in the West, unfortunately. And then parties are very dogmatic, very partisan. One would know that his party was deciding wrong but in the parliament, you always vote with your party. In Islam that is absolutely not allowed. You are responsible to God and not to the party leadership. You should always freely speak your independent view. So, by looking at Western democracy, we can get many useful things. And so it is with the economy, for example. You have the capitalistic economy. You have the socialist economy. And both of them, you can learn from. In the Sudan, we have liberalized the economy completely. And because we have liberalized it on the basis of Islam, people accepted it, although prices went up.

JD: I hear there are lots of problems with the prices going up. The people are suffering.

HT: Oh, but the government also provides them very powerful justice programs. There is a card program for the first time, where the card is taken as a tax simply to give to the poor all over the country.

JD: So there is what we would call a welfare system?

HT: It's a welfare tax, taken not from income, because anybody can deny that he had any income, but from capital itself.

JD: There are reports that there is tension in Sudan now. People feel there is pressure. Some people feel they can't talk freely. In fact, we've had to have a government person with us at all times. What's wrong? Why can't there be freedom of speech? What's happening? Is it the war in the South? What is it?

HT: Well, people are trying to build up the country. Since independence, we've had many governments, unfortunately. Most of them were miserable governments, whether they were military or civilian. So the country had developed a civil war in the South, almost a tribal war in the West and complete poverty in the East. The idea now is to try to bring the country together and not allow people to become too tribalized. If they are too tribalized, this may very well develop into a Somalia-like civil war. This would be horrible. It is not a question of religion. The civil war in the South has to be managed, not only by military action, but even if you occupy a place militarily, you have to provide it with economic development, educate people so they don't resort to violence. Someone who doesn't get a ministerial job may also take his tribe away. So, the attempt now is to establish full democracy from below, not from the top. Local government has been completely democratized, complete freedom. Trade unions now are completely free.

JD: But I have to tell you, with all respect, that I have some reports that say they are not really free. There have been some arrests—

HT: Absolutely not. Absolutely not. Completely free. And the election committees are independent. They are judges and legal officers.

JD: So, as far as you know, there have been no arrests, no imprisonments, no people rounded up because they—

HT: Of course, preventive detention has been here even during democracy.

JD: What is preventive detention?

HT: Sometimes they have people who are involved in contraband, but they can't really prove it yet. They arrest them for a while, for a month or so. They have people who think they are engaged in an ethnic, racist, military attempt, for example, or a coup, or civil war. And they arrest them until they can investigate the case, in a month or two. If they can't find anything, they release them.

JD: In a month or two? Really. Well, just to be as open as I can with you, when I hear that, I'm saying, so they arrest without any proof. And they're held for a month without any proof. And then they're let go. That, to me, is an affront against personal liberty.

HT: Oh, that might look to you because you live in a very stable, peaceful country. But look at your own country, how it behaved, for example, when the Americans first occupied that country. What did they do with the population? With the Indians? Did they manage any freedom or justice there? They just massacred the whole people. There are just the reserves now. When they conducted their civil war, were they very fair in managing their enemies? Even during the last war, they took all Americans of Japanese origin, all of them, hundreds of thousands of them, and they put them up in a camp until the end of the war. After the end of the war, the court said, this wasn't constitutional, give them some compensation. You know, in case of war and economic disturbance, you cannot apply a fair, stable, peaceful system of law. You apply some emergency measures. But you have to be fair in those emergency measures and not overapply them. Even before this government took over, the civilian government used to detain people for six months, for a year, for two, on just a suspicion, a political suspicion, or a military suspicion. And when I was taken to the detention when the military took over, there were many political detainees there.

JD: You were, of course, imprisoned for a while?

HT: Yes, for three months or so. But when we came [to power], many people were freed completely from the previous government.

So, in this country, because it's a very unstable country, economically, politically, emergency law becomes a necessity. Emergency law is applicable even in England. In the last Gulf war, there was not war in England. But all the Iraqis in England, even the students who were just in universities, they were detained. Look at the Iranians in England. They are detained over the slightest [issue]. Some of them were tried and given long-term sentences. And four years later, it was realized it was complete fabrication by the police.

JD: You may resist giving yourself a label, but in this whole sphere of Islam, from conservative to enlightened conservative to liberal to revolutionary, where do you see yourself?

HT: Oh, I don't want to qualify myself. I am not encouraged to do that in Islam. But I have learned a great deal from the West, studied there, stayed there; I have visited every Western country. I know many languages, English, French, some German, Italian, a little bit. And I have learned a lot about original Islam, its history, the Qur'an itself, traditional knowledge of Islam. And I have traveled a great deal and I am very free now. I think there is a great need of reform now and I am not bound by anything historical. I want to reform society politically so that it is completely free, not just formally free; not just a form of representation and democracy. You can have a form of democracy without true democracy at all. And you have to have a free society but also a very clean society. You can have a society that is very corrupt. And I know in the West there is a lot of corruption in the government, a lot of corruption.

In many senses I am a revolutionary because the change I work for is a complete change of social structures.

Of course the word "revolutionary" has many associations, breaking up and breaking down. But I think I can persuade society, not by using force with revolution. I can persuade women, I can persuade men to allow women to have freedom. I can persuade the government to give freedom to people. I can persuade rich people to share their wealth, persuade intelligent people to share their opinion with the masses. I'm not an elitist myself. I have a lot of education myself, more than many people in this country or in other countries. But I've had

contact with the masses, with ordinary illiterate people in the whole
country. I've been everywhere in almost every village in this country
and I like to talk down the level to them. So I'm a believer in this
general, popular, universal reform.

JD: And that makes people very afraid of you sometimes.

HT: Why should people? That's what I complain. Because wherever I
went in the West, I don't know whether they were told about me or
whether they just branded me as such, they thought I was a dangerous,
subversive revolutionary, whatever that is. And that's why I think
someone tried to kill me. I don't think he was alone. I think there was
something behind him.

JD: You think there was a conspiracy?

HT: I'm quite sure of it because he was told exactly when I was leaving.
Nobody knew. Only the government knew, because I didn't even tell
our ambassador when I was leaving.

JD: The Canadian government knew or the American government
knew?

HT: Only the Canadian government knew. Only the Canadian government knew I was going to stay in that hotel. My name wasn't in the
hotel itself. It was in a different name. But people stormed me in that
hotel. Then they stormed me in the state department. And then the
intelligence knew that I was going to be attacked on that departure.
And they told the police to ensure that this wouldn't take place but the
police just dismissed it. I don't know whether they deliberately . . . or
. . . There were some German diplomats, some American diplomats
and some English diplomats who said, well, it's our view that you are
responsible for all these Islamic movements in the whole world. If
there is a revolution anywhere, if there is a change in government, an
Islamic change in government, you must be the one behind all this.

JD: They think if they get rid of you they'll get rid of everything?

HT: I told them this is not true. This is a historical phenomenon. It's changing all over. It just happens that I speak English. I can explain it to you. I can entertain a dialogue with you over it.

You know, even in Algeria, someone told the Europeans, that this is not the Algerians, this is Hassan Turabi behind it all. But I'm not interfering in Algeria. I don't have even a TV channel over there in Algeria. I don't have money here in the Sudan. The Sudan doesn't have the money to assist anybody in the whole world.

But, I really hope, I look forward for a number of Europeans to become ready for a dialogue with Muslims instead of dismissing the whole Islamic phenomenon, which is led by elites who are Western educated. From Malaysia to Morocco, all of them are Western educated, so they are very close to you. They know your education very well, they know your culture very well.

If you are ready to engage a dialogue with them, I'm sure this is better for humanity. But if the West is still imperialist . . . Of course, we have known the West as an imperialist power. We have known how much massacre in this country, or in India or in North Africa or in Algeria, all throughout the world, how many they killed walking into the country and how many they killed before they had to walk out.

JD: Do you agree with spreading Islam through military means?

HT: Oh no, Islam, I mean the Qur'an itself prohibits forcing anyone to become a Muslim. So you don't spread it through military [force]. You defend yourself, of course, through argument or through military. It depends on how the aggression is. If it's just an aggression by words, you just reply. If it's an aggression by military, you can also defend yourself in a military manner. But the religion has to be spread freely.

JD: I'm assuming that there's not one system, political, social or otherwise, that you could identify as a model for the one you're hoping to establish here, but if there is a hybrid, a combination of them, which would there be?

HT: No, I'm trying to propose an original model which would have taken advantage of the Western model, which would have taken advantage of the other human values from the West, or from Islam or from Christianity or from wherever. And the model may not be a model which was applied in certain times of history, or in a particular time today. So I'm trying to develop my own model, economically, socially, politically, internationally.

JD: You do expect other attempts on your life?

HT: I do, I do, unfortunately.

JD: And you don't know where they're coming from?

HT: I don't know where they're coming from. Unfortunately from people who should have been very safe.

already met with her brother, Sadiq al-Mahdi, leader of the Ansar sect and the prime minister who was deposed when Colonel Omar al-Bashir seized power on June 30, 1989. It was the same coup that eventually made her husband the country's leading "spiritual advisor," as he described himself, and that turned her into the de facto spiritual first lady of Sudan. But the coup also had brought her brother house arrest and his two wives and children constant surveillance. Somehow, Wisal al-Mahdi had managed to chart a course down the middle of the family feud, while being firmly on the side of her husband.

When I arrived at her house somewhere in the heart of the sprawling city, Wisal al-Mahdi and Dr. Turabi greeted me at the door and welcomed me into the *harem,* the part of the house reserved for her to entertain female guests. But Turabi soon returned to an adjacent parlor, where he was entertaining guests of his own, all male. I had come to their house specifically to interview al-Mahdi about the status of women in an Islamic state. Tall, imposing and serious, I immediately realized that she was an impressive personality in her own right and was not the subservient, self-effacing underling I had imagined would be wed to one of the world's most feared and revered Islamic *sheikhs.*

That night she was draped from head to toe in yards and yards of flowing fabric that Sudanese women call the *thobe.* I had dared to wear a *thobe* myself, of pink flowers on a green background. I braved it part out of admiration for the feminine beauty of being enveloped in luxurious sheer fabric and part out of curiosity at how Sudanese women manage to maneuver in such attire. I did not move nearly as effortlessly, nor with as much grace as al-Mahdi, although my *thobe* had been judiciously pinned to my undergarments, while hers was simply wrapped around her body and held securely under her left arm. The *thobe* fits the basic requirements of Islamic dress, in that the hair is covered as well as the legs and arms. But the fabrics are of such striking colors that they flatter dark skin and highlight a woman's beauty, instead of mask it, which is the intention of Islamic dress. Many Sudanese women had feared that an Islamic government would force them to abandon the *thobe* for drab-colored skirts and scarves, but it seemed as if any such attempts were doomed to failure, as even the wife of the country's leading *sheikh* had not abandoned it. Despite the voluminous fabric encircling her sturdy frame, al-Mahdi had no trouble supervising the kitchen staff, setting up a buffet of several kinds of meats, rice and mounds of sweets, all the while attending her guests as well as those of her husband. I watched her with the cunning of an American reporter, searching for signs of female oppression, peppering her with questions about the suffering of the modern Muslim women. Since I never expected to set foot in Sudan again, no topic was sacred. I grilled her about the religious and political "differences" between her husband and her brother, and I even asked her if she could accept her husband taking another wife.

With a family of six children, she clearly was accustomed to verbal barrage, and she answered some of my questions with what seemed the exaggerated patience of a conscientious mother instructing a six-year-old. When we met, Sudan was in the middle of a brutal civil war in the South. Although there was concern that the United States might try to intervene in the war and support the rebels, Turabi was putting forth a good effort to improve relations between the two countries. There were rumors, which later proved to be unfounded, that Iran was using Sudan to train terrorists for attacks against the West. Turabi had visited Washington earlier in the year to refute the charges in front of a congressional subcommittee, but his eloquent English only seemed to inflame those who were convinced that he was the next *ayatollah*. Al-Mahdi had rushed to his side in Canada after he was almost killed by a fellow Sudanese and spent months helping her husband recuperate.

I got the impression that they were willing to talk to an American journalist because they felt there was still hope of bettering ties with the West, if only the West better understood Islam and the kind of state they were trying to create in Sudan. This was before Sudan was placed on the U.S. State Department's list of countries supporting terrorism and the United States began a policy of isolating it. And it was long before the United States bombed Sudan in retaliation for its connections to Osama bin Laden, who was accused of ordering the August 1998 bombings of American embassies in Tanzania and Kenya. Yet it was clear that al-Mahdi and many other women were passionately committed to the success of Turabi's Islamic experiment and were confident that such a state would bring women their fair share of power.

Obviously well educated, al-Mahdi spoke good English and French. She had traveled in the West and lived in Paris while her husband studied law at the Sorbonne. She was the great-granddaughter of the legendary Mahdi who defeated the British during the late 1880s. Her brother, Sadiq al-Mahdi, now led the Islamic sect that her great-grandfather founded in the late 1800s. But the reason she maintained her family name was not out of a sense of pride, she insisted, but in keeping with the dictates of her religion.

"In the Sudan we are called after our fathers," she said, "and by the Qur'an we should be called after our fathers." The independent identity that many Western women were now demanding by keeping their maiden names, she told me with a self-satisfied smile, was granted Muslim women thousands of years ago. Like many devout Muslim women, al-Mahdi said she saw no reason to mimic Western women in their feminist struggle, and she was even disdainful of it. Western women had lost all sense of balance in their relations with men, she said, and many had also lost all sense of decency in dress and behavior. On the contrary, Islam, she argued, grants women all the rights they need to lead happy, productive lives, both at home and in society.

During my visit to Khartoum, I met many working women, from doctors at Khartoum Hospital, to professors at Khartoum University, to the female television anchor who served as my shadow throughout my visit. Although the illiteracy rate among Sudanese women in rural areas is estimated to be 82 percent, and 40 percent in urban areas, I had seen the large numbers of female students at the university and had been impressed by the intellectual vigor among students and professors at Afhad College for Women. I had visited a training camp for a women's unit of the Popular Defense Forces and had spoken with female commanders who were readying for duty in the South. I even interviewed two women who had been elected to parliament; they told me the country had designated one-third of the seats in parliament for female delegates. They said the government was so serious about convincing men to allow women into parliament that the seats would not be filled until a woman was elected to fill them.

Although there were women working in the banks and in hotels, I did not see any female shopkeepers at the market in Omdurman, and even the person at the sewing machine who trimmed the fabric for my *thobe* was a man.

According to statistics provided by the Sudanese government, women represent about 49 percent of the population and 22.5 percent of the labor force "in the formal sector." But that figure does not count what is estimated to be an 89 percent labor rate for women in the agricultural sector, nor does it take into account the many urban women who earn money selling tea and providing beauty services, such as hair and skin care to Sudanese women who can afford it. And although Turabi and his wife told me efforts were being made to get women into public sector jobs, official estimates were that women held only 10 percent of such positions.

Turabi had assured me that the government was sincere in its efforts to break the cultural barriers that still kept many women out of public life. As I interviewed women and men in Sudan, I surmised that the government was indeed encouraging the right kind of working women—those who supported the government and who would support its programs. Women who opposed the government, whether Muslims, Christians or animists, faced the same threat as men who opposed the government, my interviews revealed. Human rights agencies had accused the government of detaining both men and women opponents without charge and of having them fired from their jobs.

Al-Mahdi had never worked outside her home. But after her children became adults, she was able to work for volunteer organizations to help orphans in Sudan and to help propagate Islam. She was secretary general of the International Organization for Muslim Women, which she helped found to educate women about the Qur'an's teachings on the role of women in society. The organization sponsored visits to Sudan by women from throughout Africa and the Middle East; during their visit, they also got a primer in Sudan's progress toward an Islamic state. Al-Mahdi said, "We give them lectures in what is happening in the Sudan so that they can reflect on it when they go back to their countries. And this will serve the purpose of what we are trying to do in the world."

What al-Mahdi was trying to do was ignite a woman's movement in the Islamic world to challenge men whom she believed misused the Qur'an to keep their wives uneducated, dependent and subservient. Although she insisted that the truth of Islam was gradually conquering tribalism and backward customs in Sudan, she said religious practices in many parts of the Islamic world were still colored by culture and tradition. Often these traditions distort the true message of Islam, especially with regard to its teachings about women.

Armed with what she believed to be the truth of the Qur'an, al-Mahdi was confident that women all over the Muslim world would win equality with men. During my visit, it seemed as if Turabi and his wife's views about the role of women were far more enlightened than Sudan's cultural tradition. Their vision of equality for women was not the same as that of a Western feminist, but it would allow women to pursue higher education, work for equal wages, participate in public life, compete for political power and even fight in the army. Such ideas are not popular in some parts of the Islamic world, and al-Mahdi told me that Saudi officials had refused to grant her a visa to promote her ideas in their country.

Although al-Mahdi considered herself an "Islamic feminist," she did not believe equality should allow women to abandon their role as primary caregivers in the home. While Western feminists work to increase their power in the workplace, Islamic feminists have goals that are centered around the home. In Sudan, for example, women parliamentarians said they had passed a law that allowed women a full year's leave of absence from their jobs to care for their newborn babies. But even more remarkable, a female legislator told me that the Sudanese parliament had passed a law mandating that new mothers be granted the leave with full pay—a major concession, considering the poor state of Sudan's economy.

I had been talking with al-Mahdi for a while and had treated myself to the abundant buffet set up on a table in Turabi's parlor when he burst into his wife's party with a bunch of dates.

"Guess where these come from?" He beamed, laying them on the table in front of us.

"I don't know . . . I have no idea," I said.

"Please, guess," he insisted.

"Washington?"

"No," he said, "just the opposite. Iraq."

They were gifts of appreciation from the Iraqi people, he said. Sudan had exported several tons of meat as a sign of solidarity with the Iraqis, over the objections of the United States. The United Nations voted to allow Sudan to export the meat, and Turabi considered it a victory over U.S. imperialism.

In some ways, though, Turabi seemed more flexible and modern on religious issues than did his wife, especially in our discussion of polygamy. Turabi sided with those scholars who argue that Islam allows polygamy under strict conditions, but actually discourage the practice. Al-Mahdi encouraged polygamy. This is an intensely debated issue among Muslim women, many of whom now argue that there is justification in the Qur'an for banning polygamy altogether. They say the Qur'an states that men can take other wives only if they are able to treat them with absolute equality. And they point to Surah 4, verse 129, which states: "Ye will not be able to deal equally between your wives, however much ye wish."

Al-Mahdi insisted that polygamy is sanctioned in Islam and that it should be practiced to help Sudan develop. Although al-Mahdi is Turabi's only wife, she said she would welcome him taking another. She giggled softly like a girl when I pressed her as to why he hadn't done so.

As for the issue of divorce, which has been denied to women in some Muslim societies, al-Mahdi believed that Islam does indeed allow a woman to divorce her husband. But while a man can divorce a woman without going to the courts, she said a woman must seek the court's intervention to ensure financial support for the children.

In Islamic law, she explained, a woman is encouraged to have a marriage contract in which she states the reasons for which she would seek divorce. Unlike in Christian doctrine, many Islamic scholars do not consider marriage sacred. It is a contract between two people, she said, albeit an immensely important one. And if a couple divorces, the father is still responsible for the full support of his children.

Although al-Mahdi was firm in her belief that Islam has the best system for the protection of women, her paramount concern was the protection of society. Women have responsibilities in society as do men, she argued. And she supported the stipulation in the Qur'an that in some judicial matters, it takes the testimony of two women to equal that of one man. Many Muslim women argue that such an injunction should be considered in light of the times, when women rarely ventured outside the home and thus were not qualified to offer reasoned testimony in court proceedings. To al-Mahdi, restrictions on women's testimony were intended to apply to women who had little experience in public life. In many parts of the world, she pointed out, women still are illiterate and rarely leave their small communities. To a Western feminist, her arguments are unreasonable. And although I challenged her on this issue for a while, it became clear to me that there was no point in pursuing the matter. She was unwilling to consider the other side of the argument, that gender is not a good basis for excluding women from court proceedings; that there are men who may not be qualified to render rational testimony but who are not excluded on the basis of their sex. Still, she did concede that such restrictions on women are not absolute.

As much as women throughout the world may share in common, my conversation with al-Mahdi revealed how much they also differ in their goals and in the methods they choose to achieve them. There is clearly a wide gap between the feminism of al-Mahdi and that of a Western woman. It is a gap unlikely to be bridged anytime soon.

As I was writing my account of this interview, NPR's "Morning Edition" aired a story about the social effects of putting newborn infants in day care. As more and more American mothers rush back to work after childbirth, researchers concluded, large numbers of babies are suffering. Many of these babies are destined to become overly aggressive as toddlers and unable to form emotional attachments as adults, they warned. Al-Mahdi would have thought such a study was not only a waste of time and money but as ridiculous as I found some of her arguments. That babies need their mothers is not only common sense, she would say, but a sacred truth, at least in the world of Islam.

INTERVIEW WITH WISAL SADIQ ABDEL RAHMAN AL-MAHDI

OCTOBER 1992, KHARTOUM, SUDAN

JD: Now, you are the wife of Dr. Hassan al-Turabi?

WM: Yes, of Sheikh Hassan al-Turabi, yes.

JD: Should I call you Mrs. Turabi, or . . .

WM: No, in the Sudan we are called after our fathers . . . and by the Qur'an we should be called after our fathers.

JD: Wisal al-Mahdi, how do you view your role, the role of a woman in Islam?

WM: Of course in Islam, there is no difference between a man and a woman. Except in specialization of their jobs in life. A woman, of course, is supposed to bring up the children and to look after the house. But in Islam, she could also participate in public life if she has time, if she has no children, has nothing to do at home, if she finds herself able to do the outside job, she can do it. In the early times of Islam, women have participated, even in war. And they have made their journey from Mecca to Medina with Prophet Muhammad, leaving their husbands behind, or leaving their fathers behind . . . and they have believed in Islam even before their brothers, believed in Islam before their menfolk believed in Islam . . . independently.

A woman could be more able than a man. It depends on the brain and the education. Education is a must on a woman as it is a must on a man, by the words of Prophet Muhammad. So, if we find ourselves able to give to the public, to give to our nation, to give to the people at large, we should.

JD: What do you think about those places, though, where women are not contributing? Where women are kept apart, where their activities are restricted?

WM: This is due to the selfishness of men. Men are selfish. They want to keep the woman at home, to deal with the jobs of the house, to take her away from public life. If she does this, they are more comfortable, of course. They can enjoy life better, but in Islam, it is not like this. Islam didn't say so. I told you women went to war with him if they were able to fight. And in one of the battles, Sheikh Muhammad praised the woman because he saw her in front of him defending him in every way that she can. And he praised her by a *hadith*, which we [still] recall. In some countries, of course, the Muslim people didn't come out of their traditions, their old traditions. In the old traditions, when the Prophet Muhammad came to the Arab peninsula, he found that little girls were buried because they were afraid that they would bring shame to the family by committing some act or another, so they buried them while they were alive, and very young. Prophet Muhammad was against this practice, and the Qur'anic verses said that women and men were equal in the eyes of God and that they were the creatures of God and that they should be educated together. Women went to the mosques.

We can see that since early Islamic times, women participated in public life. They participated in political life. They participated in economic life. They participated in family life. They participated in the different aspects of life during Medina days. After that, after some years had gone by, men took all the power in their hands and they kept the women inside. Now in most of the Muslim countries, women are kept at home. They are not supposed to go the mosques. Now, of course, a mosque in Islam is a place where we learn, like the universities now. It is a place where we legislate, where we make *Shurah* that we say our opinion about different aspects of life. And we make laws in the mosque. So if a woman doesn't go to the mosque, she is not participating in public life.

Women at the days of Islam, when Islam was at its full strength, they used to go to mosques, they used to attend the prayers with Prophet Muhammad, and they used to attend what he said, and to hear it and to narrate it. Because most of the *hadiths* of Prophet Muhammad—that is, what Prophet Muhammad said and what Prophet Muhammad educated—were passed to the other Muslim people by his wife, Aisha. And he said, take half of your religion from this lady.

JD: I don't know what question is the really appropriate question to ask in this case. So I'm going to ask you three questions and you take the one you think is the right one. Does there need to be an Islamic women's movement? Is there an Islamic women's movement? Will there be an Islamic women's movement? Which is the question I should ask?

WM: There needs to be an Islamic women's movement. I think Islam has the best code for the rights of women. It gives women the rights they long for. In Europe, women have struggled for their rights until they got it. But by Islam, this was 1,000, maybe 500 years ago, women had those rights by the word of God and by the deeds of Prophet Muhammad. So I think there should be a struggle by Muslim women to tell all the world what is happening in Islam, what Islam says, what Islam gives to women. How Islam puts women in a very high level, and it doesn't minimize the level of women as to men.

JD: Do you see the beginning of such a movement in Islam?

WM: Yes, there is a movement in Islam, by men and women. And in this movement, we uncover to the whole world what we have to offer them by telling them what Islam says about women's status.

JD: Would you tell me a little about your life? You told me you have six children. Have you ever worked? Are you working now in some capacity?

WM: Yes, I have six children. I have never worked to gain money or work which I go to office, or work which I have to do. I do voluntary work. I do work of my own. I participate in societies, in women's emancipation societies. In societies that care for orphans. And now I am the secretary general of the International Organization for Muslim Women.

In this organization, we try to bring women into Khartoum. Our headquarters is in Khartoum. We try to bring some Muslim women from different parts of the Islamic world to stay in Khartoum for about two weeks. To know about Sudan, about the experiment in Sudan with *Sharia* law; how Sudan is trying to institute *Sharia* law in all its different organizations. And they stay with us for about two weeks and they go back to their countries to reflect what is happening.

JD: So, it sounds to me that you are at the core of a women's movement. This is an international Muslim women's organization?

WM: It is the International Organization for Muslim Women.

JD: And it sounds to me like the purpose of that organization is to reeducate women throughout the Muslim world.

WM: Yes, of course.

JD: Do you believe that such a movement, such an organization, may be perceived as a threat to some countries and some regimes because it is indeed giving another version, another interpretation of the role of women?

WM: We are not threatening anybody. You must accept Islam before you abide by it. You must accept it from your whole and your own will. If not, you don't have to come into Islam. So we are not threatening anybody. We are just trying to educate the Muslim women who don't know their Islam, or who don't know how to promote Islam. And we are just trying to let these women go back to their countries and try to bring Muslim women together to make a world movement for their own happiness and for their own good in this life and the life afterwards.

JD: So what you're saying is they're simply taking a message back . . . but what I'm trying to get at is . . . are there some people who don't like a women's movement and that are working against your causes?

WM: No. Where? You mean in the different Muslim countries?

JD: I'm asking, for example, is Saudi Arabia supportive of such a group? Is Iran supportive of such an idea, of an international Muslim women's group?

WM: Yes. What I know of Iran is that the revolution which was made by Imam al-Khomeini, women participated in that revolution. Women went into the streets demonstrating against the Shah of Iran. And they made the change with the Imam al-Khomeini. So what I understand is that they are not against women. What I understand of Saudi Arabia is that they are a little bit conservative. But in Saudi Arabia now, there are educated women, who graduated from universities, and they have their own say in what is happening in Saudi Arabia. And by time [gradually], they may change the status of women in Saudi Arabia. But if they go back to the Qur'an and if they go back to the beliefs of a true Muslim, there is no upper hand over women. Men don't have an upper hand over women. Men are equals of women.

JD: If I could use a word from my culture, which is Western . . . do you consider yourself an Islamic feminist?

WM: Well, [women] are completely different. In the West, they had to fight even for the preliminary rights of women. But in Islam, thousands of years ago, we had these rights by the words of God, which are the utmost source of legislation. We had these rights by the words of Prophet Muhammad and the practice of Prophet Muhammad, who loved his wives. Who had the friends of his late wife Saidah Khadijah, he visited them, he kept friendly relations with them because they were the friends of his late wife. And he used to speak with women, women used to ask him questions. He used to reply to women. And he used to respect women.

JD: But, for example, a Western woman, a secular, Western woman, would want choice. That's the first thing she'd say. I want to be able to do what I want to do. If I want to be a career woman, that's what I'm fighting for. If I want to be a mother who works, then I want companies to help me. The choice of being what you are, is that what the Islamic woman is looking for? What does she want now?

WM: To tell the truth, a woman in Islam, as I believe, should first be responsible and care for her children, her family, because they are the ones who need her most. Because in caring for your family and caring for your children, you care for the nation and you care for the offspring which will come in later times to take care of the specialized jobs of the government and the specialized jobs of society. A woman shouldn't only look for her career. She should look first, if she has children, for the upbringing of these children, the education of these children and care for her husband and her home; and then, if her children are grown ups and they don't need her anymore, she can have spare time to give to the people around her and in public life.

JD: So to a woman in Islam, family and children are first, and everything else comes after that?

WM: I think so because nobody can replace a mother. Nobody. No nanny, no aunt, no grandmother, nobody can replace a mother. So in Islam, I should first care for my children, who are the future citizens of the Islamic society. I should first care for them and if I have time after they are grown-ups and they don't need me perhaps; if they go to schools and I have time, I can participate in public Islamic life.

JD: Looking at [Islam] from the West . . . as women . . . there are some things that are troubling. We see polygamy as being accepted, and that is very unsettling. We see that there are some restrictions on divorce. We see unsettling things such as it takes two women to equal one man in testimony. How have you resolved these things for yourself?

WM: Well, as a believer in Islam, I think that polygamy is not a bad thing at all. Because now in the West men take one wife but they have girlfriends. They have children from those girlfriends. I, myself, as a mother and a wife, I don't like my husband to go and have girlfriends. I would like him to have a clear wife there, whom he is married to by *Sharia* law like me, and her children are the half brothers of my children. This is a quiet position without any complications, without any legal complications.

JD: But there are personal complications, aren't there?

WM: With me? Not at all. Because my father used to have three wives. My grandfather had four wives. He had four wives. He was divorced from some and he had four wives. My great-grandfather had also many. . . . My brother has two wives, my uncle has four wives. Now he is as young as I am. So I don't find it strange, I am used to it. I am a believer in Islam, so as a believer in Islam, I think this is the healthiest position for a man and a woman. Because now in the West, you have a problem with girlfriends. You have a problem with wives who are not clear wives, wives whom men go to by hiding from their wives, and you have the problem of the children after the father dies. So in Islam, this position is legalized by a man having the right to marry more than one wife. I understand it. I believe in it. And I think it is very healthy and I think it is very good in the position of the Sudan, because the Sudan is a vast country, with a population of only 22 million. Every man should marry more than one wife. We will have more children. We will have more people to fill the Sudan and to cultivate the Sudan and to make the Sudanese economic position better.

JD: So you are encouraging polygamy. Do I hear you correctly?

WM: I have been encouraging it all through my life.

JD: But you're the only wife, aren't you?

WM: I am the only wife. It happens to be so. It's not me who marries, it is Hassan. He didn't decide to marry.

[LAUGHTER.]

JD: I see. But you could accept another wife?

WM: Very much. Very much.

JD: But there would be no pain at all?

WM: No pain at all. You know the great Mahdi had so many wives. When I was a child, I was brought up by those wives. They were not my great-grandmother. They were just the wives of my great-grandfather. They used to stay with us at home. They used to cook for us. They used to tell us stories when we went to sleep at night. So I have no war with the position of polygamy. I have all peace and confidence and all friendship with it. So don't ask me about polygamy, I am all for polygamy.

JD: Okay. What about divorce?

WM: Divorce in Islam and in the modern law which was passed by the attorney general in this government, a woman can divorce a man if she makes a clause in the marriage contract. Of course she has to go to court because she has to have money after that. She has to have a salary to keep her children. I think divorce, as Prophet Muhammad has said, it the most hated legitimate thing to God. Divorce is not likable in Islam because it scatters the family. It splits the family. It makes children's life uneasy. It makes the couple's life uneasy. But there is a license for divorce now in Islam. It has always been. So a man can divorce a wife and a wife can divorce a man in Islam by court.

In the case of testimony . . . you asked me about testimony and that two women are equal for one man, this is only in cases which [involve] crimes like killing and so on. In such cases, two women's voice are equal to a man, but in cases where women have more experience, like birth and conception, a woman's testimony is equal to one man's testimony. In some cases, if women know more about some situations, such as she may have been a judge and so on, her voice is equal to one man's. In some cases in which money is involved, like commerce or contracts, women we know they don't go out so much like men, they don't trade like men, they don't make contracts like men. So in such cases, a woman's testimony is half a man. This is according to circumstances. It is not because they think a woman's brain is less than a man's, but her experience in this field is less than a man's experience, that is why they don't take her word. Only two women can equal one man. It is only natural. It is only fair.

JD: It is only natural and it is only fair in certain circumstances? I don't quite get why. Why is it fair, because you're as smart as any man I've ever met?

WM: Yes, I may be as smart as any man is, if I am a judge, for example. If I go to testify in certain cases, my voice is equal to a man's testimony.

But if I am a laywoman, a woman who doesn't know anything, a woman who was just brought out of her kitchen to testify in a criminal case, she cannot . . . She is very sentimental. We know that women are sentimental. They may not even see how the man was trapped, because they saw blood or because they heard him scream. So they can not testify like a man.

JD: You believe there is something different, emotionally, about a woman?

WM: Yes. The sentiment of a woman. Women are more sentimental, especially if they are not experienced . . . if they don't go into life, if they don't get out of their houses, if they don't, for example, make contracts, if they don't travel, they can not testify like a man. That is why Islam says, in such situations, two women are equal to a man. This is not unfair on the woman. It would be unfair on society and it would be unfair on the parties who are standing before the judge if we say a woman's voice is equal to a man's.

JD: But could you envision the day as more and more women in the Sudan become more educated and capable, there would not be that need anymore . . . to say to women that one woman could stand with one man?

WM: I don't think there will be one day when all women will be as good as all men, or all men as good as all women. Because, you see, this differs from person to person, from brain to brain; from experience to experience; from education to education. So this law will be there to preserve the right of the parties who are in front of the court.

JD: But the judge has the right to weigh it?

WM: Yes, to weigh it.

JD: Political Islam, Islam as a religious force is now basically being shaped by men. I'm wondering if as women get more and more influence, what will be their effect on it? Will they make it a faith that is still tolerant and accepting of those who may not feel the same way?

WM: Well, if you want to take Islam to its earliest sources. Islam depends on the Holy Qur'an, the words of God, the words of Prophet Muhammad, the practice of Prophet Muhammad, the learning of those who are very well learned in Islam, they an make judgments if they know these sources very well. These learned sources can be men as they can be women, if women are interested in Islam and if they learn about Islam and if they dig into the sources of Islam and try to take judgment from what happened in the past of Islam and what happened in the different parts of the Islamic world. So there is no way for someone, man or woman, to change Islam. They must take it to its sources. Its sources are all very full of mercy and very far from violence. So, a man cannot change it and make it violent. A woman cannot change it and make it merciful. Because it is already full of mercy.

THREE

ANWAR HADDAM

ISLAMIC SALVATION FRONT, ALGERIA

PROFILE

IT WAS PAST 11 P.M. ON A FRIDAY when Anwar Haddam finally showed up at my home, more than an hour late. I first made contact with the representative of Algeria's Islamic Salvation Front by phone, through a friend of a friend. Even in the United States, the Front was known by its French acronym FIS (Front Islamique du Salut). Haddam suggested we talk, as soon as possible. He wanted to meet in a public place, such as a shopping mall or restaurant, but we settled on my home. And he wanted to meet that same night, at 10 P.M.

About that time, I began watching for Haddam's arrival. I saw a car appear across the street from my house and park. I expected Haddam to emerge, but no one did. Minutes passed and the car remained motionless. From my front window I was unable to see who was at the wheel. Nearly an hour passed and the car never budged. Finally it pulled away as mysteriously as it arrived. Shortly after that, Haddam arrived at my door.

A short, stout man, Haddam showed all the signs of suspicion and tension that I had come to associate with people whose lives were in danger. He was one of a four-man team serving as the FIS's leadership in exile, so he probably had reason to fear. He also had not denounced the violence being done in the name of the FIS in Algeria, and many believed he had links to some of the extremist groups that had formed since the arrest of FIS leaders there.

Haddam clearly distrusted the Western press. When I turned on my tape recorder, he turned on his. And when I tried to pry into his family, he froze. "This topic, I don't want to talk about for security reasons," he said. Even when I tried to elicit information about his life and career inside the FIS, Haddam refused to cooperate. The struggle was too important, he chided me, to reduce it to personal glory. And the leaders of the FIS were too dedicated to allow themselves to become media celebrities. He said he wanted to pursue his mission quietly and without cheapening it with vanity. His armor was impenetrable.

As one of the chief representatives for Algeria's Islamic Salvation Front in the United States and Europe, Haddam was walking a tightrope, trying to convince Western leaders to support democracy in Algeria while trying to avoid being killed by Algerian agents he believed were tracking his every step.

When I interviewed him in late 1993, Haddam was head of the parliamentary delegation of the FIS to Europe and the United States. He was born in 1954 in Tlemcen, Algeria, and studied theoretical physics at the University of Algiers. He also studied nuclear physics at Iowa State University and received a master's of science degree in 1983. He had been on the faculty of the physics department at the University of Science and Technology of Algiers since 1986 and had been involved in the Islamic movement for more than 20 years. He also was a student of Malik Ben Nabi, an Algerian Islamic scholar of considerable renown in North Africa. He was on the executive committee of the Islamic Association for Civilizational Renewal in Algeria, and in 1991 he was elected to parliament as a member of the FIS. But after elections were dissolved by the National Liberation Front, the party holding power, in 1992, Haddam left Algeria for the United States, to serve as a de facto lobbyist for FIS on Capitol Hill and in Europe. "Our main goal," he told me, "is to try to open channels in political circles throughout the Western world to try to break through this silence that

has developed around the situation in Algeria. Actually we look at it as
. . . maybe as a test . . . to the West . . . what is their intention? [What
is] the place of the Muslim world within this so-called new international order?"

Western powers were not prepared to answer that question in
1992; nor were they prepared for an Islamic victory through the ballot
box in Algeria. To the West, Islam is a threat to the stability of the
Middle East and potentially to Western influence in the region. The
fact is that the popularity of Islam as a political movement is a rejection
of Western-imposed structures and concepts. And there are basic
differences between Western philosophies and ideals espoused by
many Islamists. This is especially true when it comes to views of
human rights. Mahmood Monshipouri and Christopher G. Kukla
wrote in the article *Islam, Democracy and Human Rights: The Continuing Debate in the West:*

> The concept of rights under *Sharia* is different from, but not irrevers-
> ibly incompatible with, Western standards. While Islamic countries
> see rights as contingent entitlements and secondary to the welfare of
> the community or society, Western nations view rights as inherent
> and consider the rights of the individual to supersede the rights of
> the state or society. Because of this divergence, it is impossible to
> implement human rights strategies without the two cultures being
> cognizant of each other.
>
> . . . The West needs to concede that its ideals may not be
> desirable or practical in Islamic states."[1]

Such arguments mattered little to France, with whom Algeria fought a
bitter war for independence. France openly supported the government's cancellation of elections, fearful of an Islamic party coming to
power and turning against the West. Although the United States tried
to remain silent, it was clearly ambivalent about developments in
Algeria. The administration of President Bill Clinton eventually broke
the silence in 1994 and urged the Algerian government to begin talks
with the party it had blocked from power: "Algeria's leaders cannot

ease this crisis by overreliance on repressive policies," Assistant Secretary of State Robert Pelletreau said at a symposium in May 1994.

The crisis in Algeria began in 1992 when the National Liberation Front (Front de Libération National or FLN), backed by the army, canceled elections to prevent the FIS from gaining a majority of seats in parliament. The FIS's political popularity surprised both the outside world as well as the Algerian elite. As Remy Leveau, a professor at the Institut d'Etudes Politiques in Paris, wrote in the paper *Algeria: Adversaries in Search of Uncertain Compromises:*

> Although only recently organized, the FIS had managed to bring together in a relatively structured party the areas of influence of the numerous informal groups that claimed to be based on Islam. By using not only the network of mosques, but also teachers from various levels and disciplines, it had very rapidly built up an opposition force that could readily be stirred into action. Its electoral results reflected and added to the disarray in the camps of its opponents. Associated with the idea that it was the only party to voice an absolute opposition to an old order which had no defenders, its success was met with amazement and disbelief.[2]

The FIS's main support came from young, unemployed urban men, many of whom were educated but bitter at the lack of opportunities to use their education. As Leveau stated: "In November 1990, the number of people out of work exceeded 1.5 million and included 40 percent of young people coming onto the labor market.[3]

These unemployed youths were attracted to the FIS as an alternative to the current system and because of the radical rhetoric of some of the group's leaders. Some had promised to exact revenge against the ruling elite that many Algerians blamed for their continuing poverty and for the despotism of the Boumedienne regime. And many FIS leaders had supported calls for trials and imprisonment of officials found guilty of corruption and abuse of power. Thus many FLN leaders had reason to fear a FIS victory. Elections were delayed and then canceled; President Chadli Benjedid was forced to resign when it was feared he was weakening in favor of the Islamists; and a new High

Security Council assumed power. The council included the prime minister, the head of the armed forces and four senior government ministers. It moved quickly to ban the FIS and imprison its charismatic leaders, including its president, Abassi Madani, and deputy president, Ali Belhadj.

Violence did not erupt immediately. Moderates inside the FIS had hoped that the government could be convinced to schedule another round of elections and that it would want to avoid violence. Their hopes proved without basis, and by 1993 Algeria was plunged into what amounted to civil war. Thousands of people, including Algerian and foreign civilians, were killed in the ensuing struggle. During our meeting in the fall of 1993, journalists still were able to work in Algeria, and Haddam offered to help arrange interviews for me with FIS members there. But it soon became evident to me that a split had developed within FIS ranks and that an angry, bloodthirsty element had emerged, eager for revenge. I also learned later that Haddam had been linked to those elements, some of whom had no qualms about murdering journalists. Yet in February 1994, Haddam was quoted as calling for an end to attacks against civilians and foreigners. In our conversation, he made no attempt to hide his support for armed struggle against the government. "We are still open for dialogue to find peaceful political solution," he told me, "but we don't have any other choice."

His support for violence eventually led to his dismissal from the four-member leadership-in-exile committee, as the FIS leaders in the United States and Europe tried to distance themselves from extremists and as reports circulated that the government and FIS leaders in Algeria had begun talking.

When we spoke in my home, Haddam argued the FIS case quietly, sitting on the edge of his chair, downing the tea and cake I placed before him as if eating were a time-consuming nuisance. Haddam brought with him a big, black briefcase filled with pictures and articles about the FIS and Algeria. He brought letters from congressmen supporting his cause and the writings of leaders of the FIS, many of whom had been imprisoned.

Haddam offered this answer for those who worry that the FIS would eradicate democracy if it gained power: "It's better to have . . .

one vote one time than no vote at all. . . . Because the first time free elections ever were held in North Africa was the Algerian experiment."

Haddam said that since political parties were allowed in Algeria in 1989, the FIS has been working within the legal parameters set by the government. It has fielded candidates in local and regional elections, some of whom won and some of whom lost. The FIS accepted its victories and its defeats in these elections, he said. Abassi Madani, the FIS leader, had dedicated himself to democracy, Haddam said. Haddam said he would resign from the FIS if it backed away from democratic principles.

For opponents of Islamic groups, such assurances do little to ease concerns that the mixture of religion and politics dissolves democracy. Yet even some Islamists inside Algeria suspect the true intentions of the FIS leadership. Mahfoud Nahnah, one of the founders of the Islamic movement in Algeria, told me in an interview in Washington during the summer of 1994 that he did not trust the FIS's professed commitment to democracy. He believed that if the FIS had come to power, it would have ended democracy.

Yet even he insisted that the elections should not have been canceled and that the people had spoken. And it is hard to argue, Nahnah said, that canceling elections saved democracy in Algeria.

The struggle in Algeria represents the dilemma that all countries in the Middle East inevitably will face. Opening the doors to democracy means allowing the possibility that Islamic parties will be voted into power. And stifling democracy eventually leads to internal conflict and the threat of civil war. "Sooner or later we are sure we will get into power," Haddam told me. "Our main help is from the Algerian people. . . . The Algerian people are suffering. The Algerian people are really willing for a change."

Although the Algerian government eventually allowed elections in 1995, it refused to include FIS candidates. The elections brought neither the change Haddam said the Algerian people wanted nor satisfaction for the FIS. Today bombs continue to explode in Algeria and people continue to be killed. And FIS leaders remain either in prison or in exile, confident that they will one day come to power.

INTERVIEW WITH ANWAR HADDAM

NOVEMBER 1993, McLEAN, VIRGINIA

JD: Maybe we could begin by your telling me your name and your position.

AH: Yes, I am Anwar Haddam, elected member of parliament of Algeria. I am the head of FIS parliamentary delegation to U.S. and Europe. Our main goal is to try to open channels in political circles throughout the Western world to try to break through this silence that has developed around the situation in Algeria. Actually we look at it as an example of how . . . maybe as a test . . . actually to the West . . . what is their intention . . . the place of the Muslim world within this so-called new international order. We are really very concerned about that. How are we going to view this new century? . . . Will Islam be the new "ism"?

JD: Do you think Islam is the new "ism"?

AH: Well, it's what the West is thinking. Some people take advantage of what's happened in the last 50 years. They need a new "ism" and they thought that this would be Islam. We would like to explain to them that they have to make a difference between Communist ideology and Islam. It is totally different. In Algeria, we have been working for decades. The Algerian Islamic movement is maybe the oldest Islamic movement throughout the world.

JD: Is it?

AH: Yes. We are very concerned about Algeria, and we want to be more realistic and try to find solutions for our own people. And to try to set an example for all the Islamic movements around the world.

JD: At one point, it looked as though Algeria would be an example . . . it looked as if there would be democracy and Islamic parties would be able to participate in that democracy. Then everything fell through. Why? What do you think was the motivation behind it?

AH: Well, the motivation is that maybe some people would like . . . they don't want Islam, political Islam, to gain power through the ballot box. It would change all their theories about this new "ism": new threat for the West; who is against the so-called Western culture and so forth. We do believe that democracy and respect for human rights are human heritage. They are not [limited to] the West, Western heritage.

JD: Are you concerned that the West wants to have a monopoly on democracy? That the West seems to want to say that it must be done our way, or no way?

AH: Actually that is how one can understand the famous statement of Sheikh Ali bin Hajj, the deputy party president of the FIS.

JD: He's in prison now?

AH: Yes, he's in prison now. Some certain media quote him in just the last part of his statement saying that democracy is a saying. Actually what he was saying in his speech was that if democracy means respect for the free will of the people, if democracy means respect for minorities, we are okay. But if they would like to color it through a certain ideology—we do have our own way of life, our own ideology. That's the answer to your question. That makes difference between democracy and secularism. Between democracy as a tool, as a way of making sure the people really accept their government system, their leadership. Now, what color should be given to this government and what cultural background? We have to accept that we are . . . we have to accept the world is a plurality of cultures. This is the main point we would like to raise to the West.

JD: I'd like to talk to you a little about the idea of *Shurah* . . . in the Islamic context, I understand *Shurah* represents democracy because it represents working out the will of the people in a unified way, inside of a discussion and debate, and then coming up with a consensus.

Why do you believe that is such a difficult concept for the West to accept—a democracy that is a different system?

AH: First of all let me make qualifications. The concept of *Shurah* comes from the Qur'an and *Sunnah* and the practice of the Prophet Muhammad, peace be upon Him. It basically lets people take care of their own worldly life. Now, how it should be organized, there are some differences. Which means that we don't have specific texts to have to stick to. Now, we might have two different ideas on this . . . the Sudanese experiment.

JD: That's right, which is against parties.

AH: Maybe because they started from their own difficulties which they are facing. They had political parties maybe based on tribes. And they have so many [tribes]. How they are going to succeed, we don't know. But we do believe, since we accepted to run, we accept the system. This is the main idea. We do believe that in this modern time, this is the best way, to [ensure] that the will of the people will be respected. We have to find the guardians, guarantee, to make sure that people are really represented nationwide. This is the main difference between us and the Sudanese.

JD: The real fear, I think in the West, is that when they think of Islamists, they think of religious domination. They think of one man, one vote, one time. I would like you to tell me personally how you feel about the possibility of Islamists, your party, being voted out of office. After you win, can you be voted out of office? And whether your views represent the majority or the minority within your organization.

AH: Actually it's better to have, maybe, one vote one time than no vote at all. This is one thing. Because the first free elections ever held in North Africa was the Algerian experiment. And then we had two elections, actually; [the first were] local government [municipal] elections [held in 1990]; and we are experienced, we are managing local governments in the municipalities for more than a year and a half. Because of this genuine experiment, the Algerian people voted again for the FIS. And we should not forget that in the local government election, the rules were different from the parliamentary elections. We had what's called "proportional" elections. So we had so many municipalities, councils, so many state departments working together under the FIS leadership. There was no problem at all, even though the central government tried to take away some of the prerogatives of the municipality councils. And so people saw this genuine experiment, that's why they voted for the second time for the FIS for parliamentary elections.

JD: I see what you're saying. So there already had been a history of Islamists working in the system at a lower level?

AH: People feel that. They had experienced that for more than a year and a half. Since June 1990 we have been working. So we are not just talking like that. We practiced that. Because it was stated many times by Sheikh Abassi Madani, who said we cannot have a strong state without having strong opposition. He stated it on TV many times. It was well documented. He even stated that if the FIS would get away from this, he would be the first who would resign.

And I will state the same thing on behalf of all our elected members of parliament. We have been elected for a certain mandate, for a certain program. If somehow there would be some changes, we would be the first to resign.

JD: How old is the FIS?

AH: The multiparty is not that long in Algeria. It started by the new constitution in February 1989 . . . Our Islamic movement is indigenous; before the independence movement. In modern times, it came from the creation of Algerian Muslim Scholars Association. It was created in 1962.

JD: Who was the founder?

AH: Sheikh Abd al-Hamid Ibn Badis. Actually he was working by himself since 1913. The French people, they make big mistake, but it was good for us. While they were having the first meeting of the centennial of the colonialization of Algeria, they stated openly "now Islam is out of Algeria forever."

JD: Did they?

AH: Yes. That's what made these *ulama* get together and create this association and start a program of reconstruction of theology in society. Because it was actually financing also the Tunisian movement and the Moroccan movement. The idea of trying to reconstruct the society, to see exactly what are the problems of society. That's [what] one of our leaders, Ben Nabi, used to say. He said that people are not colonized unless they have the ability to be colonized. It's because of us. This is our approach, which differs totally, maybe, from other Islamic movements. Yes, the colonialists, they have part of this responsibility, but still, it's because of us.

JD: You allowed yourselves to be colonized?

AH: Yes, we allowed ourselves to be colonized. We allowed ourselves to be in this situation, after all. That's why our movement was always trying to let people be aware of their situation. And you know, once people get aware of their situation . . . you can get them out of it. That's why people should understand what's happening now, since more than a year and a half, actually since the fifth of May . . . that's why I was focusing on this date, the fifth of May 1992, they decided that they have to go to gain back their free will, free choice, even by the armed struggle.

JD: What do you think of the idea of armed struggle?

AH: We don't find any other solution, actually. We are still open for dialogue to find [a] peaceful political solution. But we don't have any other choice.

JD: So basically what I'm hearing is that you're saying you've been forced . . . you've been forced into any armed struggle because the government will not talk with you.

AH: And actually this is a fact. It was the Algerian Islamic movement who was behind forcing the ruling party to open to a multiparty system . . . We forced them, we suggest to them, the best way to get out is to open to a multiparty system. We were behind that. And even after the local government elections, when the government was not able to undermine the Islamic municipalities by taking many of their liberties, it tried to change the electoral vote. That's why the June 1991 event happened. You had this political struggle, political strike, to try to make them change. And people died for that. We could have done . . . at that time . . . a revolution, an Iranian-type revolution. But we refused that. We said we want to go back to the ballot box . . . And finally we won. They changed the law and we won [the] election even though our leaders were in jail. Which means that it is not a movement based on just a few members of the FIS.

JD: I have heard and read that the conditions of the jails are horrible.

AH: Oh yes, I'll give you some of the documentation of Amnesty International. Even what's happening lately, there have been more than 250 death penalties. Thirteen of them have been executed horribly. And one of them is an elected member of parliament. The situation is getting worse, actually. We did have, we still have, concentration camps in the Sahara Desert in Algeria, and no one is talking about that.

JD: What do you think the West should be doing? What should the United States be doing? And what is the reception that you personally have had as you've talked to congressmen?

AH: Well, what we are trying to ask is not to look at Islam as a new threat of "ism". We are not here trying to threaten the interests of the West. It's better for them to start, maybe, to look after their long-range interest instead of looking after their short-range interest. They have to change in their foreign policy . . . maybe it's time for the U.S. government not to deal with authoritarian regimes but to start thinking of people. But we are ready for cooperation between two civilizations, on a partnership basis. What we are sure of is that we are refusing exploitation.

JD: You think the West, or the United States, still looks to Africa for exploitation?

AH: I think so. I think so. Otherwise how come they are still supporting the ruling party? They were very active in implementing democracy in Haiti. He [Jean-Bertrand Aristide] was supposed to be a fundamentalist . . . a Christian fundamentalist? How come they implemented it there?

JD: But it's not done yet.

AH: Still—

JD: Well, they're working on it.

AH: Yes, they're working at that. And still, as you see, the Committee of Foreign Relations, they're still talking about the threat of Islam. They had a statement lately, just a few days ago. It was a good statement, anyway, but still it is not enough.

JD: How have you personally been received?

AH: Actually, these kinds of activities, I'd rather keep a low profile. I do understand it is a new administration. They are trying to shape up their foreign policy. But meanwhile, our people are suffering. So, it's very hard to explain. It's going too slow, I think.

JD: So you have been seeing congressmen?

AH: Yes.

JD: And people have been receptive?

AH: Yes, they have been receptive. But it seems that each time our case is put in the back of what's going on around the world.

JD: You're used to being in the United States. Do you think people have the wrong idea about Islam?

AH: Actually, I don't blame them, the American people. You the media, you have very powerful positions. And unfortunately, certain classes of media are not that helpful in trying to be really what they are supposed to be, that is, a bridge between our two civilizations.

JD: Were you always in politics?

AH: Actually for us, we cannot distinguish between being [an] Islamic activist and political activist. We do view Islam as a whole way of life.

JD: But did you always run for office?

AH: No, we didn't have this opportunity before. It was just one-party rule.

JD: What was your profession?

AH: I was teaching at the University of Algiers. I have been involved in the Islamic movement for almost 20 years in Algeria.

JD: And how did you get involved in the Islamic movement? How did you personally decide to take that route as opposed to a secular route?

AH: I don't know if it is a good time to talk about this, really, when my brothers are suffering . . . just to be more publicized. It should not be out of proportion. There are so many better than me.

JD: Are most of the people in the FIS intellectuals? Or do they come from all walks of life?

AH: Our movement focused mainly on two aspects: the Islamization of the intelligentsia and to have a popular basis. That's what made us successful in the political activities.

JD: How successful have you been Islamizing the intelligentsia?

AH: Actually, we have been the first to get more middle-class intellectual people to be members of the party. For instance, in our electoral list, out of 430 running for parliamentarian elections, we had more than 200 Ph.Ds. Probably more than U.S. candidates. This will show that actually the intelligentsia was ready. They are still ready to help.

JD: And what about your support with women?

AH: One may say that we won this election because of the women. This is fact, statistical fact. The majority of women actually voted for the FIS. Because, as I tell you, they have been experiencing with the local elections, people they saw, especially the women, how the FIS were dealing with them. There was no more, what you are facing here, the harassment of women in the work system. The woman has seen that they were respected as a human being.

JD: Among the people elected in the FIS, were there any women parliamentarians elected?

AH: No, because we were sure we were going to face the armed struggle. So it was not wise to let the women be represented.

JD: But the FIS has nothing against women taking a leadership role?

AH: No, if they are elected. The question is how do we see society. We have a different approach.

JD: Tell me about how you view society.

AH: Well, the problem is not men or women, men versus women . . . the problem is the whole society. The problem is that, we don't see confrontation between men and women, but complementary. We see woman as a human being, as her full contribution within the society. But we are sure that . . . we will not let her be abused or be used as sex object, or to be harassed or so. Women feel safe. That's why they voted for us.

JD: In Algeria, do many women work?

AH: Oh yes. Many of them are supporting themselves. Because one-tenth of the society has been killed because in the war of liberation. Women are used to being in active life. My sisters, most of them are medical doctors. My wife also is a medical doctor. They are active.

JD: Is your family in Algeria?

AH: This topic, I don't want to talk about for security reasons. They are not in Algeria.

JD: Are you concerned about your personal safety?

AH: Of course, but I don't care. There is a risk.

JD: There is a risk from the government?

AH: Yes . . . what we used to say . . . what is written is your fate. Whenever it is written that I will die, I will die.

JD: Yes, I thought the main danger would be if you were in Algeria. Once the exiles were out, there was not real threat outside of Algeria.

AH: I may be a special case. Because I am giving them a lot of trouble. That fact that I go directly to political centers.

JD: What do you foresee for Algeria?

AH: Two alternatives. One is they will go for an escalation of violence and so forth, which means that we have to increase the armed struggle and it will be maybe hard to implement our project and our program peacefully. Or maybe, there will be some financial—some pressure from the West. We hope it is from the United States.

JD: Do you expect that?

AH: If they are talking long-range interest, it's better for the U.S. to make pressure on the junta to go back to the free elections. I hope that they will. Now there is some talking about going back to dialogue.

JD: That's what I had heard.

AH: There are some people who are trying to do their best. One of them who was assassinated by the junta. That is Merbah, Kasi Merbah . . . he was very active in trying to reach a settlement. But he was assassinated . . . Unless there is cooperation from the West, the hardliners in the junta, they will not accept dialogue.

JD: So, the one case where the United States could show a clear commitment to democracy and improve relations with Muslims would be in Algeria?

AH: Would be in Algeria. And we are leading the movement to a proud Muslim world.

JD: Are many of the leaders of the FIS Western educated? And familiar with Western culture?

AH: Yes, they could be a bridge between our two civilizations, actually.

JD: Now tell me, what happens if you win your struggle, but with no help from the U.S.? What happens then?

AH: Well, it would depend on in what situation we would get our country. Actually, we need stability. We need a peaceful situation where we can implement our agenda. So, I don't think that we need any confrontation . . .

JD: It's just that I think . . . take the case of Iran. My concern is that if FIS wins their struggle and comes to power, but believes the West was helping to keep this [current] regime in power, there's not going to be pleasant relations between the new Islamic government and the West. And I'm just concerned about what would be the repercussions?

AH: Actually, it's very difficult for me to try to make comparisons like that. I don't want to go into this kind of discussion.

Let's say we have a totally different experience. We do insist in saying that we don't aim to establish a full theocratic system. People understand what they want after this. We don't believe that there is a divine authority, that people come to power due to that divine authority. So this is one main difference [from Iran]. The second difference that I said, in our philosophy, it's because of our situation that we are poor, that [we] have been colonized, that we are not strong enough. It's not because of the West. So basically, we are not against anybody. We are not blaming anybody. It's a totally different approach. People should understand what we are talking.

This is the message that we are trying to send . . . Sooner or later, we are sure we will get into power. Of course, it will be hard to forget, especially the French, what they are doing. So, even though there is certain hatred within the population, based on our philosophy, we will look at the situation. We will not have in our mind any enemies to be targeted . . . unless the West will build a new iron curtain between us and you, we will not build it. We are sure that we are going to be an influence in other Muslim states, especially in the area. We are the same people, in the Maghreb. Sure, the people will be influenced by our experience.

JD: Where is your biggest help coming from? Is there any country or group of people that's really there helping you?

AH: That's what bothers many people. Our main help is from the Algerian people. Really, I mean what I am saying. What people should understand, the Algerian people are suffering. The Algerian people are really willing for a change.

JD: But are there any other governments that are helping you?

AH: No, no government at all.

JD: Are there any that you really feel are opposed, are actively working against you?

AH: The French are actively working against us.

JD: What is the attraction [of Islamic parties]? People say it's an economic attraction. People say that when times are bad, they look to Islamists because they go into the community . . .

AH: That's what I'm saying. What's wrong with that? People they see. If they say that its economics that's the attraction. That means that they would like a better life. If people see that they would have better life with the Islamists, what's wrong with that? There is very much a contradiction in their thinking, actually. They say it's [an] economic situation, that's why they are supporting FIS, so let's give them the best solution economically. And there were free elections. You propose your agenda or program. The FIS proposes its program. Fifty political parties propose their programs. People have chosen this [the FIS] program. People would like better life and they believe it would be with the FIS. What's wrong with that?

JD: How many members are in the FIS? Was there ever a number count?

AH: No, it's very hard to do that. We can't.

JD: You've mentioned several writers . . . like Ben Nabi . . . would you say that his writings have influenced the founders of the FIS or the leaders now? If I had to pick some writings of people that have influenced the leaders now, who would they be?

AH: Well, let's say, Sheikh Abd al-Hamid Ibn Badis. He wrote a paper in 1938, "The Governing System in Islam." If you don't mind, in a few minutes, I will quote you something from [Ibn Badis]. "No one has the right to manage the affairs of the people without their consent. It is incumbent on the people to delegate power or to take it away. The people will not be governed except by the law that they choose and know the benefits for themselves. Therefore they obey the law because it is their own law. Not because it is imposed on them by any other authority, be it an individual or a group." He said this in January 1938. And then, when we are talking about the multiparty system, he said, "The people reserve the right to discuss their matter with those in positions and hold them accountable for their actions . . . and make sure they follow the choice of the society, not their own." Those are the founders of the Algerian Islamic movement as far as ideology is concerned. And Ben Nabi, his main idea was that people are colonized because they have the ability to be colonized.

JD: Except isn't that blaming the victim?

AH: But why do we have this mentality of being colonized? If you change the mentality of the people, you change everything. The starting point, if there would not be change in the mind of the people, there would never be intifada. Because in Palestine, there had been deep work within the population for having this intifada to change the mind of the people. The starting point is to change the mind of the people.

Did you know Abassi Medani was one of the founders of the FLN? Let me read you some of what he wrote in jail . . . just last year: "To be frank with you, even though that I am in jail, the political action, we cannot leave it, if God wills. Because political work is a part of our religion. Political work by itself is enough to achieve the Islamic system right now. If we are allowed to be free, political work is enough to make changes."

JD: But does he then go on to say that there needs to be armed struggle now?

AH: Of course, I mean, nobody can be against it. How can you be against people who are trying to get back our free choice?

FOUR

MAHFOUD NAHNAH

ISLAMIC SOCIETY MOVEMENT (HAMAS), ALGERIA

PROFILE

MAHFOUD NAHNAH, leader of Algeria's Islamic Society Movement, sat across from me in the basement of a Springfield, Virginia, town house that served as the offices of an Islamic think tank called the United Association for Studies and Research (UASR). With a plastic fork and a triangle of pita, Nahnah scooped up large portions of a chicken and rice concoction as he described the mayhem that had enveloped his homeland. His large and sturdy frame was proof that he was a hearty eater, and he wasted little time finishing the ample portions that spilled out of his take-out carton. He wore a pinkie ring of silver, in keeping with the conservative Islamic prohibition against men wearing gold, and his salt-and-pepper beard was cropped neatly. He was described to me by one Muslim scholar as the "grandfather of the Islamic movement" in Algeria, although he was as openly critical of the Islamic Salvation Front, known as the FIS, as he was of government efforts to suppress it.

Nahnah spoke no English and I tried to exchange a few pleasantries in Arabic. His face seemed to explode with delight every time I tried to communicate in his language. I was grateful that rather than being disdainful of my far less-than-perfect Arabic, Nahnah took considerable enjoyment in witnessing a foreigner trample clumsily through the grammatical landmines of classical Arabic, a language heralded for its poetic grace. The wrinkles at the corner of his eyes told me he was used to finding humor in life, and he rarely missed an opportunity to make a joke. He seemed particularly fond of plays on words and pointed out to me the phonetic similarity between his name, Nahnah, and the Arabic word for mint in the tea I was drinking—naanaa. Of course, I consistently confused the words, often calling him Mr. Mint, which never failed to elicit his hearty laugh.

Nahnah had been invited in August of 1994 to the UASR office to talk about the crisis that had ensued in Algeria since the ruling party canceled elections in 1992. The country was embroiled in a virtual civil war between the government and militants supporting the Islamic Salvation Front, which had won the first round of national elections. There was little doubt that the FIS was about to assume power in Algeria, Nahnah said. But Nahnah and his party, the Islamic Society Movement (HAMAS), opposed the FIS, and he was convinced that once the FIS gained power in Algeria, it would put an end to democracy. "That's not my conclusion," he told me shortly before his remarks at the UASR offices. "That's from reading their literature."

There were solid differences between the FIS and Nahnah's HAMAS, although they both are considered Islamic parties working to build a society based on Islamic principles. HAMAS was considered more moderate than the FIS. Nahnah's HAMAS had close ties to the international Muslim Brotherhood, while FIS leaders prided themselves on being rooted in Algeria's unique history. At least for the record, both groups said they promoted democracy.

But while leaders of FIS said they were committed to democracy and plurality, Nahnah doubted that commitment. He had watched the FIS movement and its leaders over the years, he said, and although he respected them, he was convinced they were using democracy to subvert it. He was equally convinced that FIS leaders-in-exile, such as Anwar Haddam, were supporting militant groups. At the time of this interview, Haddam was living in the United States and serving as a de facto lobbyist for the FIS with the Clinton administration and on Capitol Hill.

"I can say very clearly that Anwar Haddam is sponsoring this Islamic Armed Group," Nahnah said. "If he is sponsoring this kind of movement, that means he is sponsoring their actions. Or he has a double way of speaking." The Islamic Armed Group was one of the most notorious of the Islamic groups that split from the FIS. The Islamic Armed Group had claimed responsibility for many of the assassinations and bombings in Algeria after 1993.

Speaking in Arabic to a gathering mostly of Islamists in the United States and Western experts, Nahnah was blunt in his assessment of the causes of the violence that had torn Algeria apart. He was equally blunt when he spoke to me privately and in his written answers to questions that I sent to him in Algeria. One specifically asked him who was to blame for the violence in his country.

Nahnah explained that Algeria's one-party rule was the main reason for the explosion of violence in Algeria, a situation that he said affected even moderate Islamic groups such as his Islamic Society Movement.

"When I talked about radicalism and the transformation of radicalism to extremism, my fingers are in the fire," he told his audience at the UASR offices. "My movement suffered from that transformation very, very badly. I didn't want to touch on this part of the issue, but my aide, Sheikh al-Muslimanie, was killed, was slaughtered a few months ago by the Islamic movement. He was slaughtered with a knife."

"Two months ago, my driver was killed," Nahnah continued. "My car was stolen and he was shot to death." Nahnah said that threats had been made on his life and that he had survived several ambushes.

Nahnah was born in Algeria in 1938 and served with the National Liberation Front. Since 1960, he had been a teacher in Algeria and had long been associated with the Islamic movement there, although not with the FIS. His organization, known by its acronym HAMAS (not connected to the Palestinian HAMAS), also participated in the 1992 elections. But unlike the FIS, with a reported following of at least 3 million of Algeria's 13 million voters, Nahnah said his party had a following of only 400,000.

In his remarks at the UASR offices, Nahnah spent much of the time explaining the reasons for the popularity of the FIS and for the radicalism and violence now gripping Algerian society.

> Why are people attracted to the FIS? Is it love for Abassi Medani or Belhadj? Is it love for the FIS? Is it love for the Islamic programs and solutions? Or is it a way of taking revenge against the ruling party that took over more than 30 years ago?
>
> Some of our Arab friends know that in the big cities of Algeria, like Algiers, between 15 and 20 people live in one room . . . and they take shifts in sleeping. There is a big gap between the haves and have-nots, the elite who have all the money and the majority who have nothing. The officials in the elite can do whatever they want without any account-ability to anyone. . . . I am telling you all of these things because this is the basis for what we are experiencing right now, all this violence.

Nahnah said the Islamic movement started in Algeria more than three decades ago as an underground movement that opposed the government of Ben Bella. Nahnah had worked to bring multiparty democracy to Algeria since the repressive regime of Boumedienne. In 1976 he was arrested for working against the state and was sentenced to 15 years in prison, although he served only four years.

Algeria's governments since independence had been despotic and corrupt, Nahnah said, and the FIS's calls for seeking out corruption and punishing those responsible for it fed the anger of the people against the ruling elite.

> It is well known that Algeria produces oil and gas. Some Algerians go to Saudi Arabia and see the results of the oil wealth there and then they ask themselves what happened to our national resources. We are as rich in resources as Saudi Arabia and other countries. So they start wondering what happened to our money and our wealth.
>
> A student comes back from Europe or the United States and cannot find a house, can not find even the chalk to write with on the blackboard when he wants to teach. . . . You can find a university professor who lives in his car and hasn't even a room to go to. Sometimes he lives with a student that he teaches. And sometimes

he ends up living in the rest room of the house. . . . That's why we say that radicalism in Algeria was fed through the deteriorating economic and social condition.

Although he said he understood the roots of the violence in Algeria, Nahnah did not condone it. And although he agreed with the FIS that the government committed a grave injustice in canceling the 1992 elections, he lambasted the violent reaction that resulted.

"We always said the government had no right to steal the election from the people," he said. "But also we reject the notion that people should get their rights back by committing more injustice and atrocities. There were other solutions other than picking up arms."

Yet Nahnah maintained that the government was greatly responsible for radicalizing the FIS and for forcing young people into militancy. "People right now are very angry with the government because of its violations and atrocities and its indiscriminate killings . . . slashing the throats, without due process. . . they do not allow any chance for defense. . . . Some security people of the government take people out of their homes . . . and people are very angry." Nahnah held firm to his contention that the only hope for Algeria lay in accepting democracy, a democracy consistent with Islamic values. "We need a plan to marry democracy with Islamic values," he said. "I join the word *Shurah* [the Islamic concept of decision making through consultation] with democracy, to create *Shurahcracy*. . . . We want a home-grown plan and project that can respond to the needs of our people."

"The bottom line is to go back to the election boxes," he concluded, "and everybody should respect the results."

As the summer of 1994 was ending, there was some hope that Nahnah was about to get his wish. He had just learned that the government had agreed to a national dialogue, and he was cutting short his stay in the United States to participate in the talks. There also were signs that private talks had begun between the government and FIS leaders. The government had released some FIS members from prison and had closed all but one of the brutal desert prisons that were decried by international human rights groups.

While he was suspicious of the FIS and doubted its commitment to democracy, Nahnah knew that there would be no peace in Algeria, no chance for democracy, without its participation. He also knew that with or without the FIS, Algeria had a long and dangerous road to traverse before it would achieve anything resembling democracy.

"You here in the United States did not enjoy full democracy except after a long battle, a civil war," he told us. "Democracy in France struggled for 90 years. In Algeria, we think we can benefit from two experiences: the Islamic experience and the human experience. One civilization starts where the others stop."

As Nahnah put it, he was heading back into the "fire of the volcano" to see if he could help quench it. Still, he went back fully believing there was not much reason to trust the sincerity of any of the major parties vying for power; and there was even less reason to believe that his party would benefit. "Our plan is to participate," he said, "not to take power."

The killing of his aide and his driver were attempts to draw him into the violence, he said, and his wife and children also faced danger in Algeria. But Nahnah said he would continue to preach for dialogue and to promote peace in his country.

More than six months later, when I sent him a list of questions to get more information about his movement and his ideas, little progress had been made in resolving the crisis in Algeria. Government security agents and their opponents were still killing each other daily, and the Algerian people continued to live in a state of siege. Months later, Nahnah ran in new elections from which the FIS were excluded. Not surprisingly, his party did not win. The same people remained in power. And, not surprisingly, the violence did not end.

INTERVIEW WITH MAHFOUD NAHNAH

MARCH 1995
(WRITTEN ANSWERS FROM ALGIERS, TRANSLATED FROM ARABIC)

JD: Would you tell me a little about the Islamic Society Movement and its goals in Algeria? And how do they differ from the Islamic Salvation Front known as the FIS?

MN: The Islamic Society Movement is the daughter of Algerian society with all the burdens it carries of suffering, hope and ambition and with all the varieties of its cultural and educational backgrounds. All of this connects the Algerian people with Arabic and Islamic society as a continuation of its faith and ambition. The Algerian people are connected to African and Middle Eastern society by geography, life experience, and most of all, by the unity of fate. The Islamic Society Movement depends on three principles: *al alem* [knowledge], *al amel* [action] and *al adil* [justice]. And it has three characteristics: *al mauthoueiah* [objectivity], *al wakaeiah* [realism] and *al marhaleiah* [gradualism]. The goal of this movement is changing the system of dictatorship and oneness [one-party rule] through peaceful ways involving culture, politics and religion based on the idea of *Shurah* and the principle of democracy.

Our movement rejects using violence and aggression as a method. This movement has pressured the authorities peacefully for about a quarter of a century calling for plurality and freedom. Many of our supporters have been fired from their jobs and deprived of a means of livelihood.

Our movement's goal is to establish a society on the basis of Islam and on the characteristics of the Algerian people and to keep its identity and humanity. The movement seeks to motivate the Algerian people to build their civilization through cooperation, negotiation and living together in mutual respect and protecting religious, cultural, ethnic and linguistic minorities. We base this on the Qur'an, which says there is no compulsion in religion and you cannot dominate others.

Since it was established, the movement has always called for the independence of the legislative system and separation of political authority from religious authority; rejecting fanaticism and dictatorship. The movement insists on the necessity of mutual cooperation in decision making and in shaping public life to guarantee dignity and humanity, encouraging dialogue among both friends and opponents.

The movement seeks to establish the idea of political participation and cooperation without denigrating the efforts of those with different ideas. And the movement seeks to help the Algerian authorities recognize the necessity of participation for everybody in protecting civilization on the material, spiritual and intellectual levels. We reject revolutionary change and radical methods because we believe it is not beneficial because of the bad effects it will cause on individuals and society and the negative marks it will leave on relationships and achievements.

That's why our movement is a continuous movement and not a one-time occurrence, which would necessarily involve corruption and pollution. Whatever aggression the Algerians have inherited from the French and whatever aggressions came after that because of the dictatorial, socialist system, this aggression cannot be removed easily. Removing it needs educational, political, cultural and social efforts, double those which have gone into the self-destructive armed struggle. What we are trying to do is establish a program of moderation and balance. We recognize that there are many profound differences of opinion concerning this kind of program, but we are convinced of the necessity of combining goals with noble methods, which is the backbone of the Islamic way. We promote dialogue and nurturing the individual and society to promote balance and moderation.

JD: What about the current government in Algeria? Has it contributed to the violence? Could it have done more to prevent the catastrophe that has struck Algeria?

MN: There is no doubt that the authority which is now in Algeria is the main reason for the aggression. This relates to the ruling party, which was a cover for a political system in which the rulers could not recognize how to separate the ruling party from the authority. This intermingling between the party and the authority was so obvious that the party is the authority and the authority is the party. They have tried to deny the relationship and its role in causing the violence. On the other hand, because the crisis has reached the peak and given birth to this severe aggression, some would love to call it a newly emerging fad or blame it on the attempts at plurality which produced Islamic parties headed by the Islamic Salvation Front (FIS). The result of all this is that the two-faced political system is pointing an accusing finger at the Islamists to show the [Algerian] people and the international community that the government has no relation whatsoever with the crisis.

The government is trying to find excuses for its practices, which take a hard, radical stance and which have caused fear both inside Algeria and internationally.

To deal with such issues is very difficult, and there are differing opinions on how to deal with it. Still, the West and America are trying to find the best method to deal with it, and their efforts are still in the beginning stage. The West and America haven't seen clearly how to deal with unelected systems, and they still don't know how to deal with the Islamic tide both in Algeria and internationally. This tide really brings assurance, trust and stability to allow true development in the next millennium, which is only a few years away. Algerian authorities could have dealt with the crisis by looking wisely at the ones who created this crisis. That way the government could be fair to the citizens, unite the country and reject violence. The government would have gained popular support inside the country and internationally. This would have supported constitutional law and prevented the avalanche that has destroyed the country and benefited the arms merchants. The government could have done one thing—stage new elections. This would have been preferable to choosing a collective leadership council, importing a president and imposing an authority. It would have allowed the country's leaders to have popular support.

We in our movement see that if it was possible to achieve a peaceful solution, it could only be through allowing the people to have a voice in the system and in the people in leadership, under the framework of the principles outlined in the constitution of February 1989.

JD: What role do you feel the West should play in helping to end the bloodshed in Algeria? Specifically, what should the United States do?

MN: The best role that the West generally and America specifically can play is to announce their political neutrality. Then it should announce an increase in economic and financial cooperation and commercial trade. This announcement would cause embarrassment among all the sides engaged in the violence. Algerians have a special sensitivity to others interfering in our affairs. This nonintervention is necessary for Algeria to be able to find a way to exit from this crisis and to solve our problems without interference. We realize that democratic change would also bring with it great suffering, but we are Muslim people, we must reject spilling blood among believers.

Second, increasing economic cooperation and commercial exchange would help stop the violence because the poor economy in Algeria contributes to the disintegration of society in all aspects. Increasing financial cooperation would alleviate the economic and social suffering and protect Algeria, the heart of the Maghreb.

The Western stand has been biased and selective, which made the West lose its obligation to democracy. We are shocked at the impression the West has of Islam and of its attitudes toward dialogue and the principles of forgiveness. The West has clear excuses concerning its mistrust of Islam and Muslims because of the declarations and acts that have been exaggerated by the media, which is also biased, I am sorry to say. The West could have accepted the [Islamic] experiment in Algeria and it could have announced [its] fears and concerns. Also, the victorious Front [FIS] could have condemned officially any incorrect announcements or actions on the part of its supporters.

The victors were impatient, energized by the enthusiasm of the people. And the West hastened to judge the victory. Now they are paying the price for their impatience. In spite of that, some of the more wise people in the West are starting to recognize that among the Islamists, there are moderate examples with whom they can deal with trust. Our movement is waiting [for the West] to understand good from evil and to differentiate its interests from its noninterests.

JD: Do you believe the FIS would have become dictators? Do you think they would have established a truly democratic government? Or would they have held onto power by any means necessary, including violence?

MN: We were aware from the beginning that we were going into a very dangerous and slippery way. The announcements and the stance and the writings and the actions [coming from FIS leaders] were not encouraging as far as democracy was concerned. It did not seem to be leading the people to gaining freedom and freeing themselves of oppression. In spite of that, to issue a hasty judgment on an immature experience is not an objective way of thinking. Establishing a political system built on Islam should be centered on certain principles. If there is a detour from these principles, then the system cannot survive. First, *Shurah* [consultation] should be its principle, and democracy should be the system used to apply this principle in all aspects of life. Second, justice; third, equality. If the Islamic system lacks one of these, you cannot call it an Islamic system. Neither the people nor the political class would agree to that. This is what history tells us.

JD: Do you see any hope to end the bloodshed in Algeria?

MN: The situation in Algeria is similar to some in other parts of the world and could creep into other parts of the world if the focus remains on demolishing it [unrest] instead of curing it scientifically and objectively. The problem of aggression now in Algeria is being attacked in the name of demolishing terrorism. This makes the crisis worse. The security authorities believe they should tackle the problem by widening their base and not even trying to gain the trust of the people or limit the powers of the security agents. But they are like an army marching in place. They should use a variety of approaches to cure the problem. One of them is the law. They should use it to go after criminals, whoever has committed a crime.

JD: Do you believe Algeria eventually will have an Islamic government? Will it necessarily be opposed to Western interests?

MN: We believe Algeria is a Muslim society so it should be crowned by Muslim rule which springs from the people. Not a dictatorship and not a theocracy. What happened to Algerian society was a manifestation of dictatorship and trying to push people aside. The gap between the political system and the people has widened. People have the right to demand a system that agrees with their hopes, their characters and their goals. Any political system, whether this one now or which might come later, should be considered a guard of society, both in domestic and international interests. We believe that Algeria and other Islamic countries will be ruled by Islam, whether today or tomorrow. The Islam which will rule it is the Islam which protects man and his interests and also protects nations and countries and their interests, and which protects the political relations and diplomatic relations and strategic relations.

The West and Islam have common interests that should be protected. These interests should be maintained and developed in a way which will serve the interests of both nations. It is not logical that Islam be a factor in spreading corruption on earth. But Islam should be a factor in developing cooperation and investment. In our movement, we are concerned about establishing a mentality of living together respecting each other and participating in all the activities of society and building, whether male or female. The historic experience of Islam proves its ability to accept other believers who are different from Islam and give them a role in the political and economical society. Any political idea contrary to this is fated to international isolation.

JD: What advice would you give to Western leaders who are trying to develop a foreign policy with regard to Algeria?

MN: The Western systems and organizations are well aware of their current interests and their strategy, and they do not need our advice. But we the nations of the Third World, who are eager to be free and to exit from retardation and poverty, believe:

First, that Western countries should be obliged to maintain neutrality, which will guard the sovereignty of all nations as well as relations between nations.

Second, the West should adhere to international law which respects human rights and self-determination.

Third, it should stop selectively calling for democracy and human rights. The West should abolish its fear of Islam and reject policies based on historic hatred. It should encourage and develop within its nations the love and respect for human beings, whatever the color or belief. It should stop denigrating Islamic countries and allow them their rights to self-determination. The West should strengthen cooperation with these nations and cultivate in the minds of its people that the Islamic countries have the right to exist and to have national interests. The West should develop the awareness inside its countries that Algeria, because of its location, can play a role in keeping balance and stability in the region and continuing trust, even if its government changes.

JD: What advice would you give to Western leaders who are trying to develop a foreign policy with regard to Islamic movements?

MN: It should deal with the Islamic movement as a reality which seeks to change the policies and systems which have ruled its nations in failure. The West should correct its opinions of Islamic movements as being movements of terrorism and chaos and rebellion. It should encourage dialogue with Islamic movements on the academic and political levels. It should ease attempts to transport democratic ideas and values to our nations in general and to Algeria specifically. This would allow people to allow these values to be spread and applied. The West should be aware that Islam is the cultural storehouse and political source for all the Islamic movements, which has a great affect and role in the intellectual and cultural life.

The West should accept that Islam in Algiers is rooted among the people and springs from a belief that cannot die. It comes from an intellectuality armed with proof and facts, which makes it hard to break. It is not merely a fashion or fad, which appears in some Arab countries. Islam is not for the sake of interests, and it is not concerned with one ethnic group. It is human as long as man is on earth. It is social as long as there are people and races on earth. As the Qur'an says, we have made you nations and tribes for you to know each other.

FIVE

RACHID AL⁻GHANNOUCHI

EnNahda (The Renaissance Party), Tunisia

PROFILE

WHEN I CALLED FARJANI SAID, my London contact with *EnNahda*, Tunisia's Islamic party-in-exile, he assured me that its leader, Rachid al-Ghannouchi, was willing to talk to me, but he could not set an exact time. Once I arrived in London, Said assured me, someone would contact me. But al-Ghannouchi, Tunisia's most famous dissident, did not set specific times for his appointments, Said insisted. The sheikh had to be careful.

And so, when I arrived in London, I didn't know when or where I would meet al-Ghannouchi. I was instructed to wait for a call at my hotel. When the call came, my instructions were even more mysterious. Wait in the lobby tomorrow morning. Someone will come for you.

This script was all too familiar. It was the way I had been forced to meet many famous and infamous people in the Middle East. It's the way I met Muntassir al-Zayat, a leader of the notorious al-Gamaa al-Islamiyah in Egypt. It was also much like that when I met Yasser Arafat in Tunisia. Except the meetings were usually in the middle of the night. First would come the phone call; then my scramble to get dressed; and a foolhardy dash into a waiting car to meet a contingent of sullen, edgy men.

Like al-Ghannouchi, many Islamists who were forced underground or into exile believed their governments had sent people to kill them. They never knew when an attempt would be made on their lives, or by whom. Everyone was subject to suspicion. Staying alive meant being an unpredictable and moving target.

So as I waited in the hotel lobby for my contact, I was not sure what or whom to expect. I was told we would have lunch, but not where. And although I was given a time for our rendezvous, even that turned out not to be definite, as I waited for more than an hour. I figured arriving late was part of their security routine, but the two men who walked into the understated plushness of my London hotel seemed genuinely sorry that they had kept me waiting. One of them was Rachid al-Ghannouchi himself. And he could not have been more apologetic or more self-effacing.

For a Westerner, this is one of the most disconcerting characteristics of many Muslim men of God. We are accustomed to more elaborate signs of piety—bishops in long velvet robes or shiny-suited ministers commanding their flocks from lofty pulpits. But Muslim leaders get down on their hands and knees and press their foreheads to the dirt. Theirs is a different concept of dignity and leadership. The holiest person is one who appears the most humble. And meeting him for the first time amid the heavy damask curtains and brocade furniture, with his watery, thick-lidded eyes and his peppery gray hair and beard, Rachid al-Ghannouchi looked a humble man indeed.

They said they had planned to take me to a Lebanese restaurant near my hotel, but they discovered that it was closed. So we opted instead to lunch in the hotel's wood-paneled, dining room. I found myself staring over a white linen tablecloth as one of the world's most feared Islamists ordered seafood bisque *without* the sherry. He seemed not to notice that I ordered mine *with*.

Over lunch, with Farjani Said serving as interpreter, al-Ghannouchi told me a little of his life story and his gradual rise in the ranks of politics and Islam.

Although he described himself as a man of peace, al-Ghannouchi possessed the power to start the same kind of social unrest in Tunisia that had propelled Algeria into civil war. Many believed al-Ghannouchi's supporters in Tunisia were resorting to increasingly radical and violent tactics to overthrow the government, and they suspected his public disavowal of violence was pragmatic and superficial. If he wished to remain in England, he could not be seen as encouraging civil war in Tunisia. But even those in the Tunisian government who may have believed that al-Ghannouchi would support bloodshed feared him because of his disdain for the political status quo in the country.

At the beginning of our interview, al-Ghannouchi told me that he preferred to speak Arabic. After several years in London, he understood English well but was uncomfortable speaking it. During our meeting, he went back and forth, sometimes correcting Said's English translation and revealing that he fully understood my questions.

Al-Ghannouchi said he had not always been a committed Muslim. He was born into a poor family in 1941 in the town of al-Hammah in southern Tunisia. His early education was steeped in traditional Islamic studies at one of the prestigious Zaytouna schools, a network of schools around the country connected with the Zaytouna mosque.

Al-Ghannouchi soon found that he needed to leave Tunisia to further his educational goals, and he first went to Cairo to study at Cairo University. But relations between Egypt and Tunisia deteriorated, and al-Ghannouchi was forced to leave Egypt for Syria in 1964. It was during his four years at the University of Damascus, studying philosophy and contemplating the state of Arab societies, that al-Ghannouchi committed himself to Islamic reform.

Initially he turned to Arab nationalism as the best way to shake off colonialism and restore pride in Arab culture. He denied reports he had joined the Syrian Nationalist Social Party, while he conceded that he was greatly influenced by the pan-Arabist theories of Egypt's Gamal Nasser. Yet by the time he left Syria in 1968 with a degree in philosophy, al-Ghannouchi was convinced that the concept of Arab nationalism was flawed and that the social and political activism espoused by the Muslim Brotherhood was the only viable alternative. Israel's humiliation of Arab forces in the 1967 war was one of the prime catalysts in forcing al-Ghannouchi and other Arabs to abandon hope in secular movements and to look to their religion for solutions to social and political malaise.

As is so often the case among modern-day Islamists, al-Ghannouchi's attraction to Islam was cerebral and pragmatic. Unlike Christian clerics who experience some inner transformation, who are "born again" through some emotional revelation, al-Ghannouchi's path to Islam was through logic and the search for a political ideology. His world faced severe economic, political and social problems. He believed its leaders were elitist, carbon copies of colonialists, insecure in their own cultural identities and subservient to Western interests. Islam offered a model of a different society: one rooted in Arab culture, not European culture, and a society whose mother tongue was Arabic, not French.

He explained it this way in a speech at the University of Westminster on October 6, 1992. Ghannouchi's aides provided me with an English translation of the speech entitled "Islam and the West: Realities and Potentialities":

> During the past two centuries, the Islamic world witnessed a renaissance movement that has been successful in reviving Islam, blowing away some of the dust of decadence. . . . As a result an end was put to the Western colonial presence in most of the Muslim world, which regained some of its vividness after many decades of political despotism and cultural decline. However, the West withdrew only tactically, leaving behind agents through whom it continued to control most of the Muslim world. The agents are represented in the Westernized elites, that are cut off from the faith and interests of the masses ruled by them. Whether such elites claimed to be liberal or socialist, they all lacked popular legitimacy. The only legitimacy they had was derived from their suppression of the people and their loyalty to the West.

These feelings were in the process of being crystallized for al-Ghannouchi when he returned to Tunisia in 1969. He had spent a year in France studying philosophy at the Sorbonne and working to help poor Muslim immigrants in Parisian slums. He had witnessed the student unrest that swept through France in 1968. When he left Paris, he was convinced that Western societies offered no model for the problems facing the Arab world. Yet at home, al-Ghannouchi found that President Habib Bourguiba was determined to turn Tunisia into his version of a progressive, prosperous country. To Bourguiba, that was synonymous with Westernization and secularism. It was, as he put it, a program "to pull Tunisia away from the winds of the East." That also meant in some ways pulling Tunisia away from some of what Bourguiba considered to be the stifling influences of Islam. This even led to his attack against one of the pillars of Islam, daytime fasting during the holy month of Ramadan. He went so far as to drink a glass of orange juice on national television in the daytime during Ramadan. He also closed Zaytouna University, where al-Ghannouchi received his religious training; instituted civil codes, including one that outlawed polygamy; and absorbed the *Sharia* courts into the civil court system.

To al-Ghannouchi and others, this represented a repudiation of Tunisia's Islamic heritage and a capitulation to Western ideas of social and political progress.

Al-Ghannouchi began to crusade actively for a return to Islamic values. As a teacher in secondary schools, he used his classroom as a bully pulpit, educating his students in Islamic principles and refuting those based on materialism. He joined the Qur'anic Preservation Society, a nonpolitical organization backed by the government as a kind of concession to opponents of Bourguiba's secularism program. Initially the president supported the Islamists as a tool against his leftist opposition, but he soon found that they presented an equal if not more potent threat to his power. Al-Ghannouchi was not content simply to study the Qur'an and ancient scholars. He wanted to shake the dust off Islamic thought and make its teachings applicable to politics and modern life.

Ghannouchi talked about his concept of "modernity" at a conference at the London School of Economics on February 29, 1992.

We want modernity, contrary to the ridiculous allegations made by those adversely inclined against political Islam, but only insofar as it means absolute intellectual freedom; scientific and technological progress; and promotion of democratic ideals. However, we will accept modernity only when we dictate the pace with which it penetrates our society and not when French, British, or American interpretations impose it upon us. It is our right to adopt modernity through methods equitable to our people and their heritage.[1]

In 1981 al-Ghannouchi formed the Islamic Tendency Movement (known by its French acronym MTI) with other educated young professionals to begin putting his views into practice. They began supporting worker rights, then a major issue in Tunisia, and they began criticizing Bourguiba's government and demanding plurality in it. They also embarked on a program to convince teachers and intellectuals of the superiority of Islamic principles over Western methods as a basis for the country's educational system. Their aim was to make Islam a meaningful, vibrant force in Tunisian life. But that would soon put al-Ghannouchi at odds with the Tunisian government. In fact, only a month after the formation of MTI al-Ghannouchi and many other members were arrested and sentenced to prison, charged with fomenting unrest. Bread riots in 1984 forced Bourguiba to offer some political concessions, and he decided to free al-Ghannouchi and other political prisoners.

For al-Ghannouchi, the real break with the rulers of his country came in 1989. Two years earlier, Tunisia's former military intelligence chief, Zine al-Abidine Ben Ali, had staged a benevolent coup with the theme of restoring the country's Islamic/Arab identity. By 1989 Ben Ali was even promising free elections. Al-Ghannouchi's MTI decided to seize the opportunity to participate in what he hoped might be the beginning of democratic reform. MTI changed its name to EnNahda, or the Renaissance, and wrote a constitution detailing its philosophies on politics, economics, society and culture. At the core of its platform was strengthening Tunisia's Arab and Islamic identity, protecting civil society, improving the status of women and promoting *Shurah,* or consensus building, as a foundation of democracy. With its goals clearly stated and emphasizing its commitment to peaceful opposition, EnNahda applied for government recognition and a right to participate in elections. What the group got, al-Ghannouchi said, was a government crackdown, and al-Ghannouchi was taught a bitter lesson on the repercussions of misplaced trust. Many of those arrested were beaten and tortured, and al-Ghannouchi felt at least partly responsible for their fate, because he had urged the open test of the government's professed commitment to multiparty, free elections.

Although they were prohibited from running under the public banner of EnNahda, Islamist candidates were allowed to run as independents, competing against the ruling Constitutional Democratic Rally (RCD) and the Movement of Democratic Socialists (MSD). In the book *Islamism and Secularism in North Africa,* Michael Collins Dunn wrote:

> Although the electoral system helped guarantee that the RCD won every single seat—which seems to have embarrassed the government somewhat—EnNahda did win some 14.6 percent of the vote nationwide and in Tunis close to 30 percent. The real figures may have been higher in each case. The MDS, by contrast, hardly won votes at all, discrediting the secular opposition and giving EnNahda a credible claim to being the only real political force capable of challenging the RCD.[2]

Both EnNahda and the MDS charged that the government falsified election results. Embittered by the experience and with many of his colleagues in prison, al-Ghannouchi started a worldwide campaign to draw attention to human rights issues in Tunisia. In 1977 his Islamic Tendency Movement had helped found the Tunisian League for Human Rights.

Al-Ghannouchi said he traveled throughout North Africa and to Europe, Turkey and the Middle East, criticizing Ben Ali and calling for democracy and an end to harassment and torture of Islamists. He even visited the United States and met with some low-ranking officials in the U.S. State Department. Believing he would face imprisonment if he returned to Tunisia, al-Ghannouchi began looking for a safe haven. He found it for a while in Sudan, under the protection of Hassan al-Turabi, who exerted a strong spiritual, if not political, influence on the regime in power. Sudan even provided al-Ghannouchi a diplomatic passport. But Ben Ali also had launched an international campaign—one to isolate al-Ghannouchi. Even though al-Ghannouchi claimed he had never called for violent overthrow of the government, Ben Ali believed he still represented a threat to the country's secular government. Ben Ali convinced France to refuse al-Ghannouchi's reentry. He had visited France many times and had even studied at the Sorbonne. Sudan also found its relations with Tunisia in jeopardy, so al-Ghannouchi decided to seek asylum in Great Britain.

Al-Ghannouchi made no pretense about his asylum in London. He was there because he had nowhere else to go, and asylum in the West was much safer than asylum in an Arab country, considering al-Ghannouchi's claim that Ben Ali had ordered his assassination and even sent people to do the job during his 1993 visit to Khartoum for a conference sponsored by Hassan al-Turabi.

Despite the dangers, al-Ghannouchi said he was committed to a peaceful campaign to change the political system in Tunisia so that it would serve as an example to other governments in the Islamic world. The Tunisian government charges that al-Ghannouchi is bent on destabilizing the country and the region under the banner of religious zealotry. And the government is convinced that even if al-Ghannouchi is sincere in his commitment to nonviolence, his party attracts those who do not necessarily share the same ideals. So far the West has sided with the Tunisian government, maintaining the status quo in the region.

While there were lessons to be learned from the West, al-Ghannouchi believed that Islamic countries could develop a better system of government, one that would not separate the moral influence of religion from the political system. He found this separation of religion from state one of the most disturbing aspects of the American model of government. The influence of religion is needed most in the affairs of government, he believed, and separating it robs government of the moral principles that should be its foundation. Al-Ghannouchi also rejected the whole notion that the individual should separate religious beliefs and practices from social and political duties.

But al-Ghannouchi insisted that his main priority was to open Tunisian politics so that the people would be able to decide what kind of government they wanted in power. "We have entered the political arena in Tunisia to fight for freedoms and not to set up an Islamic state," he said in an interview with a Kuwaiti magazine. "We must respect the wishes of the masses if they decided to choose a way other than ours. We are not guardians over the people. So if our society decided one day to be an atheistic or communist one, what can we do?"[3]

Al-Ghannouchi told me he was a "democratic Islamist." He said there is no contradiction in Islam with the concept of democracy in which people choose their leaders within a system that protects freedom and human rights. In fact, Ghannouchi wrote in an article entitled "The Battle Against Islam":

> When the compatibility of Islam and democracy is in question, some Westerners and Islamists maintain, as do the diligent opponents of political Islam, that the two platforms follow divergent paths. . . . This is done by segregating Islamic government and democracy to mean 'God's rule' and the 'people's rule' respectively.
>
> . . . It is clear that 'God's rule' correlates to the rule of the people or their representatives. Islamically, these are *ahl al-hall wal-aqd,* an elective body of highly qualified and experienced scholarly individuals.
>
> . . . there is no acceptable alternative other than democracy, one that is not exclusive, recognizing all perspectives. Stability will not occur unless we have a democracy of equality that embodies the people's right to control their civil agendas without mandate; one that adheres stringently to the rotation of power; and one that strives for the fair distribution of wealth and establishment of a free-market economy.[4]

Al-Ghannouchi had spent much of his life opposing what he saw as despotic regimes, first the one-party monopoly of Habib Bourguiba and then that of Zine al-Abidine Ben Ali. While both presidents had flirted with democracy and political plurality, neither had really been willing to face the prospect of relinquishing power in free elections. Al-Ghannouchi's criticism of Tunisian authorities was echoed around the world by independent and respected human rights organizations such as Amnesty International and the Lawyers Committee for Human Rights.

In a letter to *The New York Times* on August 4, 1992, Neil Hicks, of the Lawyer's Committee for Human Rights, strongly criticized the Tunisian government for its "propaganda mill, which likes nothing better than to focus on the 'Islamic threat' while ignoring its own widespread human rights abuse." Hicks also pointed out that at least nine members of al-Ghannouchi's EnNahda party had died in police custody since May 1991 "in circumstances that strongly suggest that they were tortured to death." And Hicks argued that the trial that year of 289 EnNahda supporters, charged with plotting to overthrow the government and establish a theocratic state, violated international human rights statutes. "For example," he said, "the prosecution's evidence against the defendants relies heavily on confessions that defendants say were extracted under torture."

Al-Ghannouchi had not backed away from his role of dissident-in-exile and had doggedly directed the spotlight on the human rights situation in his country. He claimed his party enjoyed widespread support in Tunisia, but it was difficult to gauge its political support since it operated underground and was barred from participating in elections. Legal opposition parties in Tunisia remained weak and offered only superficial competition to Ben Ali. It was generally believed that al-Ghannouchi's Islamist movement represented the greatest threat, although he had consistently rejected violence as a path to bringing down the government. Al-Ghannouchi knew that not everyone associated with EnNahda could be counted on to refrain from violence. And it was feared that if Islamists in Algeria gained power by force, Islamists throughout North Africa would be incited to take the same path. In an attempt to uncover his deeper feelings, I suggested to al-Ghannouchi that oppressed people often believe they have the right to throw off oppression by armed struggle. Look at the African National Congress, I offered; Mandela was not always committed to peace. Al-Ghannouchi looked at me squarely in the eyes and answered that violence inevitably hurt the innocent.

Al-Ghannouchi seemed sincere in his distaste for violence, but he refused to criticize others who took that road, such as some in the Islamic Action Front in Algeria. Unlike Hassan al-Turabi, for example, who had a vision of a world Islamic movement, al-Ghannouchi, seemed clearly focused on reform within his own country and was hesitant to interfere in the problems of neighboring countries.

Yet shortly after the bombing of the World Trade Center in New York, al-Ghannouchi issued a statement in London condemning the act on behalf of EnNahda: "The principles and tenets of Islam can by no means provide any justification whatsoever to what has happened or may happen in the future in terms of aggression against innocent people or destruction of institutions and establishments." The statement also called on Islamic movements to condemn aggression against innocent people and urged that they "should never retreat from presenting an authentic and genuine image of Islam as a force advocating peace, tolerance and human brotherhood. . . ." The statement ended with Shurah 5, verse 3, of the Qur'an: "Help ye one another in righteousness and piety. But help ye not one another in sin and rancor."

When we retreated from the dining room to a quiet enclave in the hotel lobby, I had begun to understand how this man could have filled mosques and stirred thousands to march in the streets. He expressed his provocative ideas in a poetic, classical Arabic that was rhythmic, melodious and mesmerizing. But al-Ghannouchi also had a pronounced sense of humor. As we chatted after lunch, he became far more outgoing and animated. He was so relaxed that he dared to speak English. After the tape recorder was turned off, he even illustrated his points with jokes that had us nearly crying with laughter. But the sincerity of his convictions and his religion seemed to define all aspects of his personality. Even his jokes were related to themes of right and wrong, morality and immorality, good and evil. Finally he interrupted our banter and left to find a quiet place to pray, while I waited. In London, in exile, al-Ghannouchi's brand of religion and politics seemed tolerant, relaxed and friendly. But there are those who say that is all a ruse and that al-Ghannouchi would be far different if EnNahda came to power in Tunisia.

INTERVIEW WITH RACHID AL-GHANNOUCHI

(MOST ANSWERS TRANSLATED FROM ARABIC BY AL-GHANNOUCHI'S
ASSISTANT, FARJANI SAID)
JANUARY 1994, LONDON, ENGLAND

JD: So you say there are death threats against you?

RG: Yes. It's the Tunisian authorities.

JD: Why would people in the Tunisian government try to hurt you?

RG: This is the nature of the Tunisian authorities. In its ruthlessness, it is ruling through terrorizing people. It's a police state. We represent the main opposition force in Tunisia. And Mr. Ben Ali has worked hard to exterminate the main political figures that might represent a threat.

JD: Has anyone else been killed?

RG: Some of them are in jail now. Some of them have fled the country. Some others have resigned the political life altogether.

JD: What are you doing from here, from London, to stay politically involved in Tunisia?

RG: I try to participate and to do what I can to relieve the suffering of the people. So I convey the message of the suffering of the people to the outside world. Because Tunisia is a dark place now. It is not easy to get information out of Tunisia. Most of the people know only of Tunisia as a nice tourist place, and they think there is stability. But this is not true. It's a false picture. People are living under fear. People are governed through fear. And thousands of Tunisians are in jail and in prison. They are suffering and under torture now because of their beliefs and their opinions. It's true most of them are Islamists, but not all of them. Because there are even some leftists and liberals also in prison. So if I was inside of Tunisia, I wouldn't have many choices. I would have to accept jail and its consequences or resign political life. So I have chosen to get out of the country. It's similar to what happened in Algeria. The difference is that we have refused to act violently toward the official violence by the authorities toward our people.

JD: What is different about Tunisia and EnNahda and Algeria and the FIS? Why did EnNahda reject violence?

RG: Each movement has its own philosophy and strategy. And each kind of people has its own way to deal with problems. The Tunisian people are more peaceful and the economic situation is quite different. It didn't worsen in Tunisia to the degree that it did in Algeria.

JD: But part of the reason it has worsened in Algeria is because of the violence.

RG: But it was worsening even before that. And the history of the nationalistic movements in both countries differs. Because the nationalist movement in Algeria was very violent indeed against the French, even more so than in Tunisia. We made a lot of effort in order to restrain our people not to react in violence.

JD: So you're trying to prevent the people from resorting to violence, like in Algeria?

RG: Yes, that's right. Because everything is encouraging violence. We are neighbors with Algeria, and what's going on there has a lot of psychological impact on Tunisia. And people in Tunisia are following the news of what's happening in Algeria. Moreover, in Tunisia, you have this continuous and persistent apparatus which is torturing people and making them suffer. Hundreds of women have been systematically tortured and sexually abused. All of this is documented in Amnesty International reports. Is there any ruling party who has been ruling since 1956 until now without allowing any opponents to be in parliament or even in the local governments? It's the same breed of regimes which collapsed in Eastern Europe.

JD: What kind of support are you getting from Western governments? Are you getting any support at all?

RG: Besides my getting political asylum in Britain, nothing. Unfortunately, most of the Western support is politically for Mr. Ben Ali and it's not for the Tunisian people. The Western democracies are playing the hands of the tyrants in North Africa and in the Arab world. And this is different from the behavior of the West in Eastern Europe. The

West helped the people of Eastern Europe get democracy. But in the Arab world, it's doing the opposite. This has raised a deep question for us. Why? Is it because we are Muslims? And that we don't have the right to live in dignity and freedom and enjoying genuine democracy?

JD: Do you think that's why?

RG: This is a question. I don't have the answer, but the question is a strong one. And this question is in the minds of the ordinary people in the Arab world. Why does the West support the dictators?

JD: Is this the reason for what you said was a growing distrust of the West in the Arab world?

RG: Yes, yes. I think it is one of the main reasons. Unfortunately, the West—and I mean the policy makers, not the people—didn't get the message of what happened in Iran. The people hated the Shah and they hated anybody who was behind the Shah. Look at Algeria. According to the logic of democracy, the legitimate rulers of Algeria are in jail. But Western financial support to the current regime is still flowing. That's why in the Islamic world, there is some confusion. Why is the military regime helped in Algeria and they are confronted in Sudan? What's the reason behind it? So dictatorship is beautiful if it is against Islamists? This seems to be the Western point of view.

JD: Why do you believe there is a fear of Islam?

RG: Because they [are ignorant of] Islam. And usually people are enemies to what they [don't know]. Because all they know of Islam is an Islam that is an enemy to the West, enemy to freedom, that threatens their national interests. And this is not true. Because the people who know Islam know the mainstream of Islamic thought is a religion of love and justice between people and international cooperation which is ruled on the basis of mutual respect and interchange of interests. So this is the real picture and the other picture is false.

JD: But do you think militants are hurting the name of Islam and this is also part of the problem?

RG: Some Muslim people, militants, they bear the responsibility of presenting a very bad picture of Islam. When it's linked with bombing and assassinations and plane hijacking. But there is extremism in each civilization and in each country. Look in the United States at what you have. You have, I think, more than anybody else. To simplify the picture, look in Europe at the Nazis. There are lot of groups like that. They are minorities but they are there within the West itself. Can you portray the whole West as though it is those groups? How can you portray small groups as though they are the whole of a community which is more than one billion? Even within Islamic movements, these violent groups represent the tiny minority of the whole body. And what made their voice very loud is the Western media itself. The Western media on one hand; on the other hand, they [leaders of many countries] do not allow the other moderate groups to work, to be active within the framework of the law.

JD: I think what bothers many people in the West is that they are not sure of your commitment to a democratic system. Would you accept being voted out of office?

RG: Our movement has worked for a very long time to present an Islam that works together with democracy. This is our main approach. This is our identity as a movement. We believe, and we've said since 1981, that if the people are going to choose Communists, and you know Communists are the enemies of Islam, we should accept the verdict of the people. And we should blame ourselves and try to convince the people that what they have done is wrong. And we should protect minorities, even if they are against us. So our agenda is 100 percent democratic.

JD: Do you believe you will see an Islamic state in Tunisia within your lifetime?

RG: I hope so. The call of democracy in Tunisia is now very linked to Islam itself. So there is no genuine democracy without genuine Islam.

And they are both united in the EnNahda agenda. We entered political life in Tunisia not through the gate of the call for the institution of *Sharia* law but through the gate of the call to institute basic freedoms and democracy in Tunisia. Our assessment of the situation is not that our people need to change one kind of law with another kind of law, but we want to change the mentality of the rulers. And liberate the people from that paternalism of the government in place. The main point which distinguishes us from the rulers in place is that we want a government which is serving the people and they want a state served by the people.

JD: How big is EnNahda now? You are no longer functioning in Tunisia now, right?

RG: Our instructions are don't move. Don't do anything. We don't want more losses.

JD: But if you don't do anything, how will things change?

RG: Now they don't do anything.

JD: So there's a long-term strategy?

RG: Yes. EnNahda is like fire under the ashes.

JD: Smoldering?

RG: So any wind, any change, we'll be ready.

JD: Do you get any support from other Islamic movements. Do other people in the Islamic world offer you help?

RG: I hope that happens. But everybody has his own problems.

JD: So there's no unified—no union of Islamic thinkers?

RG: Everywhere the Islamic movement is under pressure.

JD: What about Turabi's efforts to have a Popular Arab and Islamic Conference? Is that a force to help Islamic movements? Has it helped you at all?

RG: Almost all the movements who gathered in the Sudan for the conference are suffering from oppression. Even the Sudan itself is living in a civil war, and it's strangled by this economic embargo. And it needs help, more than it can give to anyone else.

JD: Are there women in your movement? In EnNahda?

RG: This is an issue in which our movement has made new steps. Not new for us, but for other people. EnNahda is known for its strong women. They represent almost 45 percent.

JD: What drew women to EnNahda?

RG: This is an interesting question. A few weeks ago, the same question was asked by the *Times* in Britain. Why do a lot of women go to Islam, more than men? After a lot of interviews, mostly with British women, most of them said they felt Islam was providing them with something that the West doesn't provide. The West has given the woman the right to work in a job, to participate in elections, in political life. And she is free even to get drugs. But something that is not provided is that peace in the heart, in the inside. The materialistic Western life is very severe toward women, more than it is toward men. Women suffer more than men. That's why she needs some kind of security. She needs protection somehow. Not protection [because] she's very weak. But spiritually. Women are closer to the spiritual life. So this need cannot be filled by the current Western life, unless women will isolate herself and be resigned to churches or something like that. But in Islam, it doesn't push her to this drastic, severe choice. There is a balance between the materialistic needs and the spiritual needs. Between family life and life within the society. The family in Islamic society is still very strong. The family is not the mother or father or children, but it's the community as a whole. So in this context, the woman finds security and warmth in social life. And she finds caring from other people, and that caring is based on principles, not on exploitation.

JD: When a Muslim looks at the West, does he see women as being exploited?

RG: Definitely. This is very obvious. Look how women are exploited by . . . companies and used for publicity and advertising when they're young. So it's [a woman's body is] capital. It's the body and its youth. And when that woman is older, she is rejected. And nobody will bother to even see her or to care. In the second half of her life she feels that she is lost.

JD: What is it that you don't like about the American attitude of separation of religion from the state. Why is that not workable?

RG: Because the personality of the human being cannot be divided. It's one. This is one of the main problems of Western civilization. And this is a particular problem to the West, to try to divide, that is, we should be subject to two different forces. This is because when the Western man awoke and tried to use his mind to discover the world and to try to think freely, the church was a hurdle and tried to prevent that. They said the truth exists only in the Bible and that you should not seek it anywhere else. And that the way and the path to the Bible is through the priest. And from that time there were rebellions against the church. There was [a] confrontation between the freedom of the mind and its progress and between the Christian religion. But in Islam, in our history, we don't have such problems, so why make them? The Arab world and the Muslim entered into civilization through Islam, through religion. But the West entered civilization through rebellion against the church.

JD: Do you have a distinct message to convey?

RG: I don't have something special which is from me to Islam . . . but I hope that I have discovered something special from Islam. The message of Islam is not to uproot or to ban any achievements from any civilization, from wherever it comes . . . but to protect, to preserve it and to build on it. And to simplify it to try to serve the people, such as the technology itself and the progress of science, the progress of telecommunications, democracy, human rights. I believe that the message of Islam is to preserve these achievements of the other civilizations and to build on them. And to put it and to digest it within the framework of the unity and the oneness in which we believe, which is called *tawhit* in the Islamic religion.

This great principle in Islam, which rejects a lot of dualities between the body and the spirit, between the mind and the spirit, between the individual and the society, between the man and the woman, between the contemporary life and the afterlife, between the worshipping of God and the economic system, between the morals and the economy, between the West and the East . . . the main gift of Islam to this world is that it gives to all these dualities something of order and some harmony among them . . . and within the society itself . . . and within international politics . . . and between the human being and Nature itself.

JD: This explanation that you've given me sounds very acceptable, even to the Western mind. Why then do you think there is a growing divide between the West and Islam?

RG: Unfortunately, this understanding is ignored even within the Muslim world. And even the West itself doesn't get this harmony in its perception of these dualities. The modern mind is always tied to the struggle between these dualities, these opposite forces, which [in Western society] used to be represented as a struggle between the free mind and the church. And humanity couldn't liberate itself from this heritage. That's why in modern life, the word "religion" gives a bad impression because it revives the memories of a bad history, which means for them the fear that, because of religion, we are going to sacrifice this wealth, this good life, this quality life that we enjoy . . . that we are going to spoil everything for the sake of religion. So this freedom of mind, the freedom of the people to elect rulers, the freedom of expression, the freedom of movement, the freedom of women, the appreciation of art and beauty—some feel that religion means we are going to scrap all these good things. Unfortunately, this is a Western perception and a Western heritage. And because the West is the major force all over the world, which dominates the world, so people become imprisoned in this kind of thinking. And it's very difficult to think unrelated to this . . . to see and to witness that these so-called opposite things, they used to live in harmony in other civilizations . . . So in Andalusia, the arts thrived. There was progress in science, there was moderation and religious tolerance. There used to be acceptance where many minorities and communities lived in harmony within the framework of a religious principle, which is the uniqueness that Islam provides. This means that there are other people and other civilizations . . . other people and other groups that entered civilization through the gate of religion. That differs from the Western people who entered civilization through rebellion against religion.

JD: So, what I'm hearing you say is that you believe there is nothing in Islam to prohibit progress, technical progress, higher living standards or democracy?

RG: Not only does Islam not forbid it, but it encourages people to be like that. Because Islam is not a tie which is made to restrict people, but it is a force of liberation.

JD: Is there is a country today on earth that is approaching what an Islamic society should be?

RG: There is an ambition within the Islamic world to try to link itself with this picture. Unfortunately, most of the people live within the framework of a heritage of struggle between religion and civilization.

JD: So there's no state that you look to as approaching the ideal of an Islamic state?

RG: There are only some experiments, but there is no model.

JD: When you look back at the thinkers you've read, the philosophers, who stands out to you as approaching a purer understanding of Islam? Is there anyone who shaped you, whose philosophies you follow?

RG: There are a lot . . . Muhammad Iqbal from Pakistan. Hassan al-Banna, founder of the Muslim Brotherhood . . . Malik Ben Nabi of Algeria and others.

JD: And today, who do you think are the outstanding Islamic thinkers?

RG: Probably, the two sheikhs, [the late Muhammad al-] Ghazali and [Yusef al-] Qaradawi.

JD: And what's so outstanding about these two sheikhs?

RG: Qaradawi says that he is a student of Ghazali. They belong to the modern renewal school in Islam which tries to digest, to accommodate the achievements of Western civilization within Islam. At the same time, they reject the West as a model. But it doesn't mean that they feel the West is an enemy.

JD: What's wrong with the West as a model?

RG: The idea of domination. The main problem in the West is that it believes the mind can solve all problems. And that the mind doesn't need any enlightening from God. This makes the human being believe that he is superior and that he doesn't need any other force. This philosophy provides excuses for the strongest to exploit and dominate the weakest within Western society and outside the Western society. It encourages bad ideas like the domination of nature and the use of the environment without any morals at all. Moreover, the West feels there is no room for morals at all in any efforts, whether it's political activity or economic activity. This makes human desire emerge as the strongest force, as the main force which motivates the human being. So in the end, the main value for human activity is absolute power and the aim is to satisfy desire without any control or thinking how it might hurt others.

JD: So when you look at Western society, when a Muslim looks at Western society, he sees people who've abandoned God. He sees a society where people admire the rich without thinking how they got to be rich. He sees families in which mothers and fathers are not

paying enough attention to the children and guiding them. You see a
society that is bankrupt?

RG: We see a great city but without spirit, without a heart, without
light.

JD: Is there anything good that you see?

RG: It's a beautiful city. The transportation, the services are very good.
The way to solve problems within different groups within society,
promoting democracy, all of this is very beautiful. This fascinates us,
how the alternation of power can be resolved peacefully. I'm very
fascinated with that. But there is no moral substance. It's a great
machine, but without spirit.

JD: Where do you describe yourself in the whole gamut of Islamists?

RG: I feel that I'm a democratic Muslim.

JD: Is democracy to a Muslim any different from democracy to a
Western mind?

RG: It is this beautiful machine, but with that spirit that is lacking, with
that moral substance. Islam can provide the right moral substance.

JD: How do you see Muslim youths being shaped now? Are they
getting the guidance they need? Are they being alienated from the
Western world?

RG: Most of the youths in the Muslim world now, their imagination has
been captured by Islam.

JD: Why?

RG: They are looking in Islam for their identity . . . the identity that
[they] lost when [their] people followed the West blindly, so they
really become Westerners. They lost Islam and they didn't achieve

Westernization and modernization. So youths are seeking in Islam their identify. [They are] looking for justice in Islam. [They are] looking for sincerity in Islam, for honesty, within corrupted societies. So Islam is a refuge.

JD: Does this mean that Muslim youths now are more militant?

RG: The Muslims now are more than any other time willing to sacrifice. And they are most convinced that their way is the only remaining way. Because the other ways, the other solutions, have reached an impasse. There is nowhere to go. So the other examples, the other solutions, they were expected to be a remedy and they have become a part of the problem.

JD: Let's talk a little about violence and Islam. As I understand it, Islam allows violence in self-defense. Is that as you understand it? Is that the correct interpretation?

RG: Yes.

JD: Do Muslims today feel like they have to defend themselves?

RG: Yes. Muslims today believe that their countries are threatened. That their dignity is not respected. What do you expect from Palestinians when they see that after more than 50 years their homes are inhabited by strange people coming from abroad and that their lands are worked by other people? And they live in camps, struggling. And they are waiting for the United Nations to return to them their land and their homes. But they get only words, empty words. What do you expect from these desperate people but to defend themselves with all the means possible?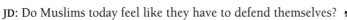

In Algeria, the people of Algeria, have made a big struggle in order to get rid of colonialism. One and a half million people have died. But after 13 years of [a] secularist regime, which is a dictatorial secularist regime, they felt their situation has worsened. So they went to Islam to get the answer. And they accepted democracy and they went to the ballot box. And they were astonished and disappointed when they found the tanks with the blessings of the West crushing those ballot boxes. So how can anybody blame such people in desperate situations if they resort to violence? When the democratic systems in the West are providing financial support to those very people who have aborted democracy?

JD: And yet you are rejecting violence in Tunisia. You're urging your people not to resort to violence. Why?

RG: For many reasons. One of them, first, I fear that I would participate in the tarnishing of the picture of Islam. For example, the Tunisian economy relies on tourism. To stop tourism is very easy. It doesn't need a lot of effort to go there and have some people make trouble with one or two tourists. But this is not right. And it would tarnish the picture of Islam in the world. You might choose violence and achieve power, but most of the time, people who achieve power through the use of violence will pursue the use of violence in order to rule. This is why we shouldn't enter a way that we don't know how to get out of. Even if we get out, it would be a huge bill paid by the people. So, it's a bad thing for the people. It's a bad thing for the picture of Islam in the world. And even if we rely on violence to achieve our goals, most of the people who will be killed won't be the people who are responsible for the corruption. The ordinary people will be the victims. They are the ones who need compassion, protection and care. This means that if we resort to violence, that we'll come to [be] a society where there will be cycle of violence and counterviolence—a civil war. And nobody can predict what will be the outcome. So we choose to be patient and that we should resist by peaceful means, through freedom of expression, through protests, through strikes, through popular means.

JD: Does this mean that you would advise the people of Algeria to abandon armed struggle?

RG: I don't put myself in their place. But each people should discover its own way to achieve freedom. I don't think that I know their country better than they do.

JD: One final question. What advice would you give to people in the West who sincerely want to try to better understand Islam and to improve the relations?

RG: First, they should try to understand Islam through its scholars, the intellectuals of Islam, and through dialogue with those people. And through the real representatives of Islamic groups. And that you should stop double-standard behavior . . . while speaking democracy and preaching it, they are supporting dictatorships. They should stop such behavior. That is why there is a doubt now in the Islamic world about whether these democracies are true and genuine democracies, or whether they are people who are talking democracies but who are not democrats. How can the taxpayer in the United States support dictatorship in Algeria? Is it right only for people in the West to enjoy freedom? Don't we Muslims have the right to a dignified life? And even if some of the policy makers no longer understand the language of morality and principles, we talk to them on the basis and grounds of mutual interest. We tell them strongly that the era of dictatorial regimes is on the brink of collapse.

The real representatives, the legitimate sons of Islam, are on their way to power, regardless whether the West accepts it or not. If it keeps preventing these legitimate forces from achieving their goals . . . and if they keep putting hurdles against them and fighting them, this means when that particular force achieves power, it will be hostile. We fear that there will not only be one Iran. But the West is helping to bring about a lot of Irans around the world.

Western intellectuals should bear in mind that this democracy which destroyed the empire of the Soviet Union is capable also of overthrowing these corrupt regimes in the Muslim world. They should bear in mind that Islam can be a friend of the West . . . moderate and tolerant. But Islam can be hard as well, and angry and seeking revenge. And the West has the power to shape this by its approach to Islam.

SIX

MUNTASSIR AL-ZAYAT

AL-GAMAA AL-ISLAMIYAH AND AL-JIHAD, EGYPT

PROFILE

I HAD VOWED NOT TO TRY to interview anyone associated with al-Gamaa al-Islamiyah (The Islamic Group) or al-Jihad (The Holy War) while I was in Cairo. Frankly, I was afraid. Instead, I had planned to interview one of their leaders in exile in Geneva. The organizations were known for their ongoing war to overthrow Egypt's government and establish an Islamic state. While they are now separate organizations with separate leaders, they united for a brief period and in 1981 succeeded in assassinating Egyptian President Anwar Sadat. Under perpetual siege from Egyptian security forces, it was feared the groups were trying to unite again to move against the current president, Hosni Mubarak.

Al-Jihad was most active in Cairo, while al-Gamaa concentrated its efforts in Upper Egypt. In February 1994 it seemed as if Egypt might be headed for civil war. Bombs had been going off in various parts of Cairo and innocent people had been hurt. In a failed attempt to kill the prime minister, Atef Sidki, two months earlier, a six-year-old girl had been killed coming out of school. Several policemen had been killed in Upper Egypt, and reports were that al-Gamaa had begun attacking tourists. Western vacationers were advised to avoid the Nile.

Egyptian authorities, determined to stop the attacks, responded with even more violence, breaking into buildings and gunning down suspected militants. In one incident the government sent more than 1,000 policemen to raid an island near Assiut, a town in Upper Egypt, launching a nightlong gun battle that ended with several people dead and injured and 40 arrested.

To make matters worse, the week before I arrived, al-Gamaa had issued a warning for tourists to leave Egypt. No problem, I thought. I'll wear Pakistani dress and no one will ever guess I'm American. The day before I arrived in Cairo, however, al-Gamaa clarified its warning. It was meant not only for Western tourists but for *all* foreigners: "This is our final warning," the statement said, "and those who read it should take it seriously. Those who do not will suffer the consequences."

So the last thing I wanted to do was defy the warning by asking for an interview with the people responsible for it. I thought long and hard about eliminating Egypt from my itinerary, but I had a long list of people to meet. The only course of action seemed to be to risk death for a few days, and get the interviews I needed.

Western embassies were taking the threat seriously and had warned expatriates to exercise caution. Security was increased on all flights into Egypt. And when I arrived at my hotel in Cairo, huge metal detectors were stationed around every door, while security guards hovered around the doors and lobby, checking bags and scrutinizing every loiterer. The atmosphere was electric.

Despite my vows to stay away from al-Gamaa and al-Jihad, the very day I arrived, I contacted a reporter from the Arab newspaper *Al Hayat* who had written a series of stories on the groups. He had good sources inside both organizations, and knew their history and could explain their motivations. It seemed he also had won their limited trust, and he was willing to help me talk to someone in both groups. We agreed to meet late that night in the hotel lobby to discuss the risks involved in arranging an interview.

At about 11 P.M., the reporter arrived. He was a tall, thin man with straight, dark hair and large, square glasses. We found a table in the lobby bar, but my companion drank only orange juice. We talked until almost 2 A.M. and he smoked cigarette after cigarette until my throat was sore from breathing his smoke. He seemed perpetually on edge and on guard, speaking slowly and in muffled tones, as if he were choosing his words carefully and did not want to be overheard. I couldn't help but wonder if my colleague himself was a member of one of the groups (which is why I have not named him), or if he believed we were being watched. And if so, by whom—members of the organizations? Egyptian intelligence? Both?

After our talk, I reconfirmed my decision not to risk a direct meeting with either al-Gamaa or al-Jihad. If my contact seemed so nervous simply talking about these groups while sipping orange juice in a hotel bar, I thought, they must be truly dangerous. The truth is, they are. Both al-Gamaa and al-Jihad believe they are fighting a war against immorality and corruption in Egypt. They believe there is no other way to clean up government and society than through *jihad*, or holy war, against the Mubarak regime, a regime that has jealously guarded power for more than a decade. News reports indicated that in a 22-month period between 1992 and 1994, 113 civilians had been killed, 7 tourists, as well as an estimated 84 policemen and 89 militants. My liaison said the number of dead was higher: more than 500 people had been killed in the past few years, including 300 police and civilians and 200 from the ranks of al-Gamaa and al-Jihad.

While al-Gamaa was working to solidify its base within society in preparation for the fall of the existing government, al-Jihad directed its efforts at infiltrating the military and winning the support of army officers for the ultimate takeover of the state.

In 1981 the organizations united and agreed to work together, with Omar Abdurrahman as their sheikh, or spiritual leader, a title bestowed on a man who is learned in Islamic doctrine. Later, differences over the sheikh's leadership role split the organizations, with al-Gamaa continuing to honor him as its spiritual leader. Al-Jihad respected the sheikh but thought he was too old and feeble to be of much use. During the brief time they worked together, al-Gamaa and al-Jihad conspired in the assassination of Sadat. Ayman Zawahri, leader of al-Jihad, spent three years in prison and then fled to Peshawar to help fight in Afghanistan. There, he worked to rebuild al-Jihad. Since most of his supporters were imprisoned in Egypt, he worked to recruit new members. Until about 1991 al-Jihad was still relatively inactive inside Egypt. While al-Gamaa had an advantage in that most of its members were in Upper Egypt and remained free, it too was inactive for many years following Sadat's assassination and the subsequent crackdown. In 1992 some of its members were accused of an attack that killed 15 Christians in Assiut. Subsequent attacks against Christians led police to begin rounding up suspected al-Gamaa members, but supposedly many devout Muslims who had nothing to do with the violence were arrested also. Many people in Assiut turned against the police, and public support for al-Gamaa increased as it turned its anger toward the police.

Both al-Jihad and al-Gamaa operated like secret brotherhoods, with hundreds of independent cells around the country. All members were encouraged to use aliases and to protect their true identifies, even from fellow members. That way if someone was arrested or tortured, he could reveal only limited information. In Peshawar, for example, Zawahri was known as Dr. Abd Al Moais.

Trust was important between members of these organizations. Young men were recruited to join after being scrutinized for months. The first qualification for recruitment was devotion to Islam, manifested by regular attendance at the mosque, observing the five daily prayers and the Muslim holy days. But inside al-Gamaa, members also were expected to commit themselves to the study of Islam and to becoming involved in their communities through social work. When a new member was recruited, he (female members usually are relatives of men already inside the organization) did not join an existing cell but was asked to form his own. Some people were members of more than one cell, but they were known in each by different aliases. Women had a place inside such organizations. According to one story, a woman went fully veiled to visit her husband in prison. Her husband escaped by walking out wearing her veil. Veiled women were also useful because they could conduct operations without being identified.

Through this system of secret cells, the organizations claimed to have thousands of dependable followers throughout Cairo. These cells, they said, were tied to hundreds of families.

The wide reach of al-Gamaa and al-Jihad represented a major problem for the government. As officials tried to crack down on the organizations, security agents often made massive arrests in communities that had fallen under the control of one of the groups.

But as Michael Collins Dunn, a Middle East expert, wrote in *Middle East Policy:* "The crackdown . . . fuels resentment in the neighborhoods, where mass roundups have occurred, and the executions have created martyrs in the eyes of those who listen to the sermons of the radical preachers." But Dunn also doubted whether the organizations were as powerful as they claimed. "While the violence is a serious challenge to the government and helps undermine the already degraded quality of life for the average resident of Cairo, there is little reason to believe that the extremists who are using violence have widespread popular support."[1]

Yet members often were respected in their communities because of their devotion to their religion and their reputation for honesty and aid to the poor and elderly. Many joined these organizations out of a desire to put their religion to work and to help change what they saw as corruption in government and immorality in society. Both organizations had drawn support from all strata of society, but especially from young, educated men who found they had limited opportunities in a system dominated by elites.

Mamoun Fandy, an Egyptian professor who was born in Upper Egypt, argued in the article "The Tensions Behind the Violence in Egypt" that, "Since Islamism is a social and political force, one can only understand it by looking at the social and political forces that produced it."[2]

Under reforms instituted by President Gamal Nasser, the children of Egyptian peasants were given the opportunity of going to free public schools, but, according to Fandy they were denied, "access to social and economic power. . . . People from working class backgrounds who were raised in the belief that Nasser had reformed Egyptian society became bitter when they realized that Nasser's revolution did not change the old order."[3]

This new educated generation grew embittered and began to criticize the Egyptian system. Fandy wrote: "During my years at Assiut University, I listened to people like Najih Ibrahim and Asim Abdul

Majid, the leaders of the Islamic movement, speak about corruption and favoritism. Ibrahim was at the top of his class in the school of medicine; Abdul Majid was his counterpart in engineering. In 1981, I heard both Ibrahim and Badul Majid were implicated in the Sadat assassination."[4]

Although experts like Fandy insisted that most of Egypt's poor did not agree with assassinations, attacking tourists and planting bombs in banks, they well understood the anger that motivated young men to join the groups responsible for such actions.

The reporter who had established numerous contacts with both organizations told me that young men and women were indeed attracted to al-Gamaa and al-Jihad out of anger and resentment over their inability to break the family network that ruled Egypt. "Al-Gamaa is the biggest," he said, "but the actions of al-Jihad are stronger." Al-Jihad preferred to save its energies for "big actions," he said, "not just minor killings. They want major assassinations." Al-Jihad reserved its attacks for military and government targets. Al-Gamaa, on the other hand, was content to strike when and where it could.

This information was enough to convince me to stay away from both groups. But the next night, I was returning late in the evening from another interview as my reporter friend drove up to the hotel. He motioned to me to get in the car, and I soon found myself speeding off to a rendezvous with the very people I had vowed not to meet. He was smoking furiously as he darted in and out of the wild Cairo traffic. Although it was already 9 P.M., my companion said we were too early for the interview, so we simply drove and drove until, finally, he parked. It was still too early, he said, so we walked at an excruciatingly fast pace, past brightly lit shop windows and deep into covered malls that were little more than dirty alleyways, crammed with stalls of sequined dresses, leather coats and bales of satiny fabric. I tried to slow down to look into some of the shops, but my escort was too tense to saunter.

"It's time," he said after half an hour of nearly jogging. We entered a doorway into a dark hall and waited for a rickety cage elevator to descend. When we arrived on the fourth floor, it was dark. My colleague rang the doorbell, but nothing happened. We waited. And waited. He suggested we continue our vigil outside. Within minutes, a small white car drove up and a big man yelled to us in Arabic.

"That's him," my guide said. "That's Muntassir al-Zayat, but that's not his car."

Muntassir al-Zayat was legal representative for both al-Gamaa and al-Jihad. He also was a member of both organizations and, when we met, he was trying to convince them to unite.

Zayat was a large, bearded man who wore an Egyptian *gallibiyah* with leather sandals. I didn't try to shake his hand, realizing that he was a strict Muslim and that unnecessary touching between men and women is discouraged. I didn't want to make him angry before we even were introduced, because one of the first things I noticed about Muntassir al-Zayat was that he was a very angry man.

He escorted us into his office, equipped with a massive desk, glass bookcases crammed with leather volumes, a new computer, several telephones and a fax machine. He spoke Arabic so slowly that I was able to make out a lot of what he said, but I was grateful that my colleague served as translator, so that there would be no confusion.

Zayat indeed was angry that night. His car had been firebombed that very night, he believed by Egyptian police. He pulled out photographs of his charred car to show me. He said neighbors told him someone poured gasoline on his car and set it afire. Within minutes it was destroyed. The police were sending him a warning, he said. And he was convinced there would be others. This information was not comforting to me. While some of the danger of entering this world lay with the people inside, a large part of the danger lay on the outside, with the determination of Egyptian authorities to crush the groups. Getting caught in the middle of a shootout between police and willing martyrs for Islam was well within the realm of possibility.

Only a few days before my meeting with Zayat, seven suspected militants were killed in a raid in a nearby Cairo suburb. And only one night after my meeting with Zayat, Egyptian police stormed an apartment in Cairo and killed three people they said were members of al-Gamaa. One of the people killed was suspected of attacking Austrian tourists in Old Cairo in December. But sitting in Zayat's office, watching the clock inch toward midnight, I knew it was too late to worry about danger.

Zayat told me some basics about his life. He was in his late thirties and was born into a large family in Aswan in Upper Egypt. As a youth he worked for Islamic causes and joined al-Jihad in 1975. He spent three years in prison when Egyptian authorities cracked down on Islamists following Sadat's assassination in 1981. Zayat said he didn't help kill Sadat, but he believed Sadat had to be killed. After prison, he completed his studies and went to law school, honing his skills for further service in the Islamist cause.

Zayat went to the United States to help successfully defend Al Sayid Nosair, who was charged with killing Rabbi Meir Kahane, the militant Jewish leader. Zayat had been lead counsel on many cases involving Islamists before Egypt's military courts.

That night Zayat was a hard man to penetrate. He was closed and bitter. But I tried to keep in mind that his car had just been firebombed and that he had reason to be angry. In truth, his hostility did not seem so much directed at me but through me. He resisted every attempt to make the interview more personal, and he absolutely refused to smile. His mind was fixed on what had happened to his car and what might happen next. Zayat believed the Egyptian government would soon try to arrest or kill him. Authorities, he said, assassinated another member of al-Gamaa and al-Jihad for speaking to the press and trying to garner public support for the cause. But Zayat said he was willing to die because he was fighting to bring democracy and Islam to Egypt.

Months later I realized that Zayat had reason to fear for his life. Another lawyer associated with Muslim militant groups had died while in police custody. Reports from Cairo said the bar association accused the government of killing Abdel-Harith Madani, charging that he had died after state security investigators in Giza gave him electric shocks, burned his body and whipped him. The death prompted nearly 2,000 lawyers, including Zayat, to stage a protest against what they said were human rights violations committed by the government against Egyptian citizens. International human rights organizations repeatedly criticized Egyptian authorities for allegedly inhumane treatment of prisoners.

Zayat himself was arrested again on May 22, 1994. Reports described him as Egypt's "most prominent Islamist lawyer," and many people suspected he would suffer Madani's fate.

Zayat told me that he had no other choice but to fight the government. If Egypt allowed Islamists to participate in the political process, he said, much of the motivation for violence would be abated. Many other people I talked to there agreed that much of the violence would end if the government allowed Islamists to vie for power at the ballot box.

Although some Islamic groups contended that they supported multiparty democracy and could accept being voted out of office, there were Islamic groups that made no pretense about their goals, which were solely for the establishment of strict Islamic rule. An example of their arguments was best exemplified by the platform of *Hizb ut-Tahrir* (Liberation Party), an extremist group that was based in London. The organization openly offered its explanation of the difference between Islam and democracy at its homepage at www.hizb-ut-tahrir on the Internet:

It is wrong to make democracy a standard for the correctness of the thoughts, or to be influenced by its concepts. Since democracy has spread in the world to the extent that its name prevailed over all popularised nations as an ideal; the oriental countries began adoption [of] it after the Western countries adopted it, despite the difference in its meaning.

. . . These thoughts are different from the Islamic thoughts of ruling both wholly and in detail. The difference between them is great, because the ruling system in Islam is the *Khalifah* system. It is a model completely distinguished from any other ruling style . . .

It is not from the people, nor from a few people or from any individual. . . . Though the *Khalifah* [common leadership for the Muslim world based on *Sharia*] system appears to be similar to the democratic system with regard to freedom of elections, voting, and to [the] voic[ing of] some opinions, it is incorrect to consider the two systems as similar because in the democratic system, these matters result from the liberties, whilst in Islam they result from the conditions of the *Khalifah* contract [obedience to *Sharia* and to a common leader]. . . . Similarly all the thoughts of Islam differ from the thoughts of democracy. They are at the same time different from aristocracy, monarchy, and of course the concept of empire. So if the

thoughts of Islam are studied they have to be studied in their capacity
as a ruling system distinguished from any other system. . . .[5]

Hizb ut-Tahrir also rejected freedom of expression as having no place
in Islam because an Islamic state had *aqueeda* (faith) as its basis; and
no opinion that violated the *aqueeda* was allowed.

The group rejected freedom of belief as well as the concept of
personal freedom, claiming that such freedom had led to social decline
and immorality in the West, while Islam set limits on human behavior.

Many inside the Egyptian government suspected that members of
al-Jihad and al-Gamaa held such views. And while many Egyptians
may have had the same fears, they did not attribute such radical ideas
to all Islamic groups and certainly not to the Muslim Brotherhood as it
existed in Egypt. There was considerable support for allowing the
Brotherhood, which was widely seen as the biggest opposition group
in the country, to participate in the political process.

In Egypt, all religious parties were banned from involvement in
politics. But even respected government supporters, such as Mustafa
al-Fikki, believed that the policy should be changed. Fikki once served
as Mubarak's secretary for information and later became director of
Cairo's diplomatic academy. Fikki was quoted in the *Mideast Mirror,* a
summary of reports in the Arab press, as saying that any group that
"has a presence on the political street" automatically enjoys "political
legitimacy." This, he said, is distinct from the "legal legitimacy" the
government grants.

Zayat would agree with that statement. But he would go one step
further in insisting that the Mubarak government had no political or
legal legitimacy since it maintained power by crushing the will of the
people. Yet Zayat indicated that both al-Gamaa and al-Jihad would have
been willing to negotiate with the government to end the violence. And,
he said, allowing even the Muslim Brotherhood to participate in
elections as a political party could help to end the cycle of bloodshed.

It's hard to know if Zayat was honest with me when we spoke. He
denied that either al-Gamaa or al-Jihad was responsible for attacks on
tourists or for planting bombs in public places. People were committing
these atrocities and blaming it on these groups, when their members
had nothing to do with them, he said. But al-Jihad was responsible for

the death of the six-year-old girl in the attack on the prime minister. Her death, he said, was an accident. I expected him to become angry at my pressing him on this issue, but instead Zayat bowed his head low over his desk and did not look at me. His sorrow, although fleeting and controlled, seemed sincere. But it was impossible for me to feel sympathy for him.

Before we parted, I felt compelled to ask why his colleagues had warned foreigners to leave Egypt. He said the warning was not meant as a threat from al-Gamaa or al-Jihad but as a warning that foreigners may be caught in the crossfire of their battle with the government. After the tape recorder was off and I was about to leave, I also asked him why he had even bothered to talk with me. His answer was piercing.

"If they kill me," he said sternly, "I want someone to say at least that I was a human being."

To the West, and certainly to Egypt's elite, Zayat and his compatriots represent the most frightening face of Islam in the modern world—angry, threatening, vengeful.

As I left Zayat, I was startled to see two young men seated silently in the outer office. Apparently they had been on guard during our entire conversation, but I had not heard them enter.

Outside, the once-bustling streets were now deserted. My escort smoked in silence as we sped back to my hotel, my thoughts focused on getting far away from the threat of men like al-Zayat.

INTERVIEW WITH MUNTASSIR AL-ZAYAT

(TRANSLATED FROM ARABIC)
FEBRUARY 1994, CAIRO, EGYPT

JD: I understand you represent two organizations that are active now in Egypt?

MZ: Yes.

JD: Can you tell me a little about the issues as the organizations see them, regarding the situation here in Egypt?

MZ: The main challenge involves the newspapers and the information media. The newspapers speak about Islam very, very bad. This is the main difficulty for the two groups, [one that] the Islamic people have been fighting [to change].

JD: So both groups have been trying to clarify the image they have in the media?

MZ: Yes.

JD: How is it that the media portraying al-Jihad and al-Gamaa al-Islamiyah, and why is that wrong?

MZ: They try to say that the two groups are terrorists and bloodthirsty. They are not like this.

JD: They are not like this? How would you describe the Gamaa and Jihad?

MZ: They try to persuade the people about the right Islam. And to help to create an Islamic state. The main problem is that the government refuses to allow them to speak to the people. No speaking in the mosques. They take the mosques of the two groups. There is reaction from that by Jihad and Gamaa. This has increased the violence . . . the action and the reaction. We know that human rights here are very, very bad . . . that the government hates the members of Gamaa and Jihad. There is torture. They put women inside jails and rape them. There is no respect for rules. All of this causes a reaction from members of the two groups, as a reaction to the actions of the government. The government and the police started to kill the members of the two groups and of other groups. These are political killings; especially big leaders of the two groups.

JD: Now, why are there two groups? What's the difference between the two groups?

MZ: Maybe the main reason is that Gamaa al-Islamiyah tries to work as an institute with the people. And the military force of Gamma used to make military actions as a reaction if anyone tried to kill the *da'wa* [Islamic missions]. The other side, al-Jihad, works for the future. They try to reach the army and the government places, and try to make them members . . .

JD: They try to infiltrate the government and win supporters?

MZ: Yes.

JD: So they have different methods of operating?

MZ: Yes.

JD: But the goal is the same?

MZ: Yes.

JD: An Islamic society, or democracy?

MZ: Islam is democracy.

JD: How will this cycle of violence stop? What must happen for it to stop?

MZ: The Egyptian government has to stop persecution of the people.

JD: That's all? I mean—

MZ: The Egyptian government must be liberated . . . They have to let the Islamists speak to the people . . . and the people will choose. This is a real democracy.

JD: Would you be satisfied . . . would you want to participate in politics?

MZ: Yes.

JD: Would they sit down with the government in a dialogue? I understand there's supposed to be a big conference?

MZ: If the government invited *Ikwan*, the Brotherhood, maybe the Jihad and al-Gamaa [will consider participating].

JD: If they thought there was an opening, a channel, they might accept it?

MZ: The government refused to let *Ikwan*, the Brothers, participate in the dialogue. Last week there was a big meeting and many people and leaders of parties were invited to speak. And they invited me to speak as a representative of al-Jihad and Gamaa. And I went and spoke. The problem is the government tries to say that Jihad and Gamaa always refuse.

JD: That's what I was told. I was told there was no way you would participate in democracy. That you want to take over the country.

MZ: There is a difference between joining the government and working with it. We will not say that this is a good government, this is a good system, this is a good regime. We will not say that. But we can join in a dialogue to explain our ideas. And the people will in the end hear from us and hear from the government and they can choose. Most of the members who will join in the dialogue agree they must abide by what the people say. Of course, we will try, if they invite us, we will try to convince the people of our ideas.

JD: And how many deaths have the Gamaa and Jihad been responsible for, on the other side? How many people have they killed?

MZ: Among the police?

JD: Yes . . . or innocent people?

MZ: Maybe 400.

JD: And do you see an end to the violence—to this killing—at all in sight?

MZ: Yes.

JD: How? Explain.

MZ: I told you at the beginning. If the government stops—

JD: But do you see this happening?

MZ: Until now, no. [We made] a small demand and the government refused. Many young people of the members of the two groups are inside the prison and jails for months and years. Why?

JD: So what is the future of Egypt as you see it? Civil war?

MZ: The Islamists will take the government.

JD: But before the Gamaa and Jihad win, there's going to be a civil war, won't there? I mean, will it descend into something like Algeria?

MZ: *En Shah Allah,* before we reach like Algeria, maybe the government will assist us to solve the problem.

JD: But why so many innocent people . . . like what happened with the six-year-old girl? How do you explain innocent deaths?

MZ: The members who did this action said they didn't want to kill the small child. They thought the school was abandoned. But the other actions, like big bombs in some squares, the two groups say that we are not doing these bombs.

JD: Oh. They say they didn't plant these bombs?

MZ: No.

JD: Do they attack tourist buses?

MZ: No.

JD: No?

MZ: When [we] do things, we send a paper saying we did it. The bombs that were put in the squares, we said we didn't do it.

JD: So other people are doing things and the Gamaa and Jihad are being blamed for it?

MZ: That's right. Maybe some people try to put the Gamaa and the Jihad in this situation and tell the people that they are killers and they are trying to kill the people.

JD: Do you think the government is doing this?

MZ: Yes.

JD: What about the recent statements to foreigners to get out of Egypt?

MZ: They declared that the Gamaa al-Islamiyah wants to make the conflict only with the government, only with the police. So they ask the foreigners to leave the country.

JD: So they're saying this so that foreigners won't get hurt?

MZ: Yes.

JD: I see. So, let's move on to the West. How do you view the United States and the Western world in its relationship with the Islamic world?

MZ: I am angry. The Islamic people here think that the United States supports Mubarak and his regime.

JD: So what would happen if indeed Islamists come to power?

MZ: The Islamic groups ask the Americans and the West, you must cooperate with the Islamic groups, with the Islamic people, and stop supporting such regimes. This would be better. [The West] would find a good relationship with Islamic groups if they give a chance to these groups to take power. But if we take power and take over the government without the agreement with the West, the relation will be very bad. We said to the Americans and we still say, your relations with the Iranians and Sudanese are very bad now. Why? Because you don't support the Islamic people from the beginning. You supported Numeiry and he was overthrown. You supported the Shah and he was overthrown.

JD: And the same is happening, you are saying, in Egypt?

MZ: The Egyptian people are religious people.

JD: I'm just wondering . . . under an Islamic society that you are trying to build, what would be different about Egypt? What changes would you make in Egypt if you came to power?

MZ: We want to create justice for the people.

JD: Economic justice? Political justice?

MZ: Everything. Islam knows economic justice, political justice, everything.

JD: What about relationships with other religions? Would there be tolerance?

MZ: Islam respects the other religions and minorities in society.

JD: One tough question. Aren't you at all concerned about being arrested yourself? Have you been arrested?

MZ: Yes.

JD: When?

MZ: After Sadat was killed.

JD: And how long were you in prison?

MZ: Three years.

JD: What were you charged with?

MZ: Nothing.

JD: You weren't charged with anything?

MZ: No.

JD: You were in prison for three years and you weren't charged with anything?

MZ: No. Many thousands were inside the prisons with no reason.

JD: Were you involved with the assassination of Sadat?

MZ: I saw that it was better for Sadat to be assassinated, but I didn't do it.

JD: Is there any chance of al-Gamaa and al-Jihad uniting?

MZ: Yes.

JD: There is a chance? They united around Sadat's assassination, right?

MZ: Yes.

JD: Why do you think there is a chance of them uniting now?

MZ: Because they have the same ideas. They take the ideas from the same source. And the way they work in Gamaa and Jihad [is] now similar. All of these reasons make me think they can achieve another union. The challenge they face now forces them to strengthen.

JD: Well, is there anything more you'd like to say?

MZ: If anyone tells you that someone shot me and that I have been killed, you have to tell the people who is Muntassir al-Zayat.

JD: But what happened to your car? Your car was bombed?

MZ: No. A big fire.

JD: And you don't know who did it?

MZ: No one knows, but someone saw a car stop near my car during the night, after midnight, and put benzene on it, set it afire and leave.

JD: Do you have any idea who did it?

MZ: I am sure that the police did it.

JD: It sounds to me like there is real war between Gamaa and Jihad and the police.

MZ: Yes. A big war.

SEVEN

SHEIKH KAMEL
AL-SHARIEF

*INTERNATIONAL ISLAMIC COUNCIL FOR DA'WA
AND RELIEF, EGYPT/JORDAN*

PROFILE

AS I WAS SAYING MY GOOD-BYES to Sheikh Yusef al-Qaradawi in Qatar, he bade me to wait a moment, then took my notebook and wrote down a man's name.

"When you are in Jordan," he told me, "talk to him." In my notebook, the sheikh had scribbled in Arabic the name Kamel al-Sharief, International Islamic Council for Da'wa and Relief. I had not heard of the organization but I had heard of Kamel al-Sharief, who had only months before been a keynote speaker at a conference in Washington, D.C., sponsored by a coalition of Islamic groups in the United States. Following Qaradawi's advice, as soon as I arrived in Amman, I made an appointment to see al-Sharief at the offices of the daily newspaper *Al Dastour* (The Constitution), where he was chairman of the board.

The offices of *Al Dastour*, one of the oldest independent newspapers in Jordan, were located on a busy highway leading from

Amman. Inside there was the usual combination of chaos and mayhem that dominates every large newspaper. As I had worked for nearly two decades at a major daily, for me the atmosphere was invigorating. The telephones were constantly buzzing, reporters were hustling around with tattered notebooks and in the background was the insistent whine of rolling presses. As I was led into the second-floor office of al-Sharief, the noise gradually faded until it was little more than a distant hum. A kindly-looking, bespectacled older man stood up from behind a large desk and extended his hand in greeting. That was my first indication of Kamel al-Sharief's religious views of moderation and pragmatism. And the picture of King Hussein, dutifully hung on the wall behind al-Sharief's desk, told me he was firmly tied to the traditional religious establishment of the Islamic world. Hussein's picture was almost as prominent as the large and exquisite desk set, whose blotter, pen and letter holders were carved of wood and inlaid with iridescent mother of pearl.

Al-Sharief struck me as a thoughtful man whose sparse gray hair and lined face gave him an air of wisdom and authority. He took obvious pleasure in discussing his religion, which he argued promoted moderation and rationality in all aspects of life. And unlike Islamists who were working in opposition to their governments in such countries as Egypt, Algeria and Tunisia, al-Sharief had strong affiliations to "official, traditional" Islam. He was one of the founders and the secretary general of the International Islamic Council for Da'wa and Relief, which was closely tied to Al Azhar University in Cairo, the seat of traditional, government-backed religious authority in the Muslim world. Among the council's member groups were those connected to numerous governments in North Africa and the Gulf under threat from reformists or revolutionary Islamic elements. But al-Sharief said he was working to spread Islam, not to overthrow governments, interfere in the internal politics of Muslim countries or revolutionize Islamic doctrine. He was active in Jordanian politics and had served the king in various capacities, including as ambassador to several European, Asian and African countries. The king had appointed him a senator from 1973 to 1974, and again in 1989. And he had served as Jordan's minister of Waqfs (religious endowments), Islamic Affairs and Holy Places from 1976 to 1984.

In the International Islamic Council for Da'wa and Relief, al-Sharief had worked to unite traditional Islamic organizations as well as the religious branches of several Muslim countries. The council was founded at the Eleventh Conference of the Convention of Islamic Research held at Al Azhar University in 1988, and it had since garnered support from many governments in the Islamic world, including Kuwait, Iraq, Dubai, Morocco, Egypt, Jordan, Qatar, the United Arab Emirates and Saudi Arabia. It also included under its umbrella many of the world's leading Islamic propagation and relief groups, including the World Muslim League, based in Mecca; the Union of Red Crescent Societies, in Riyadh; the Islamic Universities League, in Morocco; the World Assembly of Muslim Youth, in Riyadh; the International Islamic Charitable Foundation, in Kuwait; the Islamic Da'wa Organization, in Khartoum; the International Association of Islamic Banks, in Cairo; and the General Islamic Congress for Jerusalem, in Jordan.

The council's headquarters as well as its Education and Da'wa Committee were located in Cairo at Al Azhar, but the offices of other committees were spread throughout the countries supporting the organization. For example, headquarters for the General Relief Committee were in Jeddah, offices of the Data and Follow-up Committee were in Mecca, the Financing and Investment Committee was in Kuwait and the Publication and Information Committee was in Baghdad.

The council included more than 50 organizations involved in missionary or relief work outside of their own countries. Its goals were similar to those of Christian relief organizations that minister to the world's suffering people while trying to win converts. The difference was that, Muslim relief groups generally worked in areas where most people already were Muslims. Rather than win converts, al-Sharief said they worked to strengthen the faith of believers and educate them about their religion.

In unifying Muslim relief agencies, he said the council also was trying to avoid the competition so often evident among various Christian denominations as they tried to spread their special brand of Christianity through humanitarian work around the world.

As al-Sharief wrote in the council's official pamphlet explaining its mission: "Islam calls on Muslims to unify their world and assimilate their opinion. It urges the straightness of line and fights against disunity, differences and divisions." He also wrote that competition among Islamic groups would eventually hurt their most basic goal of spreading Islam as it would defeat efforts to create a united Islamic world:

> The leaders of Islamic popular movements became aware of these facts and they found that among the means leading to the coveted unity was coordination in thought, effort and action on a stable and disciplined basis. They also found the advantage of transference of Da'wa and relief work from the local sphere to the world sphere, without prejudicing the distinctive national features of each organization. Hence, there emerged, for the first time, the idea of the International Islamic Council for Da'wa and Relief. The notion was that those cooperative sister organizations comprise the elites of Muslim thinkers and large sectors of peoples. They enjoy amicable relationships with governments and leaders, and possess such informational capabilities that give them the advantage of influencing those sides, and directing them towards the unification of Muslim attitudes which shall undoubtedly serve their concerns and those of the world at large.[1]

In its bylaws, the council required member organizations to provide information about their activities, including their relief and missionary programs and the regions they served. That information was distributed to all council members, with the goal of allowing them to avoid duplication of relief services as well as excessive concentrations of preachers and missionaries in one area. The council required groups operating in the same areas to share information, storage facilities and resources. And its regulations set standards of conduct for Muslim relief workers: "Entrance to zones stricken by political or natural catastrophes in a disciplined manner free from improvisation and unrestricted competition which causes harmful and destructive allegiances of a tribal, intellectual or secular nature [is] detrimental to the general benefit; and sets the stage for the rise of atheist or secular ideas under the pretext of restoring security and stability."[2]

Through better cooperation and coordination, al-Sharief said, the council hoped to broaden the area covered by Muslim relief groups as well as increase the variety of services provided. As stated in the council's declaration of principles, one of its most important services was support for "such Islamic causes as Palestine, Bosnia and Kashmir. . . ."

Al-Sharief was an outspoken critic of the international response to the massacres of Muslims in Bosnia and of India's reported abuses of the predominantly Muslim population in Kashmir. His commitment to Palestinian struggle against Israel was natural. Al-Sharief was born in Gaza in 1926 and fought against Israel in 1948. The biographical information he provided me with said he was a member of the "Secret Resistance at the Suez Canal in 1957" and that he was awarded the Golden Order for Bravery by Egypt and the Star of Palestine Medal as well as the Order of Jordanian Star Medal and the Medal of Independence.

Islamists in Jordan were opposed to the government's peace treaty with Israel, contending that Israel had not forged a just peace with the Palestinians. Yet in Jordan, al-Sharief and his fellow Islamists maintained a stance of loyal opposition to the king and expressed their displeasure in nonviolent protest.

Al-Sharief saw his mission and the council's as a continuation of his battle to defend his faith. He was aware that Islam had many detractors in the West, and he believed it was the duty of Muslim leaders to engage such people in constructive debate. The council's statement of principles addressed this issue by requiring Muslim leaders:

> To face up to the hostile campaigns launched against Islam and Muslims in political and intellectual arenas. There shall have to be prepared scientific research on each of the topics raised. Plans shall have to be laid for cooperation among Muslim centers. New institutions may be established for following up such hostile propaganda. There shall have to be established a central leadership with substance and prestige, in order to establish contacts to promote understanding among nations based on truth, justice and mutual respect.[3]

Yet the main thrust of the council's mission remained inside the Islamic world, al-Sharief told me. With so many respected Muslim leaders working together in the International Islamic Council for Da'wa and Relief, he believed they also could help mediate problems among Muslims. Even more important, they could speak with one moral voice against the radical, violent element that he felt was hurting the name of Islam. "We have to mediate sometimes in quarrels between Muslim countries and Muslim organizations," he said. "Being a neutral body which comprises mainly elders of Islamic movements all over the world, there is a weight, you know, when we talk to people, when we try to bring them to reason, to find solutions to problems. For example, I was among a three-man delegation that went to mediate between Mauritania and Senegal during their fight. And we managed to help. We don't take all the credit, but we managed to help with that problem."

The organization also had conducted mediation between the Palestine Liberation Organization and HAMAS, the Islamic armed group fighting the Israeli occupation in the West Bank and Gaza. Again, al-Sharief said, the intervention was apolitical: "not to intervene in the political fight, only to prevent the bloodshed and to keep the differences in the realm of politics and public discourses, meetings and political action . . . to avoid violence."

Al-Sharief believed the council's united appeal would carry weight with Muslims around the world, even among those involved in violent struggles for what they considered to be the cause of Islam. As stated in the council's declaration of principles: "The more power this International Islamic Council acquires, the more respect and importance it acquires among Muslims, and consequently, the more momentum it gains to mediate for peace among the faithful, governments and organizations alike."[4]

Yet the council was created on a platform of staying out the internal politics of Muslim countries and promoting nonviolent solutions to Muslim problems, according to al-Sharief. The council's list of members did not include groups that promoted violence against authorities or that were involved in political opposition to existing governments. Such groups had as their goal opening the political system to allow the creation of an Islamic state. While al-Sharief certainly believed an Islamic state was the ideal, he was not an idealist.

"The ideal of every religion is unattainable," he told me. "Accept that. It's heaven on earth. You find in the Bible talk of Jerusalem on earth where the wolf and the lamb live together. This is the ideal. But it's good when you decide to start on the road toward the ideal. But you don't judge the people by the standard of the ideal. It's wrong to start saying you didn't reach that level, then you have to be condemned."

Al-Sharief described himself as a gradualist, a consensus builder, one who worked to avoid conflict among Muslims based on differences in dogma. "We have to say that we are Muslims, we accept Islam as our religion," he said. "We have to start from one point to unite the people, to make one solid base for our life, cooperation. And then to move from that point on targets which are attainable, which are reasonable, which are acceptable by all."

Even on the question of drinking alcohol, which the most strident of the devout would consider an offense worthy of public beating, al-Sharief took a moderate approach. He agreed that Islam prohibits Muslims from drinking, but, he said, "It is not necessary that you have to make it by law. And even if you make it by law, you might say that Muslims should not take alcohol, but you can't deprive a foreigner from his liberties, from his freedom to take it if his religion [allows it]. Even under the days of the Prophet, of the Caliphs, there were Christians who bought and sold alcohol or drank it publicly. . . . There were even Muslims who were caught doing that. There are pages in the poetry of Islam talking about wine. So there is a margin between what religion wants but what [the believers] practice."

Even on the question of Western-Islamic relations, al-Sharief took a conciliatory, peacemaking tone. Although he acknowledged the suspicion of Muslim peoples toward the intentions of Western powers because of recent colonial history, he did not dwell on those suspicions. He reminded me that the history of Muslim-West relations was not always fraught with tension and mistrust. Often, he said, "there were periods of friendship and relaxation. . . . That is why I am saying we have to stress the second type of relationship in history, not to stress always the confrontation. Stress the friendship."

Al-Sharief's creed seemed to me to express the essence of Christian dogma: Be kind to your enemies, forgive, turn the other cheek. But he said his philosophy was rooted in Islam. He understood the special concerns that govern Western attitudes toward the Muslim world, but he insisted that the West must be willing to treat that world with respect. "We have to recognize that the West has legitimate interests in our area, which has to be satisfied," he said.

Al-Sharief could be one of the Muslim world's leading peacemakers. Just as he was committed to preventing conflict among Muslims, he said he was committed to preventing conflict with the West.

Despite his opposition to the peace treaty with Israel, al-Sharief seemed to be one of the Islamic leaders most able to help build bridges between the West and the Islamic world. Not only did he articulate Muslim principles in a rational manner for Western ears, but his moderation and pragmatism could serve as a model for Muslim leaders as they face the realities of the current world order.

INTERVIEW WITH SHEIKH KAMEL AL-SHARIEF

FEBRUARY 1994, AMMAN, JORDAN

JD: Tell me, did you help found the International Islamic Council for Da'wa and Relief? Is that your creation?

KS: Not private, but I was a partner. I participated in the preparation for this organization. Because we have here the World Council for Jerusalem. I was secretary general of this organization. Its main task is to care for Jerusalem. It was based in Jerusalem but moved to Amman here. It's a nongovernment organization, of course. So my organization and others decided to form this council to serve as an umbrella to coordinate between similar organizations.

JD: Now this sounds like it's basically a social organization, not a political organization.

KS: Not political, no.

JD: So in that way it's different from the Muslim Brotherhood.

KS: It's different. We don't at all involve ourselves in internal politics. Only if we have to mediate sometimes in quarrels between Muslim countries and Muslim organizations. Being a neutral body which comprises mainly elders of Islamic movements all over the world, there is a weight, you know, when we talk to people, when we try to bring them to reason, to find solutions to problems.

JD: Have you tried to mediate, for example, between the PLO and HAMAS?

KS: Yes, we have tried. Yes, as I said, not to intervene in the political fight, only to prevent the bloodshed and keep the differences in the realm of politics and public discourses, meetings and political actions . . . to avoid violence. This is our main task, really.

JD: Obviously you felt there was a real need for such an organization, that the organizations that exist are not sufficient.

KS: No, they are sufficient in their own field. But the leaders of these organizations noticed that there was duplication of work, sometimes conflicting activities; sometimes unjustifiable competition, which wastes energy and funds. Sometimes the [group] facing the problems is weakened by their division and quarrels. So they thought it's better to have an organization which coordinates their efforts and that grows lines between them and defines fields of activities which don't contradict or conflict. This is the main task of the council.

JD: And you said there were elders from many different countries involved in this. Can you tell me some of the people that might be well known?

KS: Yes, for example, the chairman of the council is the rector of Al Azhar, which is the most prominent position; the vice president is Field Marshal Siwar al-Dahab of Sudan, head of [the Islamic Da'wa Organization] of Sudan. He's the vice chairman. And we have an executive council, which comprises many personalities, like Dr. Abdullah Naseef, the former secretary general of the World Muslim League of Mecca; Dr. Ahmed Muhammad Ali, who until recently was the governor of the Muslim Development Bank. We have the minister of the *awqaf* [religious endowment] of Saudi Arabia, minister of the *awqaf* of Egypt and the minister of *awqaf* of Qatar. So you have a large committee of this category of people.

JD: These people really must carry some weight when you all get together.

KS: Exactly. This is the idea. This is the idea. Because there are many problems. There are deep rifts sometimes, deep problems. But we do our best. We do our best.

JD: One of the reasons I'm here is the concern in the West about the mix of religion—such a dynamic force as religion, and such a dynamic force as Islam—and politics. Because sometimes it is seen that it will breed intolerance and that it will somehow radicalize countries. Could you explain what your position is on Islam as it expresses itself through politics?

KS: Well, I will just repeat what I have said in Washington recently. I was there for a few weeks. There was a meeting organized by some Muslim and Christian groups under the title of Islam and the West, Friendship Not Confrontation.

JD: Yes, it was Cooperation Not Confrontation, I was there.

KS: You were there? I was there myself. I was one of the main speakers at the dinner, which was the last night. Myself and several congressmen . . . they represented the American side and I represented the Islamic side. So, what I said was that religious studies, religious heritage, is an accumulation of historical development, sometimes friendship, sometimes enmity, sometimes neutrality, sometimes indifference. So it is the total sum which we have now in our hands. And the total sum of historical development. So, the question is not what religion tells us to do, in my opinion. It's what we want to do with our life. What we want to do, really. Do we need to live harmoniously and friendly and build a new world based on justice and fairness and good-neighborliness? If we decide that, then we will find a religious principle which will back our choice.

On the contrary, if we decide through foolishness or shortsightedness that what we want is quarrels and wars and instability, then we will find in religious principles something which will back our choice. So this is my stand. We believe now that in the world of today, the world is shrinking and becoming like a small village, that any event in one country affects [positively] or adversely other parts of the world, then we have to be prudent, we have to be careful, we have to find ways, we have to live together and to assure the legitimate interests of all parties. If we decide to go that way, then we will find that in religion which will back this choice. We will find in the Qur'an exhortations for good treatment of others, especially the Christians; freedom of religion; that dialogue can continue for generations over religious matters without anybody being obliged to change his religion.

But then what we need is to talk about the immediate needs of the age; how we can cooperate together to combat delinquency, to combat alcoholism, to preserve the family life, to preserve the ideals of the religions, then you will find in your religion that which backs you. Even the historical confrontations, if we look objectively to them, we will find that they have helped in the building of the new civilization. Even the Crusades, they were marked, no doubt, with brutality, with bloodshed, with destruction. But in the end it helped in removing the walls between different civilizations. It brought people to know each other, and everybody learned from the other. If you look objectively, you will find good things even in the ugly events. The Arab presence in Spain, for example. It also was marked with violence, but then it helped in the building of modern civilization. Even the Renaissance of Europe was called by certain thinkers the Islamic era because the Muslims helped in the translation of Greek philosophy into the modern languages. The universities of Cordoba, of Toledo, produced great scholars, popes, [who helped] all of Europe.

JD: It sounds like you are saying religion will harm government only if that's what the people want it to do. If they're looking for an excuse to make a government based on religion hostile, then they'll find it.

There's no reason why religion should be a negative force in government.

KS: It shouldn't be negative at all. But of course what you should have is a balanced compromise from both sides. Say, a social contract. Islam is the religion of the people, it's history, identity. It has many, many dear memories which press [themselves] on the minds and the hearts of the people. They have been deprived under the colonial era of living like Muslims in many ways—education, in public life. Now, in the period of independence, people want to retain, to regain their identity within religion, to live as Muslims. This is a legitimate aspiration, as I see it. Very legitimate. So, when some governments try to block this peaceful move toward Islamization in its moderate sense, in its proper sense, then the movement becomes violent. See what I mean. Where in other countries, where people are more enlightened, like in Jordan, for example. Here people are more enlightened. Even the government class sees themselves as Muslims. They share the aspirations of the people. Of course they have difficulties, they have real problems, so they go toward this object selectively and in a peaceful manner. So that creates a peaceful atmosphere in the country. You have differences but all and all it's a peaceful country, and there is a general acceptance on both sides that you will have the right to ask for a certain moderate-type Islamization. People have the right. The government has the right to be choosy, to be selective in these steps, in moving when things are ripe and correct and necessary. So this brought a balance, equilibrium in the country. In other countries, governments made it their duty to repress even the minimum demands of the people. So, it brought violence.

JD: It sounds like there is a progression toward the ideal. But what is the ideal? For example, is the ideal where there's no liquor available at all? Is the ideal that there wouldn't be X-rated movie houses, as now exist? What is the ideal Islamic state, as you see it? And you seem to be reasonable.

KS: Well, let me put it this way. The ideal in every religion is unattainable. Accept that. It's the heaven on earth. You find in the Bible talk of Jerusalem on earth where the wolf and the lamb live together.

This is the ideal. But it's good when you decide to start on the road toward the ideal. But you don't judge the people by the standard of the ideal. It's wrong to start saying you didn't reach that level, then you have to be condemned. You can't say that. But we have to say that we are Muslims, we accept Islam as our religion. We have to start from one point to unite the people, to make one solid base for our life, cooperation. And then to move from that point on targets which are attainable, which are reasonable, which are acceptable by all.

JD: So, now, when I came in, I didn't offer you my hand. You offered me your hand and I shook it. Because I didn't know whether I should or shouldn't. So I'm trying to judge. When I offered my hand to the representative of HAMAS, he wouldn't shake it. Why is that? Where does that put you? Are you more liberal?

KS: It's not that. You have in Islam both ideas. It's a question of interpretation. For example, it is in the tradition of the Prophet that he refused to shake hands with women. This is a *hadith*. But he said that he delegated one of his disciples to do the job for him. So some people like to follow the steps of the Prophet. Others say, if a disciple of the Prophet allowed himself to shake hands, then why shouldn't I do it? Especially in the modern age which [when not shaking a woman's hand] brings more confusion than solving things. If you don't shake the hand of a lady, it puts things in a bad way. But then you can't blame the other; this is his freedom. But both are acceptable. In Japan, for example, people don't shake hands. They just put their hands like this and bow. So, they are free to do that. We take it lightly. We don't make a big issue. If one of those who are the most rigid and the most fanatic sees me shaking the hand of a lady, he will not criticize me. He will say, he's free to do what he wants. It's a marginal question. It's not a basic question of the religion.

JD: That seems to be the question too among women who opt to cover. At least it doesn't seem like they look down upon the women who don't opt to cover.

KS: No, no. What we want is virtuous dress. Something modest. Like you are dressed yourself. Very good. I don't care if you cover your head or not. I am not to go about teasing people. But if a lady shows various parts of her body, we think this is wrong and it spreads immorality in society.

JD: I'd like to talk to you about the relationship between the West and Islam.

KS: Many times I have attended many rounds of dialogue, for the past 30 years. And [my participation in such dialogue] stems from my conviction that Islam basically is an open religion. First of all because it claims that it is the last religion. It is a continuation of previous religions. It is not a new religion. This is why it holds other religions with respect. It might differ with them in certain interpretations. But they recognize the Bible, the Torah of the Jews. Even they call the other prophets Muslims, in the general sense, not as followers of Muhammad but as the followers of the original meaning, which is submission to God. This is the word "Islam," total submission to God. This is why the Qur'an called Moses and Jesus Muslims. They are people who submit their will to God. So they are our prophets in this sense. They are Muslim prophets. So that makes Islam start relations with other religions from respect. This is one thing. Then, even the idea of salvation, on the day of judgment, is not confined to Muslims. Like the other religions, they make it confined to their own church or their own synagogue and they refuse to recognize the others. In Islam, everybody who does good has a share in the mercy and the grace of God. So this openness makes Muslims face these dialogues with relaxation, without any need for concessions, any complexes.

JD: But there is a certain tension that exists now between the West and the Islamic world.

KS: The tension is derived from three sources, I would say. Basically, the historical background. It was in certain times a relationship of confrontation, in history. Of course there are other periods of friendship, of relaxation. This is why I am saying we have to stress the second type of relationship in history, not to stress always the confrontation. To stress the friendship. So, the historical background was not always bright, which presented itself in literature, in memory of both sides, which you still find even in the languages. The Arabs are called Saracens. You'll find this in the collective memory. The second sources is the colonial era, which has very bad [memories] in Muslim eyes, in Muslim memory. And third, maybe, is the egoistic interests of certain Western countries. They want this part of the world to continue to be backward, to deprive it of any real advancement and [from] acquiring technological discoveries, to remain as a market for products and for cheap labor. This is another part of the problem.

JD: Is the United States one of those countries that you think has these kind of selfish interests?

KS: I think so, yes. I am talking about the government now. The government. The American people, like any other people, there are good people and bad people, like ourselves. So all in all, these motives, these inclinations lead to enmity. And this is the reason why the reaction of some Muslim groups is violent. It is not a religious-motivated violence. It is mainly political and social. People want independence, for example. People want advancement. People want modernization. People want jobs, higher standards of living. They think that the policy of the West is against all these aspirations in different ways. So here comes the violent reaction. So it is not religious, we must stress this. Why does it take a religious facade? Because it comes at a time of religious revival. It coincides with the religious revival taking place all over the world. The Muslims being Muslims, they are searching for Islam. They think Islam gives solutions for these problems because Islam calls for justice, for modesty, for honesty in government, for independence, for relations with respect between nations and people. So when these aspirations are blocked, then comes the reaction.

So this is why we believe the West should understand the aspirations of the Muslims. First understand Islam, isolated from the happenings of the moment, and go in deeper to the real spirit of Islam, which we want to develop. And to help the people who want to present a new correct type of Islam, who call for dialogue, who call for good relations.

We have to recognize that the West has legitimate interests in our area, which have to be satisfied. But the idea to have everything and deprive the other party of anything, this cannot be the human, the correct relationship. This is a self-defeating approach and will bring a violent reaction. But if the idea is to have normal relations, to have fair dealings, to have give and take, then I think compromise is not far away. This is my opinion. I genuinely believe in that. This is not just ephemeral thinking, but it's practical. Whenever I meet Western people . . . fair-minded, wise people . . . who know the needs of the age, that you can't rule people by the iron fist always and you have to find solutions with people—we usually become friends. If our ideas are so identical, so practical, then, if we can convince the others, if we can bring them to notice of leaders and people, then perhaps we are on the right path.

JD: You mentioned Sudan as one of the countries represented in your organization. Are you familiar with Dr. [Hassan] al-Turabi's efforts to have an organization of Islamists around the world? I think it's called the Popular Arab and Islamic Conference.

KS: I was in the conference myself. Oh yes, he invited me.

JD: How was it?

KS: I must say in fairness that the conference was not [advocating] violence as had been depicted outside. Not at all. Not at all. Even Hassan al-Turabi was a moderating influence. I know for sure because I met him and I met the head of state there. They are very moderate people. They are not at all against the West as was presented. This is also one of the problems which makes people believe . . . that the government of Sudan, especially Hassan al-Turabi, despite his moderation, despite his overtures, despite his extended hand to the West, but he's still under fire. He's still condemned and branded as a fundamentalist and a terrorist. That led many people all over the Muslim world to believe that the target of certain circles in the West is against Islam as such, whether it's moderate or violent. They're against any Islamic revival. And this unfortunately feeds and inflames the tendency that we should not have any hope in the West. We should not expect any fairness from the West. We should not expect any justice from the West because it's against Islam and the Muslims and they want to keep this part of the area enslaved to the West. And then the only way is to fight. Unfortunately this treatment is feeding this current in the Muslim world.

JD: But from the point of view of the West, the problem was the alleged presence of radical organizations in the country. And intelligence said there were radicals who were operating out of the Sudan.

KS: But this is not true. This is not true. The Sudanese are denying this. They are asking any, including the United Nations, any neutral body to come and investigate. But don't just listen to them [the United States] that you are terrorists and you have to be destroyed. This is the real problem. I prefer really that the Sudan, being a Muslim country, is using Islam as a mobilizing factor for the people; for decency, for honesty, even for working, for agriculture. This is why, for example, in the agriculture there is marked progress in this field because behind it some enthusiasm was introduced; that if you produce, if you reform the land, this is for the cause of Islam. So they touched the living nerve in the hearts of the people to create enthusiasm. And there are many verses in the Qur'an in the *Hadith* of the Prophet which call on people to work the land and make it like *jihad*. So for them they are using Islam to mobilize the people, to defend the country, to keep the unity of the country, to combat the separatists in the South. So when the West stands against all of these aspirations because it is Islam, because it has Islamic coloration, then the West is seen all over the Muslim world as taking a hostile stand against Islam. And this is very dangerous, very dangerous because this discredit of the moderate element, the people who want dialogue with the West, the people who want to find a compromise, people now start to call them stooges of the West. The only people who represent Islam are the radicals, the violent.

JD: So what the West is doing is undercutting the authority of the moderates?

KS: Exactly. The West is playing into the hands of the extreme element, showing that here is no compromise. There is no way at all for any dialogue, for any understanding; that the West is against Islam as such. Really, this is the problem. And the government of the Sudan wants peace. It wants good relations with others. I know for sure. I am not one who is deceived by nice talk. I go deeply in studying the situation. I know that they are ready to accept any proper solutions, respectful solutions. To assure their independence, their freedom of action, their internal reform, and they are ready to have a very good relationship with their neighbors and with the West. Al-Turabi has gone to the United States and to Canada to talk to the people there. He has spoken to them. Being a Muslim country does not mean being a hostile country to others. People are free to choose the type of government they want. If Islam serves them, if it is the only thing which can satisfy the people, let people take it. Let the people take it. I mean, communism has been accepted in many countries, different regimes, so why not Islam?

EIGHT

SAID AL-ASHMAWY

FORMER CHIEF JUSTICE OF THE SUPREME COURT, EGYPT

PROFILE

SAID AL-ASHMAWY LIVES ON A TREE-LINED STREET in the upscale section of Cairo called Zamalek. It is a fitting address for a former chief justice of Egypt's Supreme Court, as it is also home to diplomats, Western expatriates and the upper crust of Egyptian society. Zamalek is still very much a part of Cairo, with its polluted air; mangy, starving dogs; triple-parked cars and incessant, horn-honking traffic. Yet it is far more livable than other parts of Cairo where most buildings are covered with a thick layer of gray dirt and mounds of garbage rot in the streets. It is a modest oasis in the midst of some of the worst urban poverty in the world.

In his article "The Tensions Behind the Violence in Egypt," Dr. Mamoun Fandy, an Egyptian professor, described Cairo as a city of tragic contrasts. "While the old families live the life of the developed world in areas like Zamalek and Masr Al Gidida," he wrote, "millions of Cairenes live as squatters in the city's cemeteries or in slums like Ain Shams and Al-Zawia Al Hamra."[1]

This visit, in February 1994, was the second time I had talked with Justice Ashmawy at his home. The first time was less than two years before, in October of 1992. Both times, a cluster of men surrounded the door outside the building that held his second-floor apartment. And this time as before, I had to tell them who I was and whom I wanted to see.

"I'm a little early," I explained to a tall, bony man in a dirty white *gallibiyah*. He seemed to be the building's doorman. "Judge Ashmawy is not expecting me for another 20 minutes or so."

He instructed me to sit inside the doorway, in a dark corner of the large, dusty ground-floor hall, on the shaky remains of a wooden chair that no longer had a back. As it grew darker and darker outside, I watched the men as they chatted and joked. I noted the difference in their dress.

The doorman and several others wore light-colored *gallibiyahs*. One wore a white lace skullcap, identifying him as a *hajji,* a man who had made the pilgrimage to Mecca. But one younger man wore a blue running suit with white stripes running down each side. On his feet were blue, rubber, slip-on sandals. He would not have been out of place in a Little League game in the United States or at a backyard barbecue. Propped against the hood of an old, grimy car, he was having a good deal of fun teasing a boy of about 12 with straight black hair and large brown eyes who sported a baseball cap.

It would be unseemly for so many men to loiter in front of an apartment building in an upper-class neighborhood in the United States, but it was a common sight in Cairo, no matter what class. It seemed to be a natural way for men to pass the time, talking for a few hours with friends along the street. And for these men, it was also a way to divert themselves from their hunger until nightfall. Ramadan was only a few days old, and at least at the beginning, most observant, healthy Muslims try to honor the daytime fast. But in the waning hours of the day, the air becomes electric with expectancy, like the tension in the air just before a thunderstorm, as fasters lust for the feast they know awaits them.

The men did not show the least bit of curiosity toward me, and I knew it was because I was covered, dressed in a long skirt, long sleeves and a scarf. I had dressed differently in Cairo and knew how assertive Egyptian men could be, especially in groups. But this time, I seemed to be so completely out of the picture that I began to fear they had forgotten me sitting quietly in the dark.

It wasn't long before the old man in the *gallibiyah* motioned me toward the elevator. He and a younger man escorted me inside and to the door of Judge Ashmawy's apartment. I learned later that they were government security agents, assigned to guard Ashmawy and to monitor his visitors. In one of the raids on hideouts of al-Gamaa al-Islamiyah, the militant Islamic group fighting the government, Judge Ashmawy's name was found on a list of people to be assassinated. Only weeks before, an attempt had been made on the life of Atef Sidki, Egypt's prime minister, and a six-year-old girl had been killed by mistake. So the government and Ashmawy were taking the threat seriously, although Ashmawy had lived under the shadow of such danger for several years because of his controversial theories on Islam.

Ashmawy might well fall into the category of "fundamentalist" by the ill-informed in the West who still use that word. But how wrong their stereotypes would be in this case. The judge is indeed an Islamic scholar, and he also believes Islam is an all-encompassing religion that should shape all aspects of life, including government. But he is not what the term "fundamentalist" usually implies.

In his book *Political Islam,* Ashmawy explained that if the term is used, it should be understood that there are two types of "Islamic fundamentalist," one that is "activist and political" and the other that is "rational and spiritual." The first is militant, dogmatic and danger-ous, he said; the second is compassionate, tolerant and moderate. Ashmawy sees himself as the latter. In fact, he argues that extremists are themselves un-Islamic because "an essential trait of Islam is its rejection of all forms of excess and extremism."[2]

Even though Ashmawy criticizes the Egyptian government for allowing rampant corruption and for not meeting the needs of the people, he has spent a lifetime in government service. He is firmly anchored to Egypt's power structure and wields considerable influence inside the political system.

Ashmawy was born in 1934 into what he described as an "upper-middle-class family." Most of his education was in Egypt, but a needlework plaque on his living room wall with the word "Harvard" commemorated a course he took at Harvard Law School in 1978 on foreign investment in Egypt.

His career began in 1954 when he was appointed assistant to the district attorney in Alexandria and then district attorney in the same city two years later. In 1961 he became a judge and, ten years later, was named Egypt's chief prosecutor.

Probably because of his well-connected family, Ashmawy did not face problems in getting a good position. That put him in a different class from many of the Islamic activists he opposed, people who believed the existing system had failed them. According to Mamoun Fandy, himself from a peasant family in Upper Egypt, this lack of opportunity was one of the main motivations for young people who were attracted to Islamic movements.

"It is very difficult to penetrate the Cairo old-boy network," Fandy wrote. "Family connections not only exist in the universities but also constitute an important factor in promotion in high positions in government."[3]

Ashmawy had enough connections to be named a judge on the High Court in 1978; and in 1981 he became chief justice of the High Court and chief justice of the High Court for Security of State, a position from which he recently retired. Ashmawy said he retired to dedicate himself to criticizing the government and to find more time for his writing. At the time of the interview, he had already written 14 books on Islamic thought. Many consider *Political Islam* to be his best work. When it was published in 1987, Naguib Mahfuz, winner of the Nobel Peace Prize for Literature, wrote: "This book is a good example of a placid and deep voice which deals with the most critical topics which preoccupy many youngsters and adults: the rule of Allah, Islamic government, *jihad* . . . [Ashmawy] ranks with the best of our present-day thinkers in calling for constructive dialogue through which we can emerge from darkness into light."[4]

In an article published in the *Middle Eastern Studies* in July 1992, David Sagiv described *Political Islam* as Ashmawy's most important work, "not only because of the issues he deals with, but mainly for the sharp manner in which he addressed them."[5] As an example, Sagiv pointed to Ashmawy's introduction, in which the judge wrote:

> The politicization of religion or religiousness of politics are nothing
> but acts of prostitution by iniquitous men or an act of blind boorish-

ness. For these acts enable opportunism to appear as a noble act in the name of religion; they allow the exploiter to receive legitimacy by way of [Qur'anic] verses; they transform lechery into a symbol in the name of the *Sharia*, permeate perversion with an aura of sanctity and transform bloodshed, without good cause, into *jihad* bravery.[6]

These strong words summarize the convictions of a man of undeniable bravery in light of the current atmosphere in Egypt. Ashmawy's career has been marked by his outspokenness and his battle against those who would seek to, as he put it, "monopolize Islam."

Ashmawy's ideal Muslim is a "humanist and a universalist," open to all cultures, to all forms of knowledge. And he insists that tolerance of all religions is a fundamental part of his own religious philosophy.

In this regard, Ashmawy is far less hostile to Western influence than are many devout Muslims. In fact, it was clear from his home that there is much he appreciates in Western culture, music and literature.

When I arrived for our interview, the judge was pouring tea into a delicate cup and saucer of English design (he does not fast for health reasons) while the carpeted room virtually pulsated with the crescendos of what I concluded were Liszt piano sonatas. A sleek black sound system with wildly flickering red and green lights hugged one wall of his large double parlor. The waterfall of sound provided a dramatic background for the judge's eclectic collection of furniture and knickknacks. Much was inherited from his family, but a good bit of it represented souvenirs from his travels to many parts of the world. His quarters were furnished to the tastes of an intellectual and eccentric bachelor, one bold enough to mix disparate furniture styles, fabrics and colors at whim. His decorating seemed to be a clear reflection of his religious philosophy, one open to all influences and rejecting the monopoly of any one version of beauty or truth.

A large, painted eagle was perched on the corner of a French-styled desk, under the glow of a brass and crystal chandelier. Statues of Greek gods kept vigil in various corners, and several Italianate chairs flanked an overstuffed Louis XIV sofa of gold brocade. Every inch of wall and table space was covered with some treasure, from

Chinese ivory figurines, to a red enamel clock, to gilt lamps and vases, to a plate that bore a pensive portrait of the judge himself.

On one wall Ashmawy had hung two framed Arabic inscriptions that announced "God protects you from people," and "God overcomes everything." Appreciating art and culture did not exclude devotion to religion, Ashmawy believed. And he made it very clear that he was a religious man, committed to Islam. He called himself a "liberal Muslim," and an opponent of "political Islam."

To Ashmawy, all political Islamists are militants who are not to be trusted even when they claim they are in favor of plurality and democracy. They are extremists, he said, who advocate eradicating all influences of European colonialists on legal and political systems and establishing governments based on their narrow and misguided version of *Sharia*. But Ashmawy maintained that the Egyptian government as well as most others in the Middle East are in fact Islamic governments.

Although it would not be hard for Islamists to point to Egyptian laws that are not fully in keeping with traditional interpretations of Islamic law, Judge Ashmawy's argument has a point. In the 1970s, when President Anwar Sadat tried to win favor with the more radical segments of the Islamic movement in Egypt, he declared *Sharia* to be the foundation of Egyptian law.

In fact, Egyptian law allows anyone to file a lawsuit based on the "rights of God." And recently a group of Islamist lawyers filed a lawsuit on just that basis against another controversial Muslim scholar whose ideas challenged traditional interpretations of the Qur'an, as did those of Judge Ashmawy. The lawyers sued to have Dr. Nasr Hamid Abu Zeid declared an apostate because of his teachings and to have his marriage dissolved. They maintained that a Muslim woman could not be married to an apostate and that if she continued to live with him, she should be declared an adulteress. Under some interpretations of Islamic law, a woman convicted of adultery could be stoned to death. Ashmawy said the correct punishment should be public lashing, not stoning. The suit eventually was thrown out of court on a technicality, but Ashmawy and others believe the courts should not entertain such arguments because the religious laws behind them are inhumane and out of date.

Judge Ashmawy never married so he never faced the threat of such an intrusion into his private life. But he has faced his share of public censure. He has done battle in the Egyptian press with prominent Islamists, such as Fahmy Howeidi and Sheikh al-Ghazali, both well-known scholars whom many would call moderate Islamists. Ashmawy contended that these allegedly moderate Islamists had fueled extremism in Egypt. He said their impassioned diatribes against him and other liberal Islamists had incited young radicals to violence.

Calmly sipping his tea, Ashmawy reminded me of the assassination in 1992 of Dr. Farag Foda, a man who vehemently criticized Islamic militants as well as the government. Like Foda, Ashmawy believed the government was guilty of playing a dangerous game of trying to co-opt extremists by essentially accepting their narrow-minded and discriminatory philosophies about Islam.

Dr. Foda once wrote that the Egyptian authorities were guilty of passing laws that "prevent people from building churches without direct permission from the president . . . that keeps a quota system for Christians entering the police college, war college, naval college and aviation college." And, he continued, "The regime also casts a blind eye on discriminatory practices that are clearer than the light of the sun in many university departments—a regime that opens a university that is exclusively for Muslims, Al Azhar University."

"I feel sorry for my country," he said, "that it will protect my son Yasir because he is a Muslim and treat another boy unjustly because he is a Christian."[7]

Ashmawy continued to voice similar sentiments even though he knew they led to Foda's assassination. And Ashmawy blamed Foda's death not only on the militants who pulled the trigger but on all Islamic activists, whose inflammatory rhetoric, he contended, encouraged the young and vulnerable to extremism and justified murder in the name of religion.

Yet Ashmawy was at odds not only with the "activist" Islamists; he also disagreed with the theories of orthodox, conservative Islamic scholars who supported the state, including many of those at Al Azhar University. Many of them considered Ashmawy and his "liberal Islam" nothing short of heresy. They had been particularly inflamed over Ashmawy's theories on Qur'anic interpretation, in which he argued that only the parts of the Qur'an involving man's relationship with God are immutable and sacred. Ashmawy believes that everything else in the Qur'an is not sacred and is subject to change, including its guidance on man's relationship to society and to government. Much of the Qur'an is meant to be considered in its historical context, in light of the times that existed when Muhammad lived. If conditions change, then so should the interpretation of the Qur'an.

In December of 1993 he wrote for the *Middle East Times* newspaper: "In general, the Koran should be interpreted not according to the general meaning of its words but according to the historical context in which it was given. For this reason, some Koranic rulings are temporary rather than permanent. For instance, with the injunctions regarding the system of slavery, the slave harem—mentioned in the Koran but abolished by legislators across the Islamic world."[8]

Ashmawy argued that when the Qur'an says it takes two female witnesses to equal the testimony of one man, that restriction is meant only for financial transactions and it was law only because at that time women were inexperienced in such matters. Today such restrictions should not apply in societies where many women have as much financial expertise as men.

Ashmawy had proved himself a persuasive writer, steeped in Islamic history and well educated. He is a stimulating orator who presents a sturdy, imposing figure. And because of his influence with the power brokers of Egypt, his theories cannot be ignored. In fact, Ashmawy wielded considerable power during his career. Yet while he criticizes the government for tolerating corruption, Ashmawy is not really promoting democracy, at least not yet. He insists that the Egyptian masses are not ready for true democracy because they are "illiterate and uncultured." While Westerners might take comfort in Ashmawy's liberal ideas about religion, they would be troubled by his somewhat elitist attitude toward popular participation in government. Based on Ashmawy's theory, half of the world's population or more would have no say in their governments. Even in the United States, vast numbers of people would be deprived of the vote; and in South Africa, where many blacks are illiterate, majority rule would be virtually impossible.

Ashmawy's fear is that in Egypt, millions of people are so angry at what they see as rampant corruption in government, and are so poor because of it, that they are easily influenced by inflammatory rhetoric and by the promises of extremists. If these people are allowed to elect their own government, hardline Islamists stand a very good chance of coming to power. This is a chance Ashmawy believes Egypt cannot afford to take.

When I left him, the judge was about to return to work on yet another book on Islamic theory destined to excite still more controversy. He was nestled in a corner of his parlor, surrounded by his life's treasures, with books and papers stacked around him. He seemed secure and content, except that I suddenly realized he was seated in front of a large window. His stocky figure, bent over his work, cast a wide, lumpy shadow across the brocade curtains.

Outside, most of the neighborhood men had long stopped their chatting and had rushed off to begin the night's feasting. The two guards remained, however, somberly watching the black street below Judge Ashmawy's window, charged with keeping his daring and uncompromising spirit alive.

INTERVIEW WITH SAID AL-ASHMAWY

FEBRUARY 1994, CAIRO, EGYPT

JD: You have described yourself as a liberal Muslim . . .

SA: Or an enlightened Muslim.

JD: Does that mean you're at the opposite end of the spectrum from people like [Sheikh Muhammad] al-Ghazali and orthodox Muslims?

SA: Yes. These people are mostly militant Muslims, or what I call political Islam. To make distinction between them and myself or my group, I call them political Islam. While we are liberal Islam. First of all, they don't have any definition to the words of the Qur'an or the *Hadith*. These words may be interpreted in a wrong way or [out of the context of] their historical meaning. Because the word *Sharia,* for example, means a way, method and the like. Now it means the Islamic legal system, especially the jurisprudence . . . Interpreting the verses of the Qur'an [out of context in its historical meaning] is distorting the meaning of the Qur'an. The second point: They are interpreting the verses of the Qur'an with the absolute meaning of the words. In my opinion, it should be interpreted in the historical context. Once you are doing that, you are offering two Islams. Their Islam, their interpretation leads directly or indirectly to militancy . . . violence.

JD: Why does it inevitably lead to violence?

SA: There is a verse in the Qur'an they are always using. They are saying that who is ruling by what was not revealed by God is an infidel. They are condemning the government and all of society for ruling by what was not revealed by God. And it is their duty to impose their ideas. As a liberal, I believe we have many ideas and we shouldn't impose . . . And the second point, they believe that *jihad,* or holy war, is an absolute duty, and it is their duty before God to impose Islam up to their understanding over all the people, Muslims or non-Muslims. But in my opinion *jihad,* or holy war, is not holy way . . . Its meaning in Islam is to suffer. And I believe its meaning is to control yourself, to refine yourself. . . and as you fight, it is only for self-defense, not for any aggression at all.

And you are not to enforce your ideas upon others. Reality has many facets. Who can be sure that their ideas are the right ideas? I am offering my ideas and I am not sure that they are the right ideas and I am not monopolizing the truth. But they believe they are monopolizing the truth. And they are responsible to God to force it on the people. They are adopting a wrong policy, a wrong doctrine, to consider Islam, to consider politics a base of Islam. If it is a corner, or a pillar in the faith, then they turn it into *Shia,* not *Sunni.* Because the Shias of Iran only believe that politics is a pillar of Islam.

JD: So I would take it that you believe that politics and religion in Islam do not have to necessarily mix? They should be separate.

SA: I'm not separating religion and the state but religion and politics. I believe politics is a human action, and it is not sacred by any means. In Islam, there are commandments that a Muslim should share in life, but share by working, buying and selling, marriage and divorce; all these actions are civil actions, including politics. Why should politics especially be divine and sacred? They are turning civil society [into] a theocratic society.

And the last point, we have a lot of differences; I'm just giving you the main points. They don't view human rights, they believe in Islamic rights. They say that Islamic rights are before human rights. What do they mean by "Islamic rights" is not clear. And they could consider anything Islamic rights and against human rights. They don't believe in equality between people. They are stressing discrimination between people. Between believers and nonbelievers. Between Muslims and non-Muslims. Between the just and the unjust. Between the good and the evil, without putting any criteria. And the result is they can use these differences to accuse anyone of being against Islam. Beware; they are adopting a doctrine called *taquia*. *Taquia* means "to pretend." This was mentioned in the Qur'an. And it is a doctrine for the Shias. But the political Muslims are using the same thing. They are saying to you something which is not true. And they are organizing themselves as an orchestra. One may stop now. One may play his instrument. Some may take the dirty jobs. Others are justifying. Ghazali and Howeidi and Abu Malik and all others are justifying the murder of their opponents by accusing them of being heretics so that the young people may murder them . . . They issued a statement after the murder of Dr. Farag Foda. They said we are against murder, but Dr. Farag Foda went beyond all the boundaries.

JD: Why did he go beyond all the boundaries?

SA: They are not saying. They could say this about anyone. About anyone. I am, for example, offering my book, *Islamic Caliphates,* in which I couldn't invent history. But they are very mad because I offered history in a systematic way. They are offering history in an elective way, to suit their purposes. But they are not offering it in a systematic way. I am offering it to prove that political power in Islam was always theocratic power and not democratic at all; not liberal, and against the spirit of Islam and against the interest of the people. They don't like that because they are working to establish what they call an Islamic government. I believe that every government in the Islamic world is Islamic.

JD: Explain that. Egypt is an Islamic government?

SA: Yes, because it is not preventing people from prayer, from pilgrimage, from building mosques, and it is working for justice. Every government is working for justice. Islam is just.

JD: So you don't think that a government needs necessarily to enact *Sharia* law to be an Islamic government?

SA: What is *Sharia* law? I will let you know. The word *Sharia* is confused with jurisprudence. In the Qur'an, out of 6,000 verses, there are only 80 verses dealing with legal rules, and they are dealing with family law. And they are applied in Egypt. Some of them are applied over Muslims and non-Muslims. For example, inheritance law. You have in the Qur'an one rule about procedures, and it is applied in Egyptian law because it is the same in Egyptian law as in the French law and in the Roman law. Then there is one rule about social transactions. God allows you to buy and sell and forbids usury. What is usury? It is not mentioned in the Qur'an. Then it is up to the jurists to explain what is usury. And they differed a lot in the history. I have a book entitled *Usury and Interest in Islam,* and I explain how they differed a lot in history.

JD: Did they? Because I have spoken to other Islamists who say Islam prohibits any kind of interest collection.

SA: It is not true. It is not true. Usury is different from interest. Usury means four conditions. First of all it is in barter, not in dealing with money. Between two real persons, not fictitious persons. To double the debts many times, manifold in a short time. The fourth condition, which is very important, the one who failed to pay his debt was subject to be enslaved by the owner. In the time of the Prophet, the Prophet judged [whether] someone [should] be enslaved to someone else. Usury was revealed in the Qur'an mostly to prevent using others and to prevent enslaving them. If [these four conditions] are not realized, then it is not usury. And now there is no slavery. And the rate of the interest is decided by the government .

The word "Islamic law" was restricted to mean the legal rules in the Qur'an. Because the path to God is consisting of three streams, worshipings, ethical codes and legal rules, or social transactions.

Then, in Islam, out of 6,000 verses, there are 80 verses only dealing with legal rules. We have only four punishments in Islam. Some say there are six but actually in the Qur'an there are four punishments. And these punishments are to be applied if we reach a just society in which everyone can find political and economic justice. The second thing is that these four punishments are very difficult to be applied because they have a lot of procedures . . . very difficult procedures. For example, in adultery you should have four male witnesses who saw the act in a very special way which is impossible . . . and by the end, every defendant in Islam has the right to stop the execution of the punishment if he declares that he is repentant.

JD: You're saying if someone repents they should not be punished?

SA: But if someone repents then they should not be punished by stoning or lashing . . . but the government could punish him with another punishment, which is called in Islam *taazir*, or supporting, as if you are supporting by the punishment the defendant to go in the right path. Then all our criminal law, or penal law, is *taazir*. Because it is very difficult to apply the four punishments.

JD: What are the four punishments?

SA: The four punishments are cutting off the hands for theft. Lashing for accusing a woman of committing adultery. Lashing for adultery. Putting in prison or capital punishment for highway robbery. That is all mentioned in the Qur'an. Then they are not covering many things like bribery.

JD: What about murder?

SA: [Deciding punishment for] Homicide is the right of the people. [Punishment] could be dropped if the murderer or his family pays some money to the victim or his family. [Exacting punishment] is considered the right of the people, not the right of the government. Then they can [pardon a murderer] anytime by getting some compensation . . .

JD: You told me before that there were some things in the Qur'an that you believe have to be taken in their historical context.

SA: All of them. All of them. And for that you can find that some verses are temporary and not permanent. Like verses about slavery and slavery harem, concubines. It is a verse that is used by [Sheikh] Omar Abdurrahman [convicted of involvement in the bombing of the World Trade Center in New York] in the United States. "Fight them not to have trouble, till religious is victorious." It is temporary for the Prophet himself, not a permanent law.

JD: Which means that *ijtihad* [reinterpretation of Islamic law] is open. People can reinterpret and reanalyze?

SA: Yes. All the people are talking about *ijtihad* but they are not doing any new ideas. What I did in my books is that I brought new ideas. I brought [a] new method for interpreting the verses of the Koran, new methods for abrogating [nullifying] the verses of the Qur'an. Once I did that I undermined the traditional structure. I dissolved the militant doctrine. For that the traditionals like Al Azhar and the militants are against me.

JD: How do your ideas differ from the Western interpretation of religion and society?

SA: The Western interpretation is going in general terms, that religion should be only in the heart and not out of the heart. It is a relationship between man and God and that's all. The militants believe religion should control everything. But without any definition. It should control everything. Which means that you will have a theocratic society and theocratic government, theocratic law, theocratic judicial system and so on. My interpretation is that the religion should always be in the heart to control oneself and to allow him not to be an individual; first of all to harmonize himself, in himself; then to be harmonized with the family, the society, the humanity and the cosmos in general. Then I believe religion is controlling everything. I am not putting religion on the party, on the organization. The militants are putting religion on the party, on the organization and so on.

JD: When you look at Western society, you see a problem with regard to—

SA: Yes, they are cutting themselves from society and from the cosmos. I believe that the new understanding of faith or of religion, which I offered in my book, is to offer a new understanding between the militants' understanding and the Western understanding.

JD: So, you're taking the best of both?

SA: Yes. I'm putting the faith in heart, but not to stay in the heart. To be a dynamic force in the heart.

JD: But when it comes to organizing a government and organizing society, you are not opposed to using Islamic teachings to guide the legal scholars?

SA: In Islamic teaching you can find everything. Islamic teaching is supporting socialism, supporting capitalism, supporting a dictatorship, supporting liberalism, supporting theocratism. Because it is different interpretations and it is civilization with many applications. Then I'm offering the liberal interpretation of Islam. Not to force the society and the government to be a theocratic society. I believe that every government looking for justice is an Islamic government. Of course, we have some faults in every society. Here in Egypt we have corruption. In the Sudan, you have a theocratic government. Actually it is not liberal Islam. In Iran, it is government of the imams [clerics].

JD: Now, am I right in saying that there are militants here but the spectrum curves away from violence and you can find people, like you, who are liberals? So you can find people all along the spectrum?

SA: Yes, but I am sorry to say that most Muslims in Egypt especially and in many Islamic countries became fanatic and grow extremist ideas.

JD: Why?

SA: Why? Because they feel that they are oppressed . . . rejected. They have Israel and Bosnia as examples that there is a conspiracy from the West to hurt Islam.

JD: Do you agree with that?

SA: No, no. Not at all. Not at all. The Saudis used the money from the gas, from the petrol, to support their doctrine, which is a militant doctrine, the Wahhabi doctrine. The Iranians are doing the same. The CIA helped a lot, the United States helped [the militants] a lot because they used them to fight the communists. In Egypt the Nasserists were opposing President Sadat and that was the advice, to use the militants and to create a militant movement. He thought he could control it, but it went beyond his control.

JD: Can they be controlled?

SA: No, not at all. Because they are always working for themselves and they have a militant doctrine and they believe they are working for God.

JD: Can they be included in government?

SA: They are outside of any law . . . The CIA used them, and then they became a power. Israel planted HAMAS to fight the PLO and at last it is now negotiating with the PLO. But HAMAS became a bitter enemy to both. Then there are lot of elements, a lot of reasons which are [supporting] the militants all over the world. The Saudis and the Iranians are supporting every Islamic center abroad. And they are persuading even the [moderate] Muslims to be militants. The Saudis were supported by the CIA . . . and still they are supported [by the United States].

JD: So what is left to do? In all the things you mention, the one thing I did not hear you mention was democracy . . . opening up . . . plurality.

SA: Well, if you are offering now democracy in Egypt, [it will fail because] it will be used by the fascists, by the militants. Why? Because you have 60 percent of the males who are illiterate. And about 85 or 90 percent of the people who are illiterate. They are alphabetically illiterate [and] culturally illiterate. They are not cultured.

JD: What do you mean by cultured?

SA: Cultured? To have broad mind, not a short mind. To have a wide understanding, a wide view. To believe that you are not monopolizing the truth. To believe that others are there.

I believe that first of all you have to change the society to be a liberalist society . . . a liberal society. And after being a liberal society and accepting many ideas, you can offer democracy. Because democracy means pluralism. Still, most Egyptians do not believe in pluralism, in ideas. They don't believe in the other idea. The Muslim Brotherhood [is] always attacking everyone who is offering any idea that is different from their own . . . and accusing anyone either directly or indirectly of being secular, which means atheist in Egypt, which means pro-Western, which means pro-Westernized, which is a heretic.

JD: So they accuse you of being pro-Western?

SA: Yes, yes, yes. Atheist. I was accused of being atheist, Yes, you've read my book. I'm not atheist.

JD: No, it looks like you're really dedicated to the study of Islam.

SA: Yes. I am a Muslim. I am a good Muslim. But at the same time I don't believe in their doctrine. In the political Islam, traditional Islam, because it leads to militancy. Then I believe in democracy. But not before [the people] are ready for it. Otherwise it would be used by the fascists. Democracy would be undermined through democracy. Liberty will be undermined through liberty, and so on.

JD: What can the West do to improve its relationship with the Islamic world . . . with people like you?

SA: To dialogue with us. To stress our ideas. To advise the governments to take the right path by stopping corruption, by installing justice, by changing the educational system, by changing the information system and so on. We should cooperate all together because [militant Islam] is a disaster against humanity, not against Islam only. I am sacrificing myself because I am defending Islam, Egypt, humanity and civilization.

JD: And so you're setting yourself up by continuing to speak out and to publish?

SA: Yes. But my books are very well known and disseminated. In Tunisia, they are asking every student in the high school to read my book *Essence of Islam*. I always wanted to be a thinker, not a novelist or a [playwright]. This is new [being a thinker] in the East, because most writers are afraid to be thinkers because to be thinkers means to deal with some issues which are in the religious domain.

JD: And that can be dangerous?

SA: That can be dangerous.

I believe there is one religion but with many paths. And I studied Islamic law very well, and Egyptian law. And I tried to be a thinker. I published five books. The sixth book was *Roots of Islamic Law.* President Sadat was flattering the extremists and encouraging them. Then he committed many committees to codify Islamic law. I studied their work. I found that they are codifying Islamic jurisprudence which is not far removed from our Egyptian law. The only thing is that they are changing the terminology to have a theocratic legal system and theocratic judicial system. Then I published my book *Roots of Islamic Law,* carrying my new method to interpret the Qur'an and, at the same time, proving that our Egyptian law is not far removed from Islamic law. Then I was requested by some friends to simplify some ideas of the book and to publish them in a widespread newspaper called the *Akbar,* the *News.* I did. After two articles I was attacked by the Muslim Brotherhood severely.

They said that I am offering a new religion. Actually I am offering [a] new understanding for Islam. If they consider themselves the religion, then I am offering something other than what they believe in. The secretary general of the Muslim Brotherhood wrote an article in their magazine, which is called the *Dawa,* in Arabic. He said, Judge Ashmawy should stop talking by any means. It was a sign for the militants to murder me. Then in the sixth article, I said that Muslims, Christians and Jews are accepted before God, on the basis of two verses mentioned in the Qur'an.

JD: Which two?

SA: Surah 5, verse no. 69: "Those who are believers, which are the Muslims, the Jews, the Christians and the Suppines [a group who were living at the time of the Prophet] . . . who of them who has faith in God and the last day and doing well has no fear upon him and is accepted from God." I used this verse and I said we shouldn't accuse Christians and Jews of being infidels because it is mentioned in the Qur'an that we are equal; equal before God. And we shouldn't accuse each other on earth because we don't know who is right. Then the minister of the Waqf, who is in charge of religion, attacked me. He said that Christians and Jews are infidels and you should not write [otherwise]. You have to stop writing. This verse is abrogated [revised or deleted from the Qur'an by Muhammad]. I rebutted him proving to him that this verse was repeated in the Qur'an, not abrogated. And that he has no proof that it was abrogated and all the people are accepted from God, are the same in the eye of God, by the verses of the Qur'an. Then he answered me and said that I am a heretic and [spilling] my blood is lawful.

JD: When was this?

SA: It was in January 1980. The secretary general of the Muslim Brotherhood wrote in *Al Dawa* magazine that this is a *fatwa*, a legal opinion, and it should be exercised by any Muslim. I complained to President Sadat. He fired this minister. Just one year later President Sadat was murdered. But he [decided] not to codify Islamic law. And they believe I was behind not codifying Islamic law.

JD: He stopped codifying Islamic law?

SA: Yes, he stopped.

JD: Because he saw it was leading to more militancy?

SA: To more militancy. It was leading society to be a theocratic society. He was convinced of my ideas. After that I stopped, until 1983. Then I started again publishing books. I published my book *Political Islam* in 1987, which you read; and *Islamism Contre Islam*. And they were deeply, were severely mad at me. They attacked me. And Al Azhar joined them. Because I was offering new ways to interpret the Qur'an.

Two years ago, Al Azhar tried to ban five of my books in the International Book Fair. Then I challenged Al Azhar saying Al Azhar has no right to ban any book according to Egyptian law and that I am challenging the Grand Sheikh of Al Azhar to come in a live debate on TV with me . . . to say why my books are banned and I will answer him. The result was that the president himself interfered and he ordered the cancellation of Al Azhar's ban. I requested a statement from the Grand Sheikh of Al Azhar saying that Al Azhar hasn't the right to ban any book. So, to support my idea and the president's action, he was requested to do that and he did. It was published in the newspapers.

JD: One final question. When the Western people look at the Islamic world, they see only terrorists. They lump everybody together. What advice can you give them to help differentiate better so that they are not afraid of Islam?

SA: Well, first of all the bullet has a higher sound than the words. The bullet has its effect in the short run. But the word overcomes in the long term. The militants here in Egypt and in all the Islamic world are eager to make [themselves absolute judges] of Islam and to consider any other interpretation non-Islamic, secular. Like my interpretation: non-Islamic, pro-West, westernized and so on.

They are convincing the Westerners that Islam is militancy. Not everyone can search. They are always hearing about what is going on in Afghanistan, about the kidnapping in Lebanon, what happened in Iran, what is happening in Sudan, hitting tourists in Egypt, murdering the policemen in Egypt, what is happening in Algeria and so on. And the result is that this image is the only image offered to the Westerners. I am requesting people like you, the Western media, to give more space to people like me. In time we will overcome. In time the real image of Islam will appear and the bad image, the distorted image of Islam, will disappear.

NINE

BINT AL-SHATI

AL AHRAM *NEWSPAPER, EGYPT*

PROFILE

AISHA ABDEL RAHMAN IS KNOWN TO MILLIONS of Muslims as Bint al-Shati, "daughter of the coast," and columnist in the Egyptian newspaper *Al Ahram*. She is one of the best-known proponents of women's rights in Egypt and a respected Muslim scholar. Bint al-Shati described herself as "a type that is not repeated," and for a woman born into a religious family in rural Egypt in 1913, the intensity of her lifelong quest for education and independence certainly had been unique.

I met Bint al-Shati in her home in the suburb of Heliopolis, located a little less than an hour from Cairo. I was almost arrested en route when I tried to take a picture of a beautiful white house that turned out to be the residence of Hosni Mubarak. Plainclothes officers rushed up to my taxi and chastised me in furious Arabic. It's forbidden to photograph *al bait al abiath* (the White House), they shrieked as I sat cradling my camera. I expected them to take the camera and destroy my film. *"M'arif,"* I offered as a weak defense. I didn't know." My accented Arabic was enough to convince them that I was not Egyptian but simply a stupid foreigner. After they had spent their venom, they simply shooed my taxi away, satisfied that I did not fit their profile of a potential assassin.

Yet the experience was unsettling, and I was relieved to walk past the stone and iron gate and into the shady garden of Bint al-Shati's home. It seemed the most peaceful place on earth, and the smiling old woman who took my hand looked like a saint. I had first heard of al-Shati during an earlier visit to Cairo when I interviewed a sheikh at Al Azhar University, the Islamic world's oldest university, whose *muftis* (Islamic authorities) commanded great respect. I questioned him about whether women were allowed to attend Al Azhar. He told me that not only were some allowed to attend, but that recently, the university had invited a woman to lecture, an invitation that evoked a great deal of fanfare and controversy. The woman was Bint al-Shati. But she didn't get the chance to speak.

"Why not?" I asked.

"She didn't cover," the sheikh said. "Many of the sheikhs didn't like this, and they complained. Bint al-Shati burst into tears and left."

I had expected Bint al-Shati to have painful memories of the event, but she dismissed it as nothing of importance. Muslim feminists had pointed to it as an example of the misuse of Islam to try to control women. Bint al-Shati was an old woman, they argued. Even the Qur'an, they insisted, exempts women past their prime from covering. Why should the grand sheikhs of Al Azhar require more than the Qur'an?

Even though Bint al-Shati told me that she did not cover as a young woman, she did indeed drape a scarf over her hair when she went to speak at Al Azhar. But it wasn't enough, she said. Yet she told me that she had already won so many battles against male chauvinism that the catastrophe at Al Azhar was a minor irritation. She remembered when young women could not even enter the university and now they were allowed to teach there, even if they were denied the same status as men.

Bint al-Shati herself had been denied the right to enter school as a young girl. As the daughter of a sheikh in the village of Dimyat (Damietta), she was not allowed to be in the company of boys, for whom school was reserved. But she so wanted to learn that she studied in her home with her father and "his comrades," she said.

She credited her mother with supporting her desire to learn, even though her mother was illiterate. With her backing, she convinced her father to allow her to study at home, and she ended up completing courses required for primary, secondary and baccalaureate certificates. With her mother as a chaperone, she eventually went to Cairo University to continue her studies. In time she won a position as a professor of Arabic language and literature at Ayn Shams in Cairo and in Fez, Morocco.

In modern Egypt, especially in Cairo and among the middle and upper classes, it is easier for young women to pursue an education than it was for Bint al-Shati. Official government statistics indicate that in primary school, girls make up 44 percent of the enrollment and, at least according to law, primary schooling is compulsory for both boys and girls. In rural Egypt, girls are less likely to be allowed to attend school, especially if they come from poor families. Officially, the illiteracy rate is estimated to be about 50 percent, although it is undeniably higher among women, especially in rural Upper Egypt.[1]

Not surprisingly, the higher the educational level in Egypt, the lower the percentage of female students. According to government statistics, among graduates of secondary schools, only 36 percent are female. Yet that number is a significant improvement over Bint al-Shati's generation, when few women could attend secondary school and even fewer could attend a university.

Bint al-Shati was ever conscious of how unique her story was in the Arab world. She had benefited from "three revolutions," she said. "But you must pay for revolutions." The first had won women the right to learn to read and write. The second gave them the right to leave home; and the third, the right to work. Many women suffered to win those rights, she told me. And with the drama of a poet, she whispered, "Those who passed, like me, we passed on the bones . . . the smashed bones of our comrades."

In Leila Ahmed's book *Women and Gender in Islam*, she mentioned Bint al-Shati, a scholar, novelist, poet and journalist, as being one of the pioneers of working women in Egypt. Ahmed explained that such women greatly changed Egyptian society and that they faced the most resistance when they tried to move into the workplace:

> Even though progressive middle- and upper-class families (the back-ground of an overwhelming proportion of women proceeding to university) were in favor of educating their daughters, the notion of their going out in to the world to work was quite another matter; only poor women worked for a living, and it was improper for the well-to-do to work. Still, many women overcame family as well as societal resistance by arguing . . . that they wished to work not because they wanted the money but because they wanted to work.[2]

That was definitely the case for Bint al-Shati. Her motivation to pursue an education and then a scholarly career was rooted in pure intellectual exuberance, which she maintained into old age.

The office in Bint al-Shati's home was lined with tall bookcases and filled with books, many of which she had written. Her desk was covered with books and papers and though the windows were wide open, the air was so still not that not a sheet fluttered. We sat together on a long, comfortable sofa as she struggled to make herself under-stood in English. She told me she tired easily these days and sometimes found it difficult to move. I thought she had suffered a stroke, as her speech was slurred and she was sometimes difficult to understand. But she said she recently had been in a serious automobile accident and it had taken its toll on her nearly 80-year-old body. I had read that in her youth, she was smart, beautiful and virtuous.

Those characteristics were probably key to her marriage to the renowned Islamic scholar Amin al-Kholi. She became not only his third wife but his companion in Islamic study. Al-Kholi had divorced his first wife but remained married to his second wife after marrying Bint al-Shati. He died in 1966, but she said he was a powerful influence in her life. In fact, in a 1980 interview with C. Kooij published in *The Challenge of the Middle East,* she was asked if she felt any guilt toward al-Kholi's second wife. "I was very unhappy for the other family. I realized that it was cruel for them. I would have been miserable, had I been in their place. But what could I do? He was my destiny and I was his destiny. It was not a matter of happiness or unhappiness. Only my ideals were important."[3]

Expressing those ideals remained the central activity of Bint al-Shati's life. She continued to write a weekly column for the semiofficial daily *Al Ahram* and during the Muslim holy month of Ramadan, she increased her workload to produce a daily column. Her commentaries involved issues of Islamic history and law, especially with regard to the rights of women. She used the Qur'an to argue that Islam never was intended to restrict women to the home but to liberate them. Islam had never stood in the way of women's liberation, she said. The real problem had been that "the Eastern man wants to be a master."

Men who want to be masters over women have often used religion to justify their actions, she said. That has been true of Islam as it has been true of Christianity, Judaism and other religions. In her own religion, Bint al-Shati had to contend with religious scholars who believed that women should remain at home, segregated from men who were not their immediate relatives. The reasoning of many traditionalist Islamic scholars was expressed in a book I picked up in Lahore, Pakistan. *Woman and Islam* by Syed Jalal-Ud-Din Omri asserted:

> Islam assigns different spheres of activity for man and woman. The field of work of woman is her own house and of man is the world outside.[4]
>
> . . . It is no fairness to woman that she should be taken out from her natural field of work and pushed into an unnatural field of work. The first thing is [that] the pains of menstrual period, pregnancy and delivery are unavoidable. . . . The second thing is that woman is the queen of the house. She gets all the love and affection from her father, brother and husband and all the members of family and all her rights are protected in the house. If woman does not bear the responsibility of the house, she cannot claim her rights [the financial support of her husband]. Thereafter she will have to work in such a field to pass her life which will not be in fact her own field [in a profession] and where she will have to face such a partner [male co-workers] at every step who will be stronger than her. Then, it can be hardly expected that she will surpass man.[5]

While Omri conceded that Islam does not prohibit women from active participation in society, he argued that women risked a lot by doing so:

Yes, woman is seen excelling in almost all the field—social, cultural, political, educational and many other fields. In fact, she not only shows her abilities in all the activities or realms of the present day life, but also owns for herself a place of honour and merit. But, what has she done for herself and for her house? No need to ponder over the question. The answer is at hand. She has destroyed her womanliness, her sweet feminine grace . . . She has destroyed her house and her family.[6]

Bint al-Shati had fought against such attitudes all of her life. Such ideas still abound in the Islamic world, she said, yet Muslim women have become sidetracked from dispelling untruths about Islam by the obsession with dress and the veil.

"Islam is not my hands, not my face," she told me. Islam requires modesty in dress so that "when you go out, they understand you are not there to be looked at. But those who like everything out . . . that is not good."

Bint al-Shati's primary message was that men and women should not consider themselves adversaries. They should cooperate and support each other in the exploration of their talents. "He can't live without you and you can't live without him," she said. "Life can't be with one."

Yet sometimes this small, elderly woman sounded as militant as any Western feminist. As she paid tribute to the many women who dared to break through the barriers for women in Arab societies, she seemed impatient with young women who were not bold enough to continue the struggle. Egyptian women had won many victories since Bint al-Shati struggled for an education. Laws mandated a woman received pay equal to a man doing the same job, and they were entitled to the same pension and benefits. In addition, Egyptian law mandated that a woman employed for more than six months receive paid maternity leave for 50 days. Yet women were not allowed to work between the hours of 2 A.M. and 7 A.M., and by Law 137, Article 152-153, they were forbidden from being employed to do work "hazardous to health or reputation or those jobs requiring muscular strength."

As of 1994, Egyptian women had made few gains in the political arena. They won only 7 seats in the 440-seat People's Assembly, the country's parliament. Mubarak appointed another three.

Bint al-Shati believed Egyptian women should demand far more power and should not be content with token inclusion. To this pioneer, who braved a father's wrath and social scorn, it was high time for Muslim women to become more aggressive in securing the rights guaranteed them in Islam.

INTERVIEW WITH BINT AL-SHATI

FEBRUARY 1995, CAIRO, EGYPT

JD: I want to ask you a little bit about yourself, about your writing.

BA: It is a different career, because I didn't go to school. My father is an Islamic sheikh, and the daughters of these people can't go to schools. It is not allowed. So I learned everything at home, it was Islamic school.

JD: So you studied Islamic studies on your own?

BA: I studied with my father and his comrades in Damietta. I started also with Qur'an. Then, when I wanted to go to modern schools, to university, I took all of my certificates from home study . . . primary, secondary and baccalaureate. All three from home study.

JD: Do you regret not being able—

BA: Not at all, because I was different, the type is not repeated, a special type. Then when I wanted to go to modern university, it was very difficult for my father and the family [to allow it].

JD: I see. Did your family not want you to go to modern university?

BA: No, this was not allowed for the daughters of the sheikhs to go with the boys, and so I tried to go secretly . . . It was difficult, but the study was not [as] difficult as my circumstances and my [being] a woman. But my mother was always with me. I felt that she carried me.

My way was very difficult, so she helped me . . . she took me and carried me across.

JD: She supported you. Did your mother want you to become educated?

BA: No, she knows that I wanted to be educated, so she helped me.

JD: Did you have brothers and sisters?

BA: About six, but for my brothers it was not difficult for them. It was different for the daughters. There were four. I am the only one that went through to the end. They learned at home.

JD: I understand that you do a column for *Al Ahram*. What do you write about?

BA: Islamic studies, to show what is Islamic. What is woman in Islam. We don't know it. You must make differences between the law, Islam and our positions.

Because I am different from my sister, from you and everywhere else, from East to West; from upper to lower, we are different. But I deal with Islam as I know it. I can't forget what Islam gave me.

JD: I see. I understand that you were invited, one of the few women who have been invited to Al Azhar, to lecture, to speak.

BA: Yes.

JD: When you went to Al Azhar to speak, I understand that you weren't able to speak. Do you remember what happened?

BA: No, no, nothing. Some of them didn't want me to go. It was not open for girls, and they didn't want women to lecture there. But until now the academy of language [language college within Al Azhar] they don't have women. In the modern Academy of Language, we are not allowed, even now. We were the first generation to come [into universities], so it was enough for me to be in university, in the highest study.

JD: Now when you went there to lecture, I understand you didn't cover your hair?

BA: No, it was, but it was not as they wanted. So . . .

JD: What did they want? Fully covered?

BA: I don't know.

JD: Did this upset you, make you angry?

BA: Not at all. I understood and I let it pass, because we must. It was difficult for us. Even in the University of Cairo, we used to have [rulings] . . . from the Azhar and the sheikhs . . . that the girls are not to go to the University to Cairo. Not only this, but mixed study was not allowed in my age.

JD: Do you think that girls should be able to study in the university with boys?

BA: It's all right now, but still . . . you must pay for revolutions. I saw it was the most difficult revolution in our history. Because for us we had three revolutions; first to learn; second to go outdoors; third, to work. My mother doesn't read or write; [it's] *haram*. [forbidden]. To come from *haram* to what we are, we have crossed . . . Three revolutions we carried on. So [after] all we paid, it was very cheap to be refused [to speak at Al Azhar]. The first generation must pay more.

JD: Yes, yes, I see. So what you're saying is that women have gone through a revolution in the Islamic world, in Egypt. Just to be able to go out to work is a major achievement.

BA: When you get out they can't get you back. Just like a bird in a cage. We suffered much. Those who passed, like me, we passed on the bones . . . the smashed bones of our comrades.

JD: What do you think remains for women to achieve?

BA: Women should be sure that being a mother is the best work. It's not as they [men] said to us. They said that half of society can't work. We work. I think that they must know that they don't [treat] us [equal to] boys. They always look at us different from boys. So we must pay more, study more, we must have good behavior. To be good to let the society know. I don't ask for rights, I take it. Now they [women] wait [for men] to give [them their rights]. We must be learned and we must work. But till now, they don't take into account that motherhood is work.

Second, they put us in a struggle with the other sex. I can't struggle with men because we complete each other. We can't live without each other. So, it can't be a struggle between me and man. That's why we try to teach our daughters that there is not struggle. He can't live without you and you can't live without him. Life can't be with one. So, that is the second fault. Until now, it's like there is a battle between men and women.

JD: Do you see that the sheikhs and the *ulama* [Islamic scholars] and all of these people are becoming more enlightened about women?

BA: No, it is difficult to judge. Because now, everyone speaks of Islam. But you can't speak of the Islam if you don't know Islam. They try to take care of [other matters]. Because now Islam is spoiled by those who kill in the East and say they are Islamic. They are not Islamic. When they say they are Islamic, it is false. And the Western nations think that Islam is against civilizations . . . and they must make battle . . . after the [fall] of the Soviets. That Islam must be this enemy. We are not the enemy of [civilization]. We gave the world three civilizations. I can't cut my roots. Some of them think that whatever you claim from the West is modern. No, it is not modern. The mathematics is not modern. The roots are in our civilization.

JD: I wonder if you think there should be more women Islamic scholars. If women should be able to be among the sheikhs at Al Azhar?

BA: There [is] a new girls' college. But it's only for a few. We have millions every year, thousands from secondary schools.

JD: But can women go to Al Azhar?

BA: Yes, they can. It is easy [for a woman] to be a professor [now], but you can't be an *aalem*. [expert].

JD: Why can't a woman be an *aalem?*

BA: This is very difficult. I couldn't see it [happening] . . . My daughters are students and are professors now in the universities. But it is difficult for them because they are married and [the study required to become an *aalem*] would cut their life.

JD: I see, so it would be difficult for a woman unless she didn't have children and wasn't married to reach that height.

BA: Yes, some of them, they have some [qualifications to be an *aalem*], but the man doesn't want it. The Eastern man wants to be a master. And they [the women] know this. I don't want to have my man a master man. I don't want to have my husband so. I don't want it. Most of them [Muslim women] they are [content to be] the lady of the house and he is the master.

JD: So, you don't want a man to be the master over you?

BA: No. It should be cooperation. Not a struggle for position . . . for power. I don't now know what is the point. When the man is a man, for me, it is good. I am very miserable if he is not a man. But he can't be the master of the family when he is bad. But when your nature is good, you don't have any problem.

JD: You think that now in the Muslim world, women still have a struggle?

BA: Some don't understand. They struggle now over the *hijab* [head-scarf] and to go to the beach . . . really, I don't understand.

JD: You have worn the *hijab?*

BA: No, never. Because Islam is not my hands, not my face. [The intention is that] when you go out, they understand you are not to be looked at. Islam doesn't want me to be spoiled or to be attacked . . . it keeps my dignity. And if someone says anything against a woman [accuses her of adultery], he must bring four witnesses [to the act]. If he gives three only, he is to be whipped.

JD: So, when a woman goes out, does she have to cover her head?

BA: No. But those who like everything out . . . this out . . . and that out . . . for show . . . that is not good.

JD: Does Islam allow a woman to be a singer, to be a dancer?

BA: No. Why does a dancer dance?

JD: Well, like a ballet dancer?

BA: No, this is modernity. Now we [shouldn't] struggle for things that they [the West)] have. In the fourteenth century, Islam laid down human rights better [than the West has done]. Look at what American makes for Somalia and for Pakistan. They go not for civilization but to attack them. And what about Bosnia? What has happened in South Africa until two years ago?

JD: And what do you think about the relationship between the West and Islam?

BA: From our point of view, it's not easy for you. Because we are the latest religion. All the religions that came before, we respect them . . . *a min farqa baina ahad* . . . no difference between them. You can't get this from Judaism or Israel . . . We have our religion yes; our law, our behavior; but we respect all of them, from Noah, and Adam. It is easy [to coexist with other religions] . . . But not to leave my religion. Every religion has its own system and prophet. Your prophet is the Messiah, mine is Muhammad . . . not more, not less. But I respect the Messiah and Moses and Muhammad. Because we are a broad religion.

TEN

ISHAQ FARHAN

SENATOR, ISLAMIC ACTION FRONT, JORDAN

PROFILE

ISHAQ FARHAN WAS CLEARLY A VERY BUSY MAN. I could tell that immediately as he rushed into his office the morning of our interview. The photograph of him in *Who's Who in the Jordanian Parliament* showed a smiling, gray-bearded man with a checkered *kuffiyeh* draped over his head. The gray beard was the same, but the smile and the *kuffiyeh* were noticeably absent. Farhan was all business, with no time to waste. I had half an hour to ask my questions and let him get back to work.

Farhan was a senator in Jordan's Parliament and secretary general of the Islamic Action Front (IAF), considered the most powerful political party in Jordan when we met in early 1994. He was also a leading member of the Muslim Brotherhood, all of which made him one of the most influential men in the country. We met in his office on the second floor of the IAF, in the same part of town as the Islamic Hospital and the offices of the Muslim Brotherhood. He was accompanied by a stern-looking aide who sat in silence busily taking notes throughout our conversation.

Unlike Islamists in other parts of the Muslim world, Farhan said the IAF was intent on helping to maintain stability in Jordan, a country beset by so many pressures that analysts had been predicting for years that it was ripe for an explosion. There had been economic problems exacerbated by the United Nations embargo against Iraq, with which Jordan had enjoyed lucrative trade. Jordan had absorbed millions of refugees since the Gulf war, including Iraqis fleeing the economic depression in their country and Palestinians forced out of the Gulf states. Then there were the Palestinian refugees from the wars with Israel, many of whom still lived in refugee settlements in a perpetual state of anger and bitterness. Added to all of this was the strong popularity of the IAF and the Muslim Brotherhood and their opposition to King Hussein's steady moves toward peace with Israel. The Brotherhood and the IAF had been staunch supporters of the Palestinian cause and of Palestinian demands to regain the land they lost to Israel, a cause the king had long ago abandoned as futile. Despite such serious pressures, violence directed against the government had been negligible. Political analysts inside the country credited much of that to the stabilizing influence of the Islamists.

"The uniqueness of the Jordanian experiment is that so far, we have not had violent offshoots of the Islamists," Mustafa Hamarneh, a political analyst with the University of Jordan's Center for Strategic Studies, told me. "The Muslim Brotherhood has never had a history of opposition. They've always been very close to the palace. They've never advocated the overthrow of Hashemite rule or the regime. . . . The Muslim Brotherhood are very concerned about maintaining stability, and the leadership advocates nonviolence. So this is the most important political group in the country, and it advocates nonviolence."

In a survey conducted in March 1993 by Hamarneh's center on attitudes toward democracy in Jordan, the IAF was supported by about 19 percent of the population, making it the largest and most organized political party in the country. "And that support largely is among the middle class," Hamarneh said. "So to reduce the support for the Islamists . . . to a protest role is an oversimplification."

The IAF clearly had a solid base of support despite the prevalence of many secular-oriented parties and despite its being entrenched in

Jordan's establishment. Yet Islamists in Jordan were working for the same goal as Islamic political parties throughout the world: creation of an Islamic state. The difference in Jordan was that they were legal, peaceful and had a strong voice in politics. The IAF had convinced the Jordanian public of its commitment to plurality and democracy, even as members voiced their criticisms of government policies they deemed "un-Islamic."

The IAF was originally intended to be a broad-based coalition of Islamic interests, with the overall goal of establishing Islamic law in Jordan. But it ended up being dominated by the Muslim Brotherhood. In their interpretation of Islamic law, party members tried to have alcohol banned in the country but succeeded only in banning liquor from Royal Jordanian airline flights between Muslim countries. The IAF also tried to pass legislation segregating boys and girls in secondary schools. During the six-month tenure of one of its leaders, Abdallah Akayreh, as education minister, male and female employees of the ministry were segregated and fathers were banned from school functions involving girls, including their daughters. "But the king basically is opposed to these types of legislation," Hamarneh told me. "It's not by accident that not one member, female member of his family, covers."

Although many IAF and Brotherhood members advocated segregation of the sexes in schools and the workplace, that did not necessarily mean they believed that women should not pursue education and professions. Many women supported the IAF and 13 women were listed among its founding members. Yet there were no women in the offices of the IAF when I visited, and men clearly held the reins of power. As with many, although not all, of the Islamist men I interviewed, their idea of equality for women was far different from that of a Western feminist.

However much the IAF may be criticized by its opponents, or however objectionable some of its goals may seem to Western observers, the party had achieved them legally and peacefully.

Inside the IAF, there was much internal debate on many issues, including its stand opposing peace with Israel. One of the major planks of the IAF's platform had been its support of the Palestinian cause and its opposition to U.S. attempts to broker what the IAF felt was an unjust peace with Israel. Farhan seemed deeply suspicious of Western intentions in the region. He expressed serious concern about the influence of Western powers in the affairs of Middle Eastern states and recalled the legacy of colonialism that he said had made Muslims hostile toward the West.

Yet in explaining what he saw as reasons for the hostility many Islamists felt toward the governments of Western states, Farhan emphasized the need for tolerance and cooperation between cultures. He believed this desire for cooperation was not shared by the West, which he feared was intent on domination and on eradicating Islam. Like many Islamists, he bitterly criticized the West for claiming to promote pluralism while not supporting Islamists in their calls for democracy.

Farhan told me that the IAF was instrumental in helping to push the king toward democratic reform in Jordan, although it had been slow in coming. In 1989 the country held the first parliamentary elections since 1967, when the king declared martial law following the massive influx of Palestinian refugees in the wake of the war with Israel. The IAF did very well in those elections, winning 22 of the 80 seats in the parliament. On June 9, 1991, a general congress of elected representatives of all political interests in the country, including the IAF, adopted a national charter, opening the way for a restoration of political pluralism.

"It was through the national charter that representatives of all political trends in the country committed themselves to political pluralism and pledged not to use democracy to get to power and then prevent others from exercising the same right" was how a press release issued in November 1993 by the Jordan Information Bureau defined the importance of the charter in allowing the king to continue his moves toward political pluralism.

In April 1992 martial law was abolished, and in September 1992 political parties were allowed to form, the first time since 1957. Jordan's constitution now specifically protected the rights of political interests to vie for power in the kingdom, stating: "Jordanians are entitled to establish societies and political parties provided that the objects of such societies and parties are lawful, their methods peaceful and their bylaws not contrary to the provisions of the Constitution."

Yet during the decades that political parties were banned, the Muslim Brotherhood solidified its support among the people as a charitable organization. When political parties were allowed to form, the Islamic Action Front had a distinct advantage.

Because the political voices of Islamists were not smothered in Jordan, Farhan said, violence was unnecessary and extremist elements were more easily checked. Jordanians had protection against any party, Islamic or secular, completely usurping power because all parties had to acknowledge the supremacy of the constitution and, practically speaking, the supremacy of King Hussein. For his part, Farhan expressed complete loyalty to the king, whom many Islamists respected as a descendant of the Prophet Muhammad. King Hussein, in fact, appointed Farhan to the Senate.

Farhan was actually a Palestinian by birth, born in 1934 in Ain Qarem, in what was then Palestine. He had bachelor's and master's degrees in science from the American University in Beirut and a doctorate from Columbia University in New York. He told me he was a chemist by profession and spent many years teaching physics and chemistry in secondary schools. He was associate professor of Islamic Law and Education at Jordan University from 1964 to 1970 and served as the university's president from 1976 to 1978. From 1978 to 1989, Farhan was a professor of education at Yarmouk University in Jordan. In 1964 he was appointed director of curriculum development in Jordan, and in 1970 he was appointed minister of education, a post that he held in three cabinets.

Farhan also was minister of Islamic Affairs and Religious Foundations from 1970 to 1973. He seemed particularly proud of serving as president of the Royal Scientific Society and as a member of the National Consultative Council, advisors to King Hussein.

Farhan saw not the slightest conflict in his loyalty to King Hussein, his pursuit of an Islamic state in Jordan and his support for the king's moves toward democracy. This situation seemed to be typical among leading Islamists in Jordan. "You find people who are very Islamist," Hamarneh explained, "but yet they would not accept any discussion when it comes to the king."

Many Islamists felt an obligation to King Hussein because he provided them a haven in the 1970s when Egypt's Gamal Nasser and other Arab leaders were persecuting them. While many leaders were forced to reverse their policies to appease or co-opt the Islamists, King Hussein was one of the few leaders who carefully cultivated a long and close relationship with religious activists without being controlled by them. "And really, it's different with the king," Hamarneh said, "it's really different. Besides, nobody can out-Islam the man."

Although Jordanians respected the king as a descendant of the Prophet, he had not been able to avoid tensions with Islamists. For example, many of them opposed his support of Iraq in the Iran-Iraq war during the 1980s, just as they opposed his support of the Shah during the Iranian revolution. In 1986, when Syria faced its own Islamist struggle against the Assad regime, many members of Jordan's Muslim Brotherhood were arrested and harassed for their support of Syria's Muslim Brotherhood.

Yet such tensions had been rare and they had not led to violent confrontations between government forces and Islamists. Farhan reminded me that there was considerable tension between the king and leaders of the IAF over his support for changes in Jordan's election laws, changes that were designed to dilute their strength before the 1993 elections. The new election law gave each voter only one vote. Under the old system, a voter had as many votes as there were seats in his district, a situation that effectively strengthened the IAF presence in parliament as their millions of supporters cast all of their votes for IAF candidates. Farhan was one of the most vocal critics of the election law changes, but he noted that the IAF's decision to participate in the elections despite them showed its commitment to working within the democratic process. It also showed that the IAF could accept setbacks graciously, he said, even if they were unjust.

The IAF had threatened to boycott the elections, and many feared there would be a confrontation between the king and the Brotherhood. In an address to the nation on August 17, 1993 announcing the election law changes, King Hussein sent this special appeal to the IAF:

> I am concerned with safeguarding the unity of the country. I am also concerned about our sons, some of whom have been chosen to belong to a front, which they have named the Islamic Front. What I wish for them and from them is that they truly practice their historic respon-

sibilities in striving to live up to the name they have chosen, and to proceed, with God's help, toward true Islam, in fulfillment of their spiritual and worldly duties, and in the defense of that which is most precious to us against attempts to undermine and distort Islam from within the Islamic *umma* [community] and from without.

The appeal worked and a serious confrontation was avoided, or perhaps delayed. An even greater test of the relationship between the Islamists and the king may come as Jordan solidifies its ties with Israel. Many members of the Muslim Brotherhood and the IAF continued to oppose the peace treaty with Israel even after King Hussein signed it. The IAF thought the treaty was unjust to Palestinians, thousands of whom were still refugees in Jordan. But the treaty did not give Muslims control of Jerusalem, which made accepting it difficult for any Islamist. Clearly, Jordan's peace treaty with Israel had once again heightened tension between the king and the IAF. Only time would tell if that tension would grow to undermine what had been a historic relationship of respect and cooperation unparalleled in the Middle East.

INTERVIEW WITH ISHAQ FARHAN

FEBRUARY 1994, AMMAN, JORDAN

JD: What is the mission of your party in Jordan? What is the ideal you are trying to achieve in Jordan?

IF: We think that Islam is a way of life. And we think our heritage lies in the heart of the ideals and values of Islam, like in the West, you say our values—our life is the values of democracy. We think our mission is the values of Islam. And we think it is international by definition.

When we survey the democratic values, and the human rights values, and what have you, on the humanitarian and international scene, we think that the majority of these values are consistent with our ideas.

We think that the Islamic mission is our mission to our people, to try in a—in a very concise way, I can put it, to try to live our modern life, but according to our ideals, and values and heritage. And we think that if you cut the people from their heritage and values, you're just like cutting a big tree from its roots. No matter how big it is, if it has no roots, then it will not survive.

So, we think our main mission is to clear our values to our people, Islamic values, and remove the dust from them. Because many distorted values are intermixed with maybe habits, or social habits, or norms, which are not even sometimes near to Islam, or the civility of Islam.

We think our major mission is to clear up our values and let our people be aware of them. And we think that we are being in congruency with modern times. We can live our modern life also, in full efficiency, and with no contradiction with our ideals, especially when we look at ourselves as an integral part of our Arab and Islamic nation and also as an integral part of humanity. We don't want to live in isolation.

JD: Now, do you believe that Islam as a political force is threatened?

IF: Yes. I think it is threatened from two sides. The first side is the Islam as being sometimes misunderstood by Muslims themselves. The image of Islam has been distorted from the—what we call Western mouths, or Western-educated people from our people.

Besides, when political Islam began to be an issue in the Islamic nation, the West just did not understand this phenomenon. And they tried to just act upon it, or against it.

And also we see, for example, like democracy in Algeria, where the Muslims began to accept the rules of democracy and to be judged [in elections according to] the interests of the people and wishes of the people. We saw that America and France, for example, stood against the results of democracy, as if they want—if the results of democracy came in consistently with what they think—then okay, they support it. If not, then they will just—don't like it.

And we have met of course many declarations and comments from many Westerners, journalists, or thinkers, or philosophers or politicians, to say if democracy will come up . . . with an Islamic flavor, we don't like it. We don't want it. So we prefer probably dictatorship.

JD: Do you think this is one of the chief causes or one of the causes of the hostilities that—

IF: That's right. That's right. I think our people, Muslims and Arabs, are not hostile by nature. They have been subjugated by imperialism, British imperialism, French imperialism, Spanish imperialism. They did not want to be in conflict with the Americans, for example. But during the Second World War, and after that, when America began to be involved in the internal politics of our countries, unfortunately without understanding much about the anthropology of the people and the culture of the people. They just want to implement their policies by force. And the example of Israel and the strategic coopera-tion between the United States and Israel aggravated the problem. And I think if the United States did not stand by the side of Israel, many of the hostilities wouldn't have arisen between the Arabs and the Americans . . . or the American state . . . not the American people. Till now there are no such deep hostilities between the peoples, our people and the people of the United States. Many thousands and thousands of our graduates are in the States. So, they have a good picture about the technological advances and the civilization and so on. But neverthe-less, Europe has a deep history of hostility with our people, at least in the last two centuries. So, the results of these hostilities have been taken over by the American people and the fault of Europe and history has been transferred to the Americans. So, I think now the Americans are doing the job . . . I don't say naively . . . but just as a bulldozer, trying to move everything from their way without understanding the sentiments of people and the values of people. And this is aggravating the problem and making more psychological and social damages in the hearts of the people.

My suggestion is that like yourself now, and other politicians and journalists now . . . the premise and hypothesis that should replace the previous mistaken hypothesis or fallacy in the hearts of the people of the West . . . to understand that Islam and Muslims are one-quarter or one-fifth of this globe . . . 1.2 billion inhabitants. So, it is a fact of life. And even if the West wants to use all the force they have . . . all the weapons, all the nuclear weapons, they couldn't eliminate this race or this religion. This is not the way to do it. So, if they accept Muslims as part of this globe and a complete part, a sizable part, one-fourth of the world, they have to deal with it scientifically and pragmatically as here it is a fact of life. To deal with Muslims as a fact of life, not just to subjugate Muslims even to the culture of the West, although I believe the culture of Islam and the culture of the West and the culture even of the Chinese have many [things] in common. Humanity is being more and more transferred into what we might call a world culture, an international culture.

But nevertheless, the subcultures have to exist and to complement each other rather than to contradict each other. I think humanity should understand how to live with each other, acknowledging the differences: the social, the psychological, the individual, the cultural differences between each other.

See what's done in Bosnia, nobody can believe it; no human being can believe it; that just cold blood can be shed and still the only fault of the Bosnians is that they are Muslims. And everybody in this world is silent about this, although they are saying the Serbs don't have the right to do this and that. But we see the forces of the Americans are coming to Somalia just right away. The forces of the 30 nations, the European states led by the United States, to fight Iraq. Now Iraq is [isolated] for three years, they are saying we obey the United Nations rules, and so many tens and tens of United Nations groups coming and supervising and until now, they are making an embargo on the nation.

JD: Is that a big problem for you as a Muslim? The UN embargo?

IF: Yes, sure. We see the children die out of hunger. We see the people . . . and they don't have food. They have their worth just as human beings. Even if there are mistakes from the rulers, this doesn't justify killing people. And especially after the war is over. We condemn war, not just the war between Iraq and Kuwait, but any war between two Arab nations, or Muslims, or even foreigners. Nobody likes war. Everybody likes peace. But when we see the vested interests of the Americans in the petroleum . . . and we see the internal undercurrent sort of competition between the United States and Japan and Germany about our wealth and so on, as if we are just guards for them regarding this world . . . and we have some sheikhs in control here and they are just as agents for the West or the Americans, to do the job for them.

JD: Do many Islamic leaders believe that many leaders of Muslim countries are not really independent?

IF: Yes, I think that our independence is only superficial in the Arab world. And we think that American ambassadors all over the Arab world are playing bad roles and interfering in our affairs. And I don't think this is fair. So, another interpretation should be done for what they call the new world order. I'm afraid it's the world *dis*order. They are increasing disorder in the whole world rather than increasing order. So this is the roots of what we call the hostility between the West and the Islamists and Islam. And we don't think it has deep roots, especially with the Americans. With the Americans this hostility arose just after World War II. I think that as I said at the outset, the influences of the Crusades of 500 years ago between the Muslims and Europe have been transferred on the backs of the Americans.

I don't think the Arab nation will for long be fragmented. We look for a sort of united Arab states, like the United States of America. They fought each other in a civil war for years and years and then they found pragmatically that they should live together in a sort of federation and so on. And I think this is the future of the Arab world. If the world will be order instead of disorder, America and Europe should look on the Arabs and the Muslims as one nation instead of keeping to fragment them. Now the United States is trying to fragment Iraq into three states, south, north and middle; and also, we think that a conspiracy on Syria is behind the scenes to fragment it . . . and even the simple unity between Jordanians and Palestinians, we think many unseen figures are trying to disrupt these people, which are one nation. And it's proved to be a very good unity in the last 30, 40 years.

JD: It seems to me that in Jordan, there's a relatively low level of violence, of religiously motivated violence. To what do you credit that?

IF: Well, I credit it to three main factors. The first factor is our Islamic values, which are peaceful. We condemn violence. In Islamic ideology, to kill one person is like killing all of humanity. This is a verse of the Qur'an. No matter what his religion is, Islam is against killing a cat, let alone a man.

JD: So why do they keep doing this in Egypt?

IF: The system is doing it. There is a low score of intelligence among those who are doing it against the higher echelon. This comes to the second factor in Jordan that our king has some wisdom, has experience and he knows how to deal with his people. He has credibility. The third factor is the Islamic movement factor, which is a factor of stability rather than instability. We consider our national unity, our stability of the country as a prime strategy in our political Islam strategy.

JD: So unlike what is feared, that if you allow Islamic parties to participate in government, they will destabilize it, the fact is that they stabilize it?

IF: They stabilize it more. I think it would stabilize it more. We have tried to have some ministers in the last cabinet . . . two or three years ago. And we proved to people that our ministers are more human and more value centered and more near to the people than other non-Islamic ministers, for example, or a minister who does not really care about Islamic ideals.

JD: But certainly you were not happy about the latest changes in the law in which you lost some of your power?

IF: Sure. Well, we think this change in the election law has done great damage to us. We were about to boycott the elections. But because we care about our country, because we care about national unity, because we care about dealing with politics pragmatically, we thought that it was not wise to boycott the elections, although it was meant to cut some of our political power. We think in the long run, democracy should be reinforced and become a way of thinking and a way of life. In the long run, distorted laws, or bad laws, as we call them, can be changed through democratic channels.

JD: So, you're committed to democracy?

IF: That's right.

ELEVEN

IBRAHIM GHOSHEH

HAMAS, WEST BANK AND GAZA

PROFILE

Allah is its Goal.

The Messenger is its Leader

The Qur'an as its Constitution

Jihad as its methodology, and

Death for the sake of Allah is its most coveted desire.

—Motto of the Islamic Resistance Movement[1]

IN FEBRUARY 1994 Ibrahim Ghosheh conducted his work as spokesman for the Islamic Resistance Movement, known by its acronym HAMAS, from the offices of the Muslim Brotherhood in Amman, Jordan. While HAMAS was not supposed to have a legal or official status in Jordan, the fact was that there was still a close relationship between the Brotherhood in Amman and HAMAS, although it was perhaps not as close as during the 1980s, when HAMAS first surfaced in the West Bank and Gaza as an offshoot of the Jordanian Muslim Brotherhood. I first contacted Ghosheh by faxing a request from Washington to the Brotherhood's offices in Amman to meet him. I was not surprised when he agreed to meet me in their offices. The Muslim Brotherhood's headquarters were on the second floor of a four-story building, only a short, tree-lined walk from the Marriott Hotel where I was staying.

On another floor was a pharmacy and medical clinic. Across the street was the Islamic Hospital, and around the corner were the offices of the Islamic Action Front, the most powerful political party in Jordan, another creation of the Muslim Brotherhood. And just as the Islamic movement in Jordan built its political foundation by providing medical services to families, giving money and comfort to the elderly and the poor, HAMAS had been doing the same in the West Bank. Yet both the charitable and the militant aspects of HAMAS had been sources of anxiety for the Palestine Liberation Organization (PLO). PLO leaders had long been concerned about HAMAS's activities in the West Bank and Gaza. HAMAS had been the PLO's direct rival among Palestinians and opposed peace talks with Israel. Most of all, HAMAS had opposed the PLO for following a secular path to the liberation of Palestine and for compromising on the return of what it contended was Arab land held by the state of Israel. There had been allegations that Israel actually helped strengthen HAMAS in order to undercut the PLO and weaken the Palestinian resistance.

Yet it had long been apparent that HAMAS could be as dangerous, if not more so, than the fighters of the PLO. As Robert Satloff described it in a paper published by the Washington Institute for Near East Policy in October 1988:

> To the Israelis, busily combating the pre-intifada diplomatic gains of Palestinian nationalism on the international level and the guerrilla threat internally, Islam appeared as part of the solution, not part of the problem. Support for Islam—or at least indifference to its growth—was viewed as coming at the expense of the more feared nationalist groups. As a result, successive Israeli officials readily gave permission for the construction of new mosques and for the registra- tion of Islamic charitable organizations as legally functioning public associations.[2]

Ghosheh emphatically denied that there was any cooperation between HAMAS and Israel at any point. The people who would solidify

HAMAS as an organization originally worked underground as members of the Muslim Brotherhood based in Jordan, he said. The Brotherhood was not taking an active role in resisting Israeli occupation because it was busy preparing itself by gaining the support of the people and building cadres of fighters. The Brotherhood's initial passivity toward the occupation may have misled Israeli officials into believing that devotion to religion would divert Palestinians away from their quest for a state. If so, they were wrong. While Ghosheh did not credit HAMAS with actually igniting the intifada, he did credit Muslim activists inside Gaza and the West Bank with encouraging it weeks before Fatah leaders joined the resistance.

Although the Palestine Liberation Organization would dispute Ghosheh's version of this story, it was clear that the intifada solidified HAMAS as a distinct organization with close ties to the Brotherhood and with support from its members in Jordan. HAMAS was formed by Sheikh Ahmed Yassin and other Palestinians who gradually came to believe there was no solution to their problem other than fighting Israel. Inside the larger Brotherhood at the time, many still were not ready to condone all-out violence, although they shared the anger and frustration of their more militant brothers. HAMAS's inroads against the PLO were due partly to its social programs and partly due to popular frustration at the PLO's inability to relieve the suffering of its people under occupation. Eventually the PLO came to fear HAMAS almost as much as the Israelis, especially after the Gulf war, when the rich Gulf states cut off their funding to the PLO, almost bankrupting it, while HAMAS continued to enjoy financial support from its backers. Ghosheh said that much of this financial support came from payments offered by Muslims inside the Occupied Territories as well as around the world, including in the United States. The PLO also received financial support from Palestinians and Arabs worldwide. But Muslims everywhere wanted not only to help HAMAS's social aid programs for Palestinians inside the West Bank and Gaza; many also wanted to help them maintain the struggle against Israel.

HAMAS's *jihad* against Israel was the foundation of its popularity with the Palestinian people and especially with youths searching for a way out of the daily misery of occupation. During the bleakest hours of the peace process, when the meetings seemed to be endless shams and there was little hope of a breakthrough, HAMAS's popularity was at its highest. More and more, Palestinians were ready to accept the hard and angry message of HAMAS: that the only hope lay in *jihad* and that negotiating peace with Israel was treason.

Ghosheh was one of the most important people in HAMAS. He was a small, intense man who spoke quickly, even in English. Like many middle-age Palestinian men, Ghosheh had spent his life consumed with the cause of recapturing the land Palestinians lost to Israel. As all-encompassing as that cause may appear, however, Ghosheh had an even greater one—Islam. In HAMAS, he was able to work for both. Ghosheh took pains to explain that Islamic movements throughout the world, from the Muslim Brotherhood in Jordan and Egypt to the Jamaat-i-Islami in Pakistan, all supported HAMAS's struggle. That struggle involved not only Palestinians, he said; it was an "Arabic and Islamic" cause.

"Understand," he said, "the issue is important for the Palestinians and for Arabs and Muslims. Because Jerusalem, the Al Akhsa mosque is not only for the Palestinian; it is for all the Muslims all over the world." Ghosheh was about 11 years old when Israel declared itself a state. At that time he lived in East Jerusalem, while the Jews controlled the western part of the city. He remembered the fighting around Jerusalem, "especially on the walls." Memories of Arabs fighting Jews had been etched in Ghosheh's psyche. They were why he first joined the Islamic movement in Egypt as a teenager in the 1950s—to continue the battle for his homeland. He was a young and angry engineering student then, not unlike another Palestinian fighter whose name became synonymous with the Palestinian cause. In fact, Ghosheh said he and Yasser Arafat were friends during the days when they both studied engineering in Cairo. They both were members of the Muslim Brotherhood, but Ghosheh never strayed from the strict Islamic path in pursuing their goal of liberating Palestine from Israeli control.

Although Arafat professed to be a devout Muslim, he had little patience for those who would want to fashion an Islamic state in Palestine. When I interviewed him in Tunis in 1989, he declared emphatically that the country he envisioned would be a secular democracy, and he expressed contempt for those who would divide the

Palestinian people along religious lines. "It should be known that even Fatah, when it started, started from the Islamic movement in the '50s," Ghosheh said. "And even Arafat himself . . . when he was chosen as a leader of the Palestinian students, [it was] we, the Islamic movement young people, who chose [him]."

During his university days in Egypt, Ghosheh worked underground with the Muslim Brotherhood, which had been banned by the Pan-Arab nationalist president Gamal Nasser. Ghosheh saw the real turning point for the Islamic movement after Israel's victory in 1967, which was a major defeat for Arab nationalism. "People started to say, why we are defeated?" he remembered. "Is it because we are away from Islam? After that time, we started in the Occupied Territories, in the West Bank and Gaza Strip, to build our foundation in schools, health clinics, clubs and so on, to train the young people and to prepare them."

In 1989, after decades of involvement in the Islamic movement, Ghosheh was "recruited" to serve as a spokesman for HAMAS in Jordan. He was a member of HAMAS's consultative council, the decision makers and leaders. His command of English probably contributed to his recruitment as its spokesman, along with his decades-long commitment to the goals for which HAMAS had become infamous—turning the clock back far past 1947, when Israel was created.

Although Ghosheh could hardly have been surprised that HAMAS's reputation in the West was that of a feared terrorist movement, he actually seemed taken aback when I referred to it as a "militant" organization. Except for our discussion of whether Israel initially supported HAMAS, it was the tensest moment of our interview.

In fact, he angrily contested the United States including HAMAS on the list of terrorist organizations. HAMAS never engaged in acts like those committed against tourists in Egypt, he argued. Ghosheh also said that HAMAS had never attacked anyone outside of land occupied by Israel. The latter statement, at least, seemed to be true.

Yet HAMAS had claimed responsibility for attacks in Israel that killed innocent people. In February of 1996, a spate of suicide bombers killed dozens of people within a few days, among them children and elderly Israelis.

It could hardly be contested that HAMAS had provided a haven for angry young men who were prepared to kill and to die. HAMAS supporters, as well as those of groups within the Palestine Liberation Organization, had been connected to attacks against fellow Palestinians whom they accused of collaborating with Israeli authorities. Men acting in the name of HAMAS's independent military wing, the Izzeddin al-Qassam brigade, had attacked Israeli settlers, Israeli border policemen and soldiers. The brigade was named after a Syrian-born sheikh who formed resistance cells to fight the British occupation of Palestine. He was killed by British authorities in 1935, and many Palestinians considered him a martyr.

Before March 1994 the brigade may have tried to restrict its attacks to Israeli military targets. According to Islamic researcher Ahmad Rashad, "Qassam cells appear to be striving for a disciplined, organized guerilla mechanism, rather than an instrument of random violence . . . HAMAS may applaud isolated incidents against civilians, yet such cases are not usually planned by Qassam cells."[3]

Whoever planned them, the leadership of HAMAS had claimed responsibility for random acts against civilians. One of its worst campaigns of violence came only a month after I spoke to Ghosheh. In March 1994 Baruch Goldstein, a former Israeli soldier, opened fire in a crowded mosque in Hebron, killing an estimated 42 Muslims and wounding another 150. Izzeddin al-Qassam began a campaign to kill an equal number of Israelis to atone for the massacre. In one HAMAS operation, a man named Ra'ed Zakarneh volunteered to drive a car fitted with explosives into an Israeli bus in the town of Afula. That suicide bombing killed nine Israeli civilians and injured 52. A second attack soon followed in the Israeli town of Hadera. Four more Israelis were reported killed and 30 wounded.

In early 1994 it appeared that HAMAS was at a crossroads and its leaders were trying to decide which road to take, whether to cooperate with the PLO in making peace with Israel or to escalate their activities into full-scale civil war. Exacting revenge and righting the wrongs of occupation was a recurring theme in HAMAS's history and one that seemed to drive Ghosheh and many of its leaders. Ghosheh lost what he said was a 1,000-year heritage when Israel seized East Jerusalem. That's how long he said his ancestors owned their land in Jerusalem, land that now was part of the state of Israel. But Ghosheh had not seen his home since 1967, when Israel occupied all of Jerusalem and the West Bank of the Jordan River. A civil engineer, Ghosheh was working at the time with Jordan on a scheme to prevent Israel from siphoning the waters of the Yarmouk River. After Israel's stunning military victory, a victory that represented disaster for Ghosheh and hundreds of thousands of other Palestinians who became refugees in Amman, all of his work was for naught.

Yet Ghosheh was convinced that his children would once again live on the land that his parents plowed. He was convinced that although the battle with Israel may be long, it must be won. Just as the Christians conquered Jerusalem and remained for hundreds of years until they were forced back to Europe, he told me, so would be the fate of the European Jews who were now living on the land of his forefathers.

When I spoke with Ghosheh in February 1994, Arafat and Rabin had already stunned the world by shaking hands on international television, and HAMAS's leaders were debating whether they should adopt a more pragmatic position. Even as Ghosheh castigated Arafat and the PLO for weakening their resolve to fight Israel until it relinquished all Arab land, he also conceded that HAMAS had resolved not to work actively against the PLO's efforts to make peace with Israel. HAMAS, Ghosheh said, also was honoring an agreement worked out with the PLO to stop the cycle of Palestinian fratricide: of HAMAS youths and Fatah youths killing each other in the streets of Gaza. Hundreds of youths had died as a result of the war between the PLO and HAMAS that raged for months. At one point, Israeli officials noted that more Palestinians were being killed by each other than by Israeli soldiers. But on April 23, 1994, the PLO's Fatah Hawks and al-Qassam guerrillas announced publicly that they had signed a peace pact "to end the violence in Palestinian society."

The Palestinian truce was only one sign of major changes inside HAMAS. When I asked Ghosheh if he could envision peace with Israel, he could not bring himself to say no outright. Other HAMAS leaders went even further after it became clear that Israeli troops would indeed pull out of Gaza and Jericho, in what was hoped to be the first stage of their eventual withdrawal from the Occupied Territories. HAMAS's bureau chief in Damascus, Musa Abu Marzuq, indicated in an interview with an Amman weekly that he could envision peace if Israel pulled out of the Occupied Territories and dismantled its settlements there. And as the initial Israeli pullout seemed certain, reports circulated of meetings between Israeli officials and those of HAMAS. Supposedly HAMAS's leaders were contemplating negotiations with Israel and political participation inside the Palestinian autonomous region. Yet the glimmer of hope that HAMAS might compromise proved fleeting. In the spring of 1994 Israel began an all-out attack on HAMAS, killing and arresting many of its members. In May 1994, under pressure from Israel, King Hussein, who was eyeing his own peace treaty with Israel, declared HAMAS an illegal organization. Jordan withdrew Ghosheh's passport, along with that of Muhammad Nazzal, HAMAS's chief representative. Jordanian officials also ordered both men to curb their activities and to stop issuing statements claiming responsibility for attacks inside the Occupied Territories. They also were asked to decide their status inside Jordan, whether as Palestinian refugees or whether they would accept Jordanian citizenship and obey Jordanian laws.

The choice could not have been a hard one for Ghosheh, who had spent his life in the Palestinian cause. "I am living in Amman, I have my family in Amman and my children," he told me, "but I am ready to leave everything to return back to Jerusalem, my city."

After Israel's pullout from Gaza and Jericho, HAMAS began an internal debate on how to respond to PLO rule, and it seemed as if the moderates had won out. Directives were issued that there would be no political activity inside of mosques, and there were signs that HAMAS would participate in elections when they were scheduled. But that optimism was short-lived. Although several members broke ranks and ran in Palestinian elections as independents, HAMAS chose not to participate as a political organization.

The sad truth may be, that for people like Ghosheh, who are consumed with anger and hatred, compromise is not possible, and they will continue to be a thorn in the side of any authority that tries to bring peace between Arabs and Israelis. For men like Ghosheh, as long as Israel survives, peace can come only in martyrdom.

INTERVIEW WITH IBRAHIM GHOSHEH

FEBRUARY 1994, AMMAN, JORDAN

JD: Could we begin by your telling us your name, your position and a little bit about your organization here in Jordan and the West Bank?

IG: In the name of God, the Merciful, the Compassionate . . . Ibrahim Ghosheh, civil engineer, I am spokesman for HAMAS. Everyone knows about HAMAS. It is a Palestinian Islamic movement. It is founded in the Occupied Territory and Gaza Strip. It is working for the liberation of Palestine, of course, all Palestine. And its struggle for freedom. All its operations against the army, the occupation army and those settlers who are with weapons. We are working as a struggling movement. We are strugglers for freedom, actually. Thank you.

JD: Are you a typical member of HAMAS? Why are you here and not in the West Bank?

IG: I am one of the Islamic movement members. I have been attached since the '50s. My profession is civil engineer. I work in building and dams and so forth. And five years ago, I was recruited to work for HAMAS as a spokesman. I am from Jerusalem. Born there and raised there. I was unable to return back to Jerusalem since 1967. My family is well known in Jerusalem. Now, in HAMAS, we are doing our best, if we are not able to return back to Jerusalem, that the sons of our sons one day will return back to Jerusalem . . . which is an Arabic, Islamic city.

JD: Now tell me how old you are and what are your memories of leaving? What happened?

IG: I am 57 years old. I remember well the days of 1948. I was a young boy. I know well the fighting between Arab Muslims and the Jews in Jerusalem, especially on the walls of Jerusalem. And you know, everyone knows that the west part of Jerusalem was under the control of the Israelis in 1948 during the days of Ben Gurion. And the east part of

Jerusalem was under the control of the Israelis in 1967. I used to live in Jerusalem, in the old city of Jerusalem. And afterward outside of Jerusalem. And in 1967 exactly, I was working on a dam on a river, Yarmouk. You know this project was not to let the Israelis take the water of the Jordan and the Yarmouk. And that time, every week, I return to my house in Jerusalem. But on the fifth of June, when the war started, within two, three days, Israel was able to beat the Arabs and to split its area three times the area of the old Jerusalem. So, I continued my work in the east part of Jordan. Of course Jordan at that time was from the east bank to the west bank, together. From that time I am living in Jordan.

JD: So your family was well known. You had a home. How long did your family live in Jerusalem?

IG: My family lived in Jerusalem, according to my memory, more than 1,000 years.

JD: More than 1,000 years?

IG: Yes, you know we lived in the ancient part of Jerusalem. And till now, there is part of my family still there. And we even, our grandfather participated with Saladin in the twelfth century when the Europeans attacked this area . . . the same as they are doing by the Jews . . . and I am sure that the result will be the same also. That this land will be freed and liberated as it was liberated 800 years ago.

JD: Now how strong is HAMAS here and in the West Bank?

IG: You see, HAMAS is strong in the West Bank and Gaza. It is strong because it is working on two roots, one of them, eastern root, the other one is national root. And you know its policy is well known, very clear, and very strict. And so many of the Palestinian people attach to HAMAS, especially when they are frustrated with what is going on with what is called the peace process, the Gaza-Jericho accord. So, its organization, its foundations are there in towns and villages and in the camps of the refugees. So, it's impossible for Rabin or others to remove the roots of HAMAS. Now, outside the occupied territories, there are some symbols, like myself, who gave services to HAMAS inside, especially in the media, in political movements and in trying also to have a channel to the people in Jordan and others. Added to this, that although there is no organization for HAMAS outside the Occupied Territories, but Islamic movements, to a certain extent, they are supporters of HAMAS . . . Muslim Brotherhood in Jordan, Muslim Brotherhood in Egypt, Jamaat-i-Islami, for example, in Pakistan. They are supporters of HAMAS. And it is important that HAMAS does not deal with the Palestinian issue as a Palestinian one only. It deals with it as an Arabic and Islamic [issue]. So, when we meet with the people, or with the decision makers in Arab and Islamic countries, we put it like this: Understand the issue is important for the Palestinians and for Arabs and Muslims. Because Jerusalem, the Al Akhsa mosque is not only for the Palestinians. It is for all the Muslims all over the world.

JD: Your group, HAMAS, is known in the United States as being a militant organization. Do you agree with that, and can you explain what has led to this militancy?

IG: First of all, can you express to me what do you mean by militancy?

JD: We mean you are an organization that is engaged in an armed struggle.

IG: No, this is not right, in general. Because HAMAS is an Islamic movement, it is going to execute Islam in all the fields of Islam. One of the most important fields in Islam is *jihad,* especially if the land of the Muslims is occupied by others. Then the Muslims have the duty, and it is in our religion called *fareetha* to practice *jihad* against occupation. So we cannot say that HAMAS is only fighting. HAMAS is working to try to make a nation like the Palestinian, to stand on their legs. First of all to get rid of the occupation. Second to build an Islamic state based on the principles of Islam. This is exactly HAMAS.

You know, one of the important things is that we are not against the religion of the Jews or, of course, the Christians. Anyone who visits the Occupied Territories will find that the Jews and the Christians were living in Palestine for centuries. No one touched them. Because, according to our Islam, we have to believe in Moses and Christ, as we believe in Jesus, as we believe in our Prophet Mohammed. So, we are against the Jews because they came to our country, took it by force, kicked us out. Now there are four million Palestinians outside. Everyday they are killing the children, women and our people. So, if any nation has the right to struggle against occupation—if the Europeans have the right to struggle against occupation of the Nazis in the middle of the century; or even for the Americans who have the right to struggle against the British, who were seizing Americans at that time—this is the same thing. And this is the real picture of the conflict between the Palestinians and the Israelis.

JD: Now, as a young man, you joined HAMAS, but you had an option to join other organizations. You could have joined, I guess, the PLO. What led you to this channel? And what's leading so many young people to join the HAMAS movement?

IG: When I was young, I actually joined the Islamic movement. It should be known that even Fatah, when it started, started from the Islamic movement in the '50s. And even Arafat himself . . . now I am contradicting his political perspective, but in the '50s, we were together, friends. Because in the '50s, I was learning engineering and he was learning engineering. He was before me. But when he was chosen as a leader of the Palestinian students, [it was] we, the Islamic movement young people, who chose [him] to be as a leader of this association. Of course, in that time, 1950s, when Nasser [cracked down on] the Muslim Brotherhood and they were sent to prison and some of them killed and some of them went underground, Arafat and others like Abu Jihad [Khalil Wazir] and others started to formulate Fatah. And when they started, they actually took the first cadres from Muslim Brotherhood. This is a fact.

JD: So the Fatah movement also came from the same roots as HAMAS.

IG: Yes. That's right. But after . . . 1968, Fatah has started to open its windows and doors to all ideologies. Marxists, nationalists. And by time, Fatah has been [moved] away from the track of Islam. And in spite of that, Islamic movement continued to support Fatah. When Fatah was struggling against the occupation, against Israel . . . actually, when Fatah has started in 1965, before the occupation of the West Bank and Gaza Strip, they were aiming to liberate Jaffa, Haifa, Led, Ramallah and so on. But we are sorry to say their aims were changed. And now HAMAS actually now is following with the same aims as Fatah of 1967. Now we have many reports from the Occupied Territories that some of the Fatah people, young people, they want to attach to HAMAS because they discover that HAMAS is now going on the same road which Fatah started. Sometimes we laugh about that. Because we say if Fatah had started by taking our cadres, now, this time, it's time to take back those cadres into HAMAS.

JD: Do you have any idea of how many people are involved with HAMAS?

IG: You see, I can't give numbers. But according to the latest statistics now you can say 50 percent of the Palestinian people, outside and inside, are supporting HAMAS. One week ago, the most [recent] election was in Gaza Strip for engineers [the engineers' syndicate]. HAMAS, the Islamic [movement] headed by HAMAS, got about 47 percent. Fatah got 45 percent. And the other groups took the remnant, which is about 8 percent. These elections give an idea about the power of each faction. Now, inside the Occupied Territories and outside, of course, HAMAS and Fatah are the strongest. They are shoulder to shoulder. By time, HAMAS is getting more support from the Palestinian people. Because many people were frustrated with Arafat. Although Arafat started the struggle against Zionism . . . he has lost the road completely. Now he's after what's called autonomy.

JD: To talk about the peace process: Do you see any way at all that you could make peace, that HAMAS could make peace with the state of Israel?

IG: Regarding autonomy our position is known. We are against autonomy. One of the reasons is that this autonomy does not give one square inch of Palestine. All the land is for the Israelis, none for the

Palestinian. Of course our [view of] the conflict between Arab and Israelis, or Muslim and Israelis, or Palestinian and Israelis, and sometime it's the same issue, [is that] it's a question of just and fair. Any nation in the world, if they are allowed to be deported from their land and live in tents for now more than 45 years, these people have a very big longing for their land. For example, for me, I am living in Amman. I have my family in Amman and my children, but I am ready to leave everything to return back to Jerusalem, my city.

JD: You're not living in the refugee camps, are you?

IG: No, no, I am not in refugee camps. Because I explain that when the war in 1967 started, I was an engineer working here in Jordan. We do not like to fight because we like fighting. Palestinian people want to live in peace. But what is the description of this peace? What is the specification of this peace? Any peace without returning the four million Palestinians to their land and their homes is a false peace, is a superficial peace. It will not continue even if this agreement of Gaza and Jericho, by the support of the United States, maybe it will move, but we are sorry it will not continue, it will stop. Because this is against the nature, against the laws of the world, against the laws of Allah. Now, this big mistake is not because of the mistake of the Jews, it is the mistake of Britain, of the United States, of the world. Now, in order to solve this problem in the right way, they want to deceive the world. They want to deceive themselves by saying an agreement was signed and everything is okay. Now, five months after this signature, approximately, does the intifada stop? Does the conflict stop? Do these young people who want to return back to their country, this longing, stop? No. And it will continue.

We in HAMAS say that the conflict between Islam and Zionism is a long one. It will take decades. We are sure of that. One day the Europeans came to this country and they stayed 200 years and they were turned back. And we are sure that this state of Israel will not continue. Because it is against the nature of the area, against the people. No one will accept them. Take, for example, the Egyptians. Now it is 15 years after the signing of Camp David. Till now, it is known that those Egyptians who visited Israel are less than 1,000. And this, what is called, normalization, everybody knows that the Egyptian people do not want this normalization. So many of the media [are trying] to deceive the world so that we are coming to the future where everything will be settled in the Middle East. This is not right. And we are sorry to say that they deceive themselves.

JD: If I understand what you're saying, you won't be settled until the Palestinians will be able to go back to Jaffa and there isn't an Israeli state. Is that correct? Am I understanding you correctly?

IG: Yes. Of course, now the planners of the Israelis, they will not allow the refugees to return back. And they will not even allow those who were deported in 1967 to go back, it's number about 800,000. On the contrary, now the planners are planning to bring more immigrants from Russia and from other places. Even the president of Israel, [Ezer] Weizman, he put it clear. He said by the end of the century we want to double the population of the Jews in Palestine. They are going to bring about maybe three million by the end of this century. Israel, by the aid of America, wants to control all the area. Palestine now is over. It is under their control. But they want to control all of this area . . .

Maybe in Europe for centuries they were oppressed, but why are we to pay this price? On the contrary, the Muslim world opened their arms to the Jews when they were dismissed from Spain. This is well known. Now the Jews want to get the Muslims to pay for their oppression, which was in Europe and Russia and other places.

JD: Where are you getting your support from? Are other Arab countries giving you support? How are your funding your opposition?

IG: HAMAS is an organization built from faith and principles. If the young people are prepared on this foundation, they are very strong and they are very brave. So this is on the contrary to those men of Arafat who work because they are supported by money. This is a big difference. So these young people, and girls, they are complete, because they are actually, it is as if they are praying to God . . . same thing. In Islam, praying to God [is] not only in *salah* [worship], or in fasting, but also in work. If you work and you work for the sake of

God, you are also exercising your praying. So many Muslims outside Palestine support HAMAS by money, by *zakat*. This support goes to the people inside, to the families, those who are in prisons and so on.

JD: Tell me a little about that. What is your social work inside the West Bank?

IG: You see, whether his house is blasted, or whether he is killed, HAMAS tries to help as it can. We can't say we are able to compensate him for the total amount of his house, maybe it's $100,000, in order to help him continue living. We hope that the Islamic world, the Islamic people, to help us more. It's no secret that HAMAS is trying its best to make its ties with Muslims everywhere more stronger to support the *jihad* in Palestine.

JD: What countries are your biggest supporters? Jordan or—

IG: There are many Muslims in Jordan, in the Gulf, in Saudi Arabia, in Turkey, in Pakistan, in Yemen. Many of them put their *zakat* to help us.

JD: Now, you said there were young women associated with HAMAS helping the organization. Would you talk a little about what role women play in your organization?

IG: The most acclaimed, the most role they play inside the territory is that as a mother, as a wife and as a daughter. We have many mothers whose sons are in prison or killed, or outside; and wives, the same thing. They continue raising the family, take care of the family when the man is outside. They are strong enough. Also now, they participate in facing the media and express the oppression which happens against their husbands or their sons. And of course, some of them participate in some operations against the occupation.

JD: Are you saying that some women actually serve as soldiers?

IG: Yes, some of them. Because you know the struggle is not for the men only. And we know that in our history, in Islam, women have participated with our Prophet Muhammad in struggling against those who were against him in Mecca.

JD: What if there really is an agreement that comes out of Gaza and Jericho and there is an autonomous region? Will HAMAS try to participate in elections and in the governing of that region?

IG: Regarding the agreement, I [said] that the future of that agreement is not very clear and we will not be surprised if this agreement falls down. And maybe this is one of the reasons the United States started to activate another track, which is the Syrian track. And everybody knows that this agreement was signed in Oslo, away from the United States. This agreement has many gaps in it. And even the Israelis have found that it is very difficult to be implemented on the ground. And also many gaps [were] obvious from Arafat himself—whether he is able to take the power and run this agreement. It is very obvious that now the future of this agreement is, as we say in Arabic, very much in the wind.

JD: Yes, but if it *were* to succeed?

IG: Of course, we are not for autonomy. We will not participate in elections. If we are against autonomy, of course we will be against the mechanism of this autonomy. And now election is a way to execute this. If it happens we are going to convince the people not to participate, but without using violence.

JD: Now is this different, because one of the things that was happening in the territories was that Palestinians were fighting Palestinians? Has that stopped?

IG: Yes.

JD: And if so, what's the reason?

IG: We are very pleased because since the signing of this agreement until now, there was not any conflict between HAMAS and Fatah. You know we just stand back and let Fatah do what it liked. We were depending that the negative signs will start to appear inside the camp of Arafat. And this is exactly what happened. Now, everyone knows that there are many resignations of Fatah and there is also what is called misunderstanding between Fatah and its people because of the agreement. So we are pleased that this conflict did not happen and we will do our best not to have any struggle with Palestinian people.

We hope Arafat will not also push his people to initiate any kind of a struggle. We are convinced now that he has many problems; that he is not going to think of us. He is in a mess, as you say. So we do believe in democracy. On the contrary, when Arafat, years ago, [began] to participate in PNC [Palestine National Congress], we said we are ready to participate, but there should be an election. Because he gives us only 18 seats of about 480, which is about 4 percent. We said we do believe in election. And what the Palestinian people chose as the weight of HAMAS, we will accept it. But it should be free election.

JD: What's the future for HAMAS now?

IG: Once I heard some specialist from the Zionists. They were having dialogue on Israeli TV. And one of them said that HAMAS is like the pioneers of the Zionism. How the pioneers of Zionism were planning to have a state and a land. Actually HAMAS wants their land, their country. We are sure that this is not easy. Now the power is with Israel. But no one can say that this strength will continue. We see what happened to the USSR. And now I know that there are many cracks in the Israeli community, many cracks. I don't want to go into the details of it. We will continue. This is very important.

. . . How long it will take, we don't know. But the most important thing is that it not stop. So this is the actual struggle between HAMAS and Zionism. This is actually the real battle. Now there is a strategy for HAMAS, which is the uprising of Islam around the area. There are projects everywhere, the Muslims, the Islamic movements trying to reach power. We are sure that where the Muslims reach power, this will be very big support for HAMAS. For example, if Egypt, if the Muslims reach power, this will be very big support.

JD: So you are getting support from and are supporting the movement in Egypt?

IG: Actually, we have no power to support them. But we are with the Muslims if they reach power, like Sudan, like Iran, like in the future, if Egypt and Tunisia and Algeria. This is very important for the project and its future.

JD: But in the territories, for example, when the HAMAS people strike, do you try to avoid striking innocent people? I mean, maybe you don't think anybody is innocent. But do you only try to attack the military people? What is your attitude on who you will strike?

IG: Yes. HAMAS now, we are sorry to say that, the foreign ministry of the United States put HAMAS on the list of terrorism. This is not fair, this is not right, and we hope they will take it out. Because HAMAS has no operation outside the Occupied Territories. Nothing. This is very important. The second thing is that HAMAS is struggling against the soldiers, the forces. And the settlers, actually, who are equipped with weapons. They are the other army of the Israelis. We don't say that there aren't some mistakes. But mainly HAMAS is aiming to fight against the tools of occupation, which is the soldiers, who kill the children, who blast the houses, who strip the Palestinians of their dignity and so forth.

JD: Well, then certainly you don't agree with Egyptians who are attacking foreigners?

IG: Yes. You see, HAMAS is believing in Islam as Islam. We do believe that Islam from our Qur'an and from our Prophet Muhammad does not allow to attack any innocents. You have the right to attack those who oppress you, who take your country and so on. But tourists who come from outside and they want to see Egypt and you kill them, we call this nonsense. And this is one of the things that, if Mubarak wants to solve the problem, he should allow for Muslim Brotherhood. He should make them legal. Now they are not legal. These people know Islam well. Many of the educated people are their leaders. If these people are allowed, we are sure that these terrorists will be to the minimum. Because they will express their Islam. And the second thing, the solution of Egypt and Algiers and Tunisia and others, in Islam we all it *Shurah,* or in West we call it democracy. Let the people choose what they want, even if they are Muslims . . . Now the United States people and the West, they should be brave . . . to allow the people of this area to choose their life, not to intervene in their life. If they want to choose Islam, let them choose Islam. And not to say that Islam, if it comes to power, will be against democracy. This is not right. But the majority of the people are Muslims. Sure, Islam will continue. We believe in the other opinion, in other religions. Any place in the Islamic community, you will find many [minority] religions, till now. I am sorry to say that this is contrary to what happened in Spain, for example. When the Catholics took the power, they let all of them [believers in other religions] either to be killed or to be dismissed.

JD: Do you think this is why things have not erupted into violence in Jordan, because Islamists have participation in government?

IG: Yes, this is right. Because you know the Muslim Brotherhood here in Jordan, they are wise. They know Islam well. Also, the regime here is also wise. There is also, what you say, some contradictions. But usually it is solved peacefully. And this is very important. This example in Jordan, if it is chosen in Egypt and in Algeria and in other places, then many souls will not be lost.

JD: One difficult question. Since I work in this field I hear many things and I must ask you a difficult question. I have heard that Israel actually supported HAMAS initially as a way to get at Fatah, to stop Fatah, to make the Palestinians fight each other.

IG: This question is not difficult. It's well known. Even I read about dialogue between Arafat and Rabin. And one time Arafat told Rabin, you are the reason for the uprising of HAMAS. If you ask it to a young man, he is difficult to answer. But for me, I have relations for more than 40 years. I know well the history of the Islamic movement in the area, from the '50s until 1967, was under pressure from Nasserism.

They were not allowed even to go outside. I myself, when I was in Egypt, I was working underground. Because if any mistake happen, I would go either to prison or to be dismissed. This is during the days of Abdel Nasser. So actually, Islamic movement, we continued to work underground until 1967.

After 1967, all the community, Arab world, after defeat of Nasser and defeat of Arab nationality, the people started to say, why we are defeated? Is it because we are away from Islam? So they started to study Islam, to ask about Islam. After that time, we started in the Occupied Territories, in the West Bank and Gaza Strip, to build our foundation in schools, health clinics, clubs and so on, to train the young people and to prepare them. It was decision from the Islamic movement not to start struggling against Israel before we prepare. So it took us from after 1967 to the end of the '70s, you can say 15 years. After that, when there was a foundation ready, Islamic movements started to rise. And anyone who wanted to study the world would notice that after '80s, the universities in Gaza, in Bir Zeit in Nablus, there started to arise what is called Islamic bloc by the students. And they started to compete with Fatah in elections in that time. And at that time, the idea to start *jihad* started. And this happened with Sheikh Ahmad Yassin when he was sent to prison in 1982. So at that time we started to prepare ourselves.

When intifada happened in 1987, there was a decision within the Islamic movement that, if the situation is good, we have to participate in the intifada. So there was a decision taken by the leaders of the Muslim Brotherhood at that time to participate in the intifada. And the Muslims were the first who participated in intifada. After two weeks, the people of Arafat started to participate in intifada. So, it is not right to say that Israeli was . . . it was decision of Islamic movement not to struggle if you are not prepared. We have to prepare ourselves. This is the reason exactly.

JD: So you never got any encouragement or money or anything like that from Israeli sources?

IG: No, not at all. At all.

JD: Let's talk about the relationship as you see it between the Western world and the Islamic people. How do you see that relationship now?

IG: I think that until now, the relationship is not ordinary. We want it to be ordinary.

JD: By ordinary, you mean a good relationship?

IG: Yes. Yes. How to be ordinary, we have to understand the West well and the West has to understand us well. There are two things that should not affect the idea of the West toward the Muslims. One of them, the lobby of the Jews. I want to say frankly, if this affection is stopped, the West will be helped to understand us better. For example, to say that all Islamic movements are terrorists. This is exactly Rabin. And since Rabin is fighting against HAMAS, this means he should be supported by the West. The second thing, the history, I mean, the differences in religion between Christianity and Islam, should not affect relations. Of course, in history there was conflict between Islam and Christianity. But we do believe the origin of Christianity is the same as origins of Islam. Nothing differs. Also, we want that the West, when they want to study our Islam, not to follow some lies and say these Arab Muslims want everyone to marry more than four and also that they are living with camels, and those things which are away from facts. This is important to understand. Now, the religion in the area should be left to the decision of the people. If [it's] the decision of the people, they want to choose Islam, [this should not] be stopped by the West, as it happens now in Algeria. This is [a] very obvious example for this. We are sure if anyone studies Islam well, he will notice and discover that Islam does believe in others. We don't say that we are better than others. The principles of Islam do not differentiate between black and the white, between the rich and the poor.

It is very important for us to have ties with the West. We cannot build our area without the help of the West. We want to develop our areas. We will depend on each other. And the West also will depend on our sources, like oil and so on. We do appreciate the West also to help us in technology and trying to live better life. And we think that many traditions and principles in our area, we think the West is in need of [them]. Anyone who come to this area will notice the family is very strong and that man is very respected. We do not live the material life only. We do believe in the spirit.

TWELVE

Sheikh Yusef Abdullah al-Qaradawi

University of Qatar

Profile

THE BRIGHT FEBRUARY MORNING that I met Sheikh Yusef al-Qaradawi, I had to begin our interview with a sincere thank you. Had it had not been for his considerable influence in Qatar and his renown as one of the world's leading Islamic thinkers, I might never have entered the country.

I had not slept in more than 24 hours when I greeted the sheikh at his office in Doha University. I still do not know why I was refused an immediate visa at the Doha airport, as the Qatari embassy had assured me. All I know is that when I arrived at the airport it was almost midnight and a line of nearly 50 people stood between me and the official passing out entry visas from a tiny window. When I finally found myself at the head of the line, the man behind the counter motioned me to a chair and told me to wait. For me, he said, there was no visa. With all the righteous indignation of an offended American, I demanded to know why. Was it because I was a woman traveling alone? Was I improperly dressed, even though I was completely covered with a scarf? Was there some developing problem between the United States and the Gulf? I threatened to call the American embassy and did. The embassy official who rushed to the airport in the middle of the night offered moral support but confessed he was unable to help. In desperation, I ranted and raved and, in a bid to win sympathy, asked the man behind the visa window if he would like to see his mother treated in such a manner. Nothing helped. Only when I mentioned the name of Sheikh Yusef al-Qaradawi did I notice the official raise his eyebrows and look up from the stack of papers on his desk. Then a skinny, black-haired policeman sidled toward me with a cup of coffee and offered it to me with a smile.

"I think we make mistake." He grinned like an embarrassed schoolboy. The name of Yusef al-Qaradawi had made a difference.

"You know Sheikh Qaradawi?" he asked, in eager broken English. "How you know him? He important man. Good man. Not to worry. Call him. He help. No problem."

Sheikh al-Qaradawi did indeed help, although it was hours before I realized it. At 7 A.M., airport officials arrived with profuse apologies and ushered me into the cushiony comfort of the VIP waiting room while they prepared my visa. Then they ushered me into my own luxury van, down the immaculately clean thoroughfares of Doha, past the blue waters of the Gulf and into the Sheraton Hotel. I wanted nothing but sleep yet I had less than half an hour to prepare for my meeting with the sheikh.

Among Islamic scholars, al-Qaradawi is considered one of the leading moderates. His name is known throughout the Islamic world for his writing and lectures promoting restraint in religious matters; and after several hours of questioning him, neither his demeanor nor his conversation betrayed those themes. Yet in some of al-Qaradawi's writings, he had expressed opinions that could easily be considered radical, from a Western perspective.

Al-Qaradawi had written more than 50 books, including the well-known *The Lawful and the Prohibited in Islam* and *The Priorities of the Islamic Movement in the Coming Phase*. But it was his book *Islamic Awakening: Between Rejection & Extremism* that interested me most. He had written the book for Muslim youths, who by the millions were looking to Islam for an identity distinct from the Western world and for a solution to the many ills plaguing their societies. The book was especially intended for those youths who believed Islam justified expressing their rage and frustration through acts of violence.

In the book, al-Qaradawi offered potent arguments against extremism in religion, citing a well-known *hadith*, or saying of the Prophet Muhammad: "Beware of excessiveness in religion. [People] before you have perished as a result of excessiveness."

Al-Qaradawi was born in Egypt in 1926, and by the time he was ten years old he had memorized the Qur'an. His entire educational study had been devoted to Islam. He graduated in 1953 from the College of Fundamentals of Religion at Al Azhar University, the Islamic world's foremost institution of religious study. In 1973 he obtained a doctorate in Islamic jurisprudence from Al Azhar, assuring him a place in the intellectual hierarchy of Islamic scholarship. He accepted a coveted post in the Islamic Culture Department of the university and later founded several colleges devoted to Islamic study. When I met him, he was director of the Center for Sunnah and Sirah (Tradition and Life History of the Prophet Muhammad), which he had helped found at the University of Qatar.

The university was deserted the day I met al-Qaradawi. His office was located inside one of several buildings that were undergoing extensive renovation. Yet his large, yellow office was an orderly haven of efficiency. He wore a white turban, glasses and a long, brown robe. His carefully trimmed gray and black beard made me recall the discussion in his book *The Lawful and the Prohibited in Islam*. In it, the sheikh examined the *Hadith* (authoritative collection of the sayings and deeds of the Prophet Muhammad) and maintained that Islam encouraged Muslim men to grow neat beards as a distinguishing feature, to differentiate them from Christians and Jews.

I also couldn't help but recall that in the book the sheikh discussed the opinions of Islamic scholars on such subjects as whether women should pluck their eyebrows. They shouldn't, he said, because they would too closely resemble "harlots." Yet he concluded that dying the hair was permissible for both Muslim men and women—again, as a distinguishing feature, to set them apart from the other "people of the book," as Muslims have historically referred to Jews and Christians. Al-Qaradawi quoted Ibn Taymiyyah, a noted Islamic writer and scholar, who lived in the fourteenth century: "The Qur'an, the Sunnah and the consensus of Muslim scholars all teach Muslims to be distinct from non-believers and in general to avoid resembling them. Anything which is likely to cause corruption in a hidden and diffuse manner is related to this matter and is likewise prohibited. The imitation of the appearance of non-believers will lead to imitation of their immoral behavior and evil qualities—indeed of their beliefs."[1]

In *The Lawful and Prohibited in Islam*, al-Qaradawi explained that Muslims were forbidden from racism, nationalism and chauvinism: "It is not permissible for a believer in Allah and the Last Day to support his people without regard for whether they are right or wrong, just or unjust." [2]

Al-Qaradawi also discussed everything from dress to capital punishment. For example, he declared men were prohibited, barring exceptional circumstances or medical necessity, from wearing gold and silk. He discussed the reasons why Muslim women were encouraged to dress modestly, and he argued in favor of their right to demand divorce. He decided that there was indeed a place for music and art in a religious society, and he tackled tough issues such as contraception, concluding that it was sanctioned in Islam, but the consent of the woman was mandatory. Abortion, he said, was not to be considered a legal birth control method, although it was permitted in medical emergencies: "While Islam permits preventing pregnancy for valid reasons, it does not allow doing violence to the pregnancy once it occurs. Muslim jurists agree unanimously that after the foetus is completely formed and has been given a soul, aborting it is *haram*. It is also a crime, the commission of which is prohibited to the Muslim because it constitutes an offense against a complete, live human being."[3]

The key word in this opinion is "complete." Some Islamic scholars believed that abortions could be performed lawfully in the first trimester, especially for medical reasons. Al-Qaradawi went even further in saying that abortion was allowed at any stage if the life of the mother was threatened. And, in *The Lawful and the Prohibited*, he quoted a ruling issued by Sheikh Shaltut, a former scholar at Al Azhar: "For the mother is the origin of the foetus; moreover, she is established in life, with duties and responsibilities, and she is also a pillar of the family. It would not be possible to sacrifice her life for the life of a foetus which has not yet acquired a personality and which has no responsibilities or obligations to fulfill."[4]

In *The Lawful and the Prohibited,* al-Qaradawi quoted the Islamic scholar Imam al-Ghazali, who wrote in his book *Al-Nikah (Marriage).*

> Contraception is not like abortion. Abortion is a crime against an existing being. Now, existence has stages. The first stages of existence are the settling of the semen in the womb and its mixing with the secretions of the womb. It is then ready to receive life. Disturbing it is a crime. When it develops further and becomes a lump, aborting it is a greater crime. When it acquires a soul and its creation is completed, the crime becomes more grievous. The crime reaches a maximum seriousness when it is committed after it [the foetus] is separated [from the mother] alive.[5]

While there would seem to have been some contradiction between al-Gazali's opinion that abortion at any stage was a crime and al-Qaradawi's assertion that some abortions were allowed, there was actually much agreement between the two scholars. Al-Qaradawi agreed that abortion at any stage was a crime, just as stealing a loaf of bread would be a crime even if the thief were near starvation. But he considered such a crime a justifiable offense, just as in his opinion abortion would be justifiable under strict circumstances.

Al-Qaradawi also delved into other controversial issues, such as masturbation, and ended up disagreeing with the teachings of many Christian churches. He concluded that Islam allowed masturbation as a way to prevent men from lusting after women, but he suggested that fasting was the preferable way to control the male sexual appetite. In his chapter "The Sexual Relationship," al-Qaradawi discussed frankly and openly several sexual issues, claiming that Islam took a more moderate approach to such matters: "The Qur'an does not neglect the sensual aspects and the physical relationship between husband and wife. It guides human beings to the best path, fulfilling the demands of the sexual urge while avoiding harmful or deviant practices."[6]

We did not, of course, discuss such things during our conversation. Instead we focused on what al-Qaradawi called "the true message

of Islam." He spoke in calm, measured Arabic and was seated behind
a large desk and in front of rows of bookcases lined with leather-bound
books, with several younger colleagues in rapt attention, one of whom
served as a diligent and exacting translator.

He said he was dedicated to "the middle way in Islam." He did not
advocate establishing Islamic states through violent revolution, but
through gradual change, noting that God created the universe in
gradual steps that took seven days to complete. Al-Qaradawi never
raised his voice or gesticulated wildly, as so many of the devout are
wont to do. And when he quoted the Prophet Muhammad, his voice
was almost a whisper: "'Beware of going deeply into religion with no
basics, with no footing, because if you do such a thing, you will distort
more than you interpret.'"

In *Islamic Awakening Between Rejection and Extremism,* al-
Qaradawi explained what he believed were the signs of extremism in
religion:

> The first indication of extremism is bigotry, the rigidity which makes
> a person obstinately and intolerantly devoted to his own opinions
> and prejudices. Bigotry deprives him of the clarity of vision regarding
> the interests of other human beings, the purposes of legislation, or
> the circumstances of the age. Such a person does not allow opportu-
> nity for dialogue with others so that he may compare his opinion
> with theirs, and chooses to follow what appears to him most sound.[7]

Excessiveness in such practices as prayer, fasting and religious rituals
were other signs of extremism, al-Qaradawi contended. Even the
Prophet, he said, when asked to choose between two options, "always
chose the easiest unless it was a sin."

In *Islamic Awakening,* he wrote: "In the field of *da'wa* [propaga-
tion of Islam], there is no place for violence and coarseness. That is
evidenced by the following *hadith*: 'Allah loves kindness in all
matters.'"[8]

Al-Qaradawi also strongly criticized violence among Muslims,
and he quoted the Prophet Muhammad, who warned that if a Muslim
died fighting another Muslim, both of them were equally guilty:

"When two Muslims draw weapons against each other, they are at the brink of Hell. If one of them kills the other, they both enter it together."[9]

It would be easy to miss nuances in al-Qaradawi's religious stand, however. His definition of extremism did not include people with strong opinions and strict religious standards, especially if they did not resort to violence or try to impose their standards on others.

Some of al-Qaradawi's own teachings would seem extreme to Westerners. For example, he agreed that a Muslim who was guilty of being a *kafir* (blasphemer) would be subject to the harshest penalty under Muslim law, death. According to al-Qaradawi, to be declared a *kafir*, a person would have to deny that Allah was God, that Muhammad was his Prophet, or that the Qur'an was the revelation of Allah.

Sheikh Muhammad al-Ghazali, the Egyptian religious scholar and authority who died in March 1996, ignited debate within Islamic circles on the question of apostasy following his testimony in July 1993 at the trial of 13 Islamic militants accused of killing the Egyptian writer Farag Foda. Foda was an outspoken critic of radical Islamists, who accused him of apostasy. Al-Ghazali ruled that an apostate should be given time to repent, but if he doesn't change, Islamic scholars such as al-Qaradawi generally agree that killing an apostate is lawful under Islamic law.

Yet some scholars disagreed with al-Qaradawi, contending that in the Qur'an, an apostate is threatened with punishment in the next world only. Al-Ghazali told the court he personally believed an apostate should be given a life sentence. And even among those who believed that apostasy deserved death, there was disagreement over how it should be carried out and by whom. Some contended that any Muslim could carry out the punishment, whereas others argued it should be undertaken solely by an authority, such as a state.

Al-Qaradawi complained that people often were wrongly condemned as blasphemers for the slightest affront or for breaking religious taboos against drinking and gambling. Under al-Qaradawi's strict definition of a *kafir*, it would be difficult for a Muslim to be so condemned without intentional and blatant blasphemy. It could be argued that any Muslim who acted in such a manner with knowledge of the penalties could be deemed mentally ill, thus exempt from punishment. Such penalties only applied to Muslims who were guilty of *kufr* [blasphemy], al-Qaradawi contended. They did not apply to non-Muslims, he said. And he noted that anyone who professes "there is no God but Allah" has embraced Islam "and consequently his life and property should be granted safety."

In the United States, where freedom of speech is even more sacred than freedom of religion, any person who would support a law allowing someone to be killed because of offensive speech would certainly be considered extreme. Thus, from a Western perspective, al-Qaradawi, one of the Islamic world's leading intellectuals, might not appear very moderate. Yet among Islamic activists, his views on this issue were indeed considered so. Among Islamists, there could be no greater crime than offending the faithful and denigrating God. Even the act of murder was not considered so serious an offense as a Muslim denouncing God.

Critics of Islamists, including many more secular-oriented Muslims, see such opinions as fodder for radicals who would issue death warrants against novelists such as Salman Rushdie or condemn writers such as Bangladesh's Taslima Nasrin for expressing her opinion about Islamic law. Nasrin was forced to go into hiding when she allegedly was misquoted by a newspaper columnist as saying the Qur'an should be changed.

Issues such as blasphemy are precisely why many people, including many Muslims, fear even moderate Islamists in control of government. They believe leaders such as al-Qaradawi, if allowed to implement their dogma, would move to enact severe restrictions on speech and personal liberties.

Yet al-Qaradawi served an important role within the ranks of Islamic activists. He had undertaken the important mission of trying to restrain the violent elements within the ranks of Islamists, with teaching based soundly in the Qur'an. To youths in Islamic movements, his was one of the most respected of all voices. And most of his teaching channeled their passions away from an outer *jihad* to an inner *jihad* of self-control and peace.

INTERVIEW WITH SHEIKH ABDULLAH YUSEF AL-QARADAWI

FEBRUARY 1994, DOHA, QATAR

JD: Since you clearly are one of the leading Islamic thinkers today, could you tell us a little bit about the path that you've taken in your life that has led you deeper into Islamic thought? How did you begin, who guided you?

YQ: This current, or path that I've dedicated myself to in the last few years and for a long time, is what we call "the middle way" in Islam, and it's not my phrase, it's from Islam itself. As the Qur'an itself says, "We made you the middle nation."

JD: When you say middle, do you mean moderate?

YQ: Yes. Our Qur'an invites us to risk moderation in Islam. As the Qur'an says, "Try not to tip the scale, and do not take too much from it either;" maintain balance. As well, our Prophet, peace be upon Him, says, "Beware of going deeply into religion with no basics, with no footing, because if you do such a thing you will distort more than you interpret."

Secondly, I was raised in a school that served Islam, founded by a man distinguished by his moderation, who believed in establishing relations with all parties, as different as they may be. And this man, Hassan al-Banna, was "a community/nation in himself," may he rest in peace. He believed in dealing with all people, some of his consultants were Christians, and they were among the prominent ones. He also believed in building bridges among Sunnis and Shias. I met some of them at meetings in Cairo about these things. It was due to Hassan al-Banna that I adopted my moderate ideas.

The third factor that has influenced my personality is that I am among those born moderate by temperament; this was given to me by God almighty. This is one of my gifts. I am at the other end of the spectrum from people who are distinguished by going to extremes, either to the left or the right. My stance is in the middle of these two groups.

JD: About the theme of moderation: Are you concerned that extremists may be threatening Islam? What's the motivation behind this theme of moderation?

YQ: The power of this current emerges from a number of sources. First, it agrees with the spirit of Islam, as I said before. Second, this current is older, having more established roots than the other currents, which are rootless and will not last for long. With time they will vanish. Third, moderation has the broadest base; it has more people, public opinion, behind it. Violent movements have no basis, except when the media depicts it. Moderation in Egypt is preferred by all people, as it is in Algeria, Morocco and Sudan. It fits with people's instincts.

JD: So what you are saying is that the true message of Islam is a moderate force, that is all-encompassing in life. Is that a correct interpretation? Furthermore, what is the Islamic movement today? Are there really several?

YQ: The true message of Islam is peace. Islam invites all nations to come together, as the Qur'an says. "We made you people and tribes to know each other, in every way." Therefore, our Prophet, peace be upon Him, considered the Hudaibiyah treaty of truce, concluded in 628, between Muslims and nonbelievers, a bright victory. Muslims did not see it this way at the time, but the Qur'an recognized it as a victory for Islam.

JD: What was the agreement about?

YQ: As mentioned before, the Prophet and his companions, peace be upon Him, wanted to go to Mecca to make *umra* [the lesser pilgrimage], and they went peacefully, but when they got there the *mushriqin* [pagans] and *kuffar* [nonbelievers] refused to let them in. The Muslims then promised the Prophet that they would fight the *kuffar*. They gave their word outside of Mecca, at a well called al-Hudaibiyah, under a famous tree mentioned in the Qur'an.

There were some negotiations between the two parties, but the treaty and truce lasted for the next ten years. The agreement was that Muslims would not make the lesser pilgrimage that year but instead the next year. The Qur'an considered this as a victory, but a peaceful one, won by common sense and good words, not by arms. As the Qur'an says, "We gave you a bright victory." The Medinans asked the Prophet if this was really a victory. The Prophet said that it was.

JD: I have to ask you: Aren't there some occasions when Muslims must fight? For example, when governments are corrupt?

YQ: When this thing started in Algeria and the materialist force stood against this, the Islamists tried to express themselves in different ways, other than violence, because it wouldn't have led to anything good. So they went to the streets, made strikes, issued decrees. There were some moderates among the Salvation Front [FIS] leaders, such as Mr. Abd al-Qadir al-Hishami, he tried to halt the tide, to convince leaders to halt the tide, to try to be peaceful. When the activities of the Salvation Front were restricted and the prominent leaders were taken to prison, it was natural for something to happen. Nobody ever agrees on injustice. The fact imposes itself that the moderates may try to do something to avoid bloodshed in the streets. They tried to convince their youth to try to be patient, not to be violent.

Among the people who were on the path to dialogue, not on the path to violence, were Mahfoud Nahnah, president of the Islamic Society Movement, and Abdullah Jadallah, president of the Islamic Renaissance party. They tried to find a solution to this dilemma through peaceful negotiations.

JD: I want to talk about Islamic youths, and your particular message to them.

YQ: First, youth and their message represent an important stage in Islamic history. I consider youth to be the future of the *umma* [worldwide Islamic community], the human wealth if I may say so. They are even more important than material, for example, oil, wealth. Nations are measured by gold, money wealth, but youth are the skeleton and the backbone of the Islamic nation. They are also the pillar of the Islamic awakening. This is clear in Egypt, Sudan, in Algeria, and in the Gulf. Youth are the in the majority of those doing the pilgrimages, filling the mosques, and reading Islamic books. Muslim women are taking the *hijab*, on their own accord, even against the pressures of their parents, simply because they love Islam. As we know, the Islamic awakening is based on youth. They are known for their hot-bloodedness, their pushiness, because they feel the injustices of the world. Because of the technology, the material civilization [science and technology] of the West, they feel this sense of injustice, which forces them to violence and extremes. What interests me is this phase of the last two decades. I am trying to analyze the awakening of youth and to set it on a moderate course. I think there is no need for violence, because the Islamic call is spreading every day, for example from the Egyptian syndicates, lawyers, engineers, et cetera, most of whom are Islamists. Why the violence? Those who resort to it have nothing solid in their hands. Violence is their last resort. I am trying to help the youth build themselves mentally through culture, spiritually and religiously through worship, morally by virtue, physically through sports, and socially by serving everyone in society, through clinics and dispensaries.

JD: So you are channeling the energy of youth into constructive things in society?

YQ: Yes. But I would like to make something clear; it is very important that youth should not only indulge themselves in political life, they should be interested in the life of society as well. That means if a Muslim is a doctor, he should establish a clinic to help people, free of charge, if he's a teacher; he should teach. Everyone in his field should participate in their own way.

JD: I think what people in the West find so fascinating about what's happening in the Islamic world is that unlike in the West, where young people seem to be turning away from religion and turning away even from morality, young people here seem to be doing the opposite.

YQ: We must be honest: statistics say that only 5 percent of Christians in the West go to church. Even when they go it is not necessarily for religion but may be for social reasons. In Muslim countries, even those who usually disobey Islam come closer to it when they hear some preaching from a mosque; they come quickly to Islam. As we know, Islam does not impose anything on humans either against their instincts or their minds. The Holy Qur'an says to try to bring your proof, argument, if you are really truthful. The Islamic teachings, although they are somewhat rigid . . . they compel Muslims to go to the mosque five times a day . . . yet Muslims find peace in them. In doing so, the Muslim escapes material life and goes toward his soul. Islam is a religion that presents people [with] a way to wash his body, a spiritual cure for the mind and [helps] him balance this life with the afterlife. Islam gives balance between the mind and the heart, the spiritual and material, the soul and the body, this world and the afterlife. You cannot find this balance in other religions, only in Islam.

JD: What about relations with the West; what can the West do to improve relations with Islam?

YQ: First, we want the West to recognize our right to exist and the right of Muslims to live their religion. It is better for the West that Muslims should be religious, hold to their religion and try to be moral . . . rather than being amoral, atheist, with no grounding, nothing to hold on to. This is the first point, that the West should let Muslims apply *Sharia* in their lives. If they are good Muslims, how could the West mind?

The second thing is that we have to make the West see that life can stem from more than one culture, one civilization. This variety is in the interest of humanity, not against it. But we cannot put one civilization or religion above others in the world. There must be this variety. The Muslims had this civilization before; they had different elements, technically and religiously. There were Christians and Jews in early Islamic civilization; they contributed to building Islamic civilization. That's why we say that it's okay that there is diversity in the number of religions and civilizations in the world. Relations among them should be of dialogue, not conflict. We Muslims have this diversity due to the will of God. As the Qur'an says, had God wanted people to be one nation He could have done it. Instead He gave them freedom to choose and interact. Every man thinks that the right is with him and the others are wrong. Muslims believe that God will account for his deeds in the afterlife. As the Qur'an says, God is ours and yours, you have your deeds and we have ours. There is no judgment until God gathers us together in the afterlife. God, not I, will make every man accountable.

Thirdly, the West is powerful, the master of the world situation, militarily, economically and politically. Therefore, if it wants to improve its image it should . . . When Muslims look to the West they see that it is prejudiced against them in many ways. We have the conflict between the Arabs and Israel, in which the West is with Israel. It is also clear in Bosnia-Hercegovina, even for the least thing—lifting the embargo on arms—they are against Muslims in every way, although they speak about "New World Order." They should deal with us as they deal with the rest of the world, not with a double standard. They go with democracy everywhere, but when it comes to the Islamic world it is different; they are against Muslims, they are with dictatorships and with the regimes against the people. As in Algeria, when most of the people said yes to the Muslims, but the West erased the votes of Muslims.

Also in Iraq, the West wants Iraq to destroy all the weapons it has, but it won't do the same with Israel. Elsewhere, voting corruption has been encouraged by the West.

Fourthly, it is better for the West, in dealing with Islamic areas, not be satisfied only with reports which come to them through intelligence and security agencies. They should be in touch with the real thing; they should come and see things the way they are.

JD: Sometimes it's confusing which is the right Islam, because there are so many different movements. Is there any attempt to unify the different Islamic philosophies so that they can be easier to grasp? Is there a world united movement?

YQ: Islam has some main sources which are recognized by all Muslims, Sunni and Shia alike. All believe in one God, the afterlife, the importance of prayer, of *zakat* [charity tax], and the pilgrimage. They forbid adultery, usury, wine and intoxicants. Differences among them should happen, because their intellects differ one from the other. You cannot put them in one pot, they will be different. The Qur'an approves of this. We have the Golden Rule, it says that we should cooperate in what we agree upon. But also we should excuse one another on things that we disagree about. We may differ among each other.

Many people talk about a unified Islamic movement, but this should not be, because intellects differ, and this is a good sign. God has created the universe full of differences, yet in harmony. We should try only to compromise, to find something in common among different religious schools, especially their bases, without destroying their differences.

THIRTEEN

KHURSHID AHMAD

SENATOR, ISLAMIC ACTION FRONT, PAKISTAN

PROFILE

KHURSHID AHMAD GREETED ME at his home in Islamabad with a warm smile and a weak handshake. That he took my hand at all was a sign of openness and moderation in the inner circle of committed Islamists. It was not a firm grasp, and I suspected he would have preferred not to touch me at all, but Islam teaches that Muslims sometimes must choose the lesser of two evils. For Khurshid Ahmad, it was a choice between potentially offending a guest in his home or mildly breaching the Islamist disapproval of shaking a woman's hand.

From his writings and our interview, it was clear that Ahmad was a devout but pragmatic Islamist, one who realized the necessity of compromise in an imperfect world. As a representative of the Pakistan Islamic Front (PIF) in the Senate, Khurshid Ahmad was a minority voice in his country's political arena, one that was a distant third to the two powerful political dynasties—Benazir Bhutto's Pakistan People's Party and Nawaz al-Sharif's Pakistan Muslim League (PML). Yet the PIF was the strongest and most organized Islamic party in the country, founded by the powerful Jamaat-i-Islami movement to work inside the political structure to establish a "true" Islamic Republic of Pakistan. As

Khurshid Ahmad and his colleagues in the PIF saw it, neither of the two main parties were moving quickly enough in ensuring that Pakistan's laws fully conformed with Islamic law.

As vice president, or deputy *ameer,* of Jamaat-i-Islami, Ahmad was instrumental in helping to found the PIF in May 1993. Before deciding to launch its own political party, the Jamaat had worked with the Pakistan Muslim League, and Khurshid Ahmad had been a member of the cabinet of Zia al-Haq. Al-Haq seized power in 1977 from Prime Minister Zulfikar Ali Bhutto and wooed Islamists to secure his own power base. But by the time the Muslim League, led by Prime Minister Nawaz Sharif, faced Benazir Bhutto's PPP in the 1993 elections, the Jamaat had lost all faith in both parties.

Resurgence, the Jamaat's publication, described the PIF in its June 1993 issue as a "movement to end corruption and political exploitation by providing God fearing and Islam loving leadership to the nation." That was two months before national elections for the National Assembly in which the PIF won only 3 of the 201 seats reserved for Muslims. (Pakistan set aside 10 seats for non-Muslims.) Bhutto's PPP won 86 and Sharif's PML won 72. It was a bitter disappointment for the PIF, which had been confident that the Pakistani people wanted an alternative to what was widely seen as rampant corruption in both of the main parties.

"With the population having 75 percent illiteracy rate, it is difficult to change the traditional course of the politics but not impossible," the party officially stated in *Resurgence* following its defeat. But although the new PIF party campaigned heavily, it formed only two months before the election and in a country where "barons, feudal lords, rich and influential families and people still command authority over peasants and poor people living in rural areas." The PIF was forced to concede that Pakistan's poor, among whom it had expected to win a strong political base, was still very much allied to the two main parties. And it would take more than a few months of heavy campaigning to convince them there was a viable alternative. Ahmad was committed to helping the PIF strengthen its standing with Pakistan's 53 million registered voters. Yet he had another huge commitment as well, one that frequently forced him to leave Pakistan for Europe.

Ahmad was a Westward-looking Islamist. He had traveled widely in the United States and Europe; he even lived for ten years in Great Britain before returning to Pakistan in 1978 to accept the post in Zia al-Haq's cabinet. But Ahmad's attraction to the West was not based on admiration or imitation of Western culture. In fact, the opposite was true. Khurshid Ahmad saw the West as desperately in need of Islam's moral influence. But he also believed that world stability depended on good relations between East and West. As Maulana Maudoodi, one of the greatest Islamic thinkers of the modern world, wrote in the foreword to Ahmad's book *Islam and the West:* "The call of our times, is that, with a view to achieving world peace and international amity, mutual relationship among different nations be reconstructed . . . the need for the establishment of a relationship of the people of Europe and America with the Islamic fraternity, on new foundations of good will and good cheer, stands out as of paramount significance."[1]

Ahmad believed the Islamic da'wa (propagation of the faith) should not be confined to the Middle East but should be spread throughout the world, even in the United States and Europe. Ahmad was associated with the Islamic Foundation based in Leicester, England; and from 1973 to 1978, he was its director general, charged with leading the organization's efforts to spread the Islamic message in Europe. When I spoke to him, Ahmad was president of the International Association for Islamic Economics, a branch of the Islamic Foundation. He was also on the academic advisory board of the Institute of Comparative, Political and Economic Systems at Georgetown University in Washington, D.C., and was associated with Islamic organizations in Africa and the Middle East. He considered Islam not only a religion but a code of life.

Ahmad had earned a reputation as a leading Islamic economic theorist, helping to develop an Islamic concept of business and finance in the modern world. As he wrote in the pamphlet "Economic Development in an Islamic Framework":

> The major contribution of Islam lies in making human life and effort purposive and value-oriented. The transformation it seeks to bring about in human attitudes and *pari passu* in that of the social sciences is to move them from a stance of pseudo-value-neutrality towards

open and manifest value-commitment and value-fulfillment. . . .

    We must reject the archetype of capitalism and socialism.. Both
these models of development are incompatible with our value system
. . . both are exploitative and unjust and fail to treat man as man, as
God's vicegerent on earth. Both have been unable to meet in their
own realms the basic economic, social, political and moral challenges
of our time and the real needs of a humane society and a just
economy.[2]

As he explained in the pamphlet, an Islamic-oriented economic system
would make "human resource development" a top priority:

This would include inculcation of correct attitudes and aspirations,
development of character and personality, education and training
producing skills needed for different activities, promotion of knowledge and research, and evolution of mechanisms for responsible and
creative participation by the common people in key developmental
activities, in decision-making at all levels and finally in sharing the
fruits of development.[3]

Development in an Islamic system would not be profit oriented but
people oriented, he believed. Production would be guided along the
lines of what was best for society. That would mean that factories
would be encouraged to produce abundant supplies of food and
necessities for living, but "the production of those things whose use is
forbidden in Islam would not be allowed; those whose use is discouraged, their production would be discouraged, and all that is essential
and useful would be given priority and encouragement," according to
Ahmad. Alcohol production would be prohibited, as most probably
would be cigarette production. As Ahmad outlined them, priority
production would entail:

- Abundant production and supply of food and basic items
  of necessity (including construction material for building
  houses and roads and basic raw materials) at reasonably
  cheap prices.

- Defense requirements of the Muslim world.
- Self sufficiency in the production of basic capital goods.[4]

Islam prohibits usury and, thus, assessing interest payments on loans is against Islamic law. Ahmad was credited with encouraging the establishment of Islamic banks that did not charge interest, and their number and rate of success seemed to be growing. But the basis of the Islamic concept of economy is justice, he argued, which encompasses redistribution of wealth when necessary through levying of taxes, zakat. And supposedly no one would be allowed to become rich by exploiting others. As Ahmad explained it, the concept of morality and duty to God as well as to society is very much at the heart of his concept of an Islamic economic system, and morality is what many Muslims find lacking in Western capitalism.

Ahmad had been formulating his theories of the ideal Islamic state and its economy ever since he joined the Islamic youth movement, the Islami Jamiat-i-Tulaba, in 1949. His family had moved to the newly created state of Pakistan one year earlier, from their home in New Delhi, India, where Ahmad was born in 1932. His father, Aziz Ahmad, was a successful businessman who became active in the Muslim League. In New Delhi, Khurshid Ahmad participated in public demonstrations in support of Pakistan's independence. And when his father moved the family to Karachi in 1948, Ahmad was quick to become involved in the Islamic movement.

He soon met Maulana Maudoodi and was so impressed with his vision of Islam and society that he committed himself to Islamic study and activism. Khurshid Ahmad said his activism with the Jamaat's student movement shaped the course of his life. He spent three years as president of the organization, editing several of its publications, before he joined the Jamaat-i-Islami as a full member in 1956. Today Ahmad is one of the world's most respected Islamist leaders.

He lived in a pleasant, tree-lined section of Pakistan's modern capital, Islamabad. The whitewashed stone walls of his villa opened to a spacious courtyard. Inside the voices of children created a pleasant cacophony, and I was greeted at the door by one of his sons, a lanky, dark-haired boy of about 11. He escorted me into a modestly furnished living room that was large enough to hold several seating enclaves of stuffed sofas and upholstered chairs. I can remember no pictures on the walls and very little decoration at all. I interpreted the austerity as a sign that Ahmad agreed with Maulana Maudoodi's philosophy that art inevitably leads to idol worship. I imagined that Khurshid Ahmad's living room had been the setting for many meetings of the hierarchy of the Jamaat-i-Islami and its political arm, the Pakistan Islamic Front. Once again we were in the midst of a power blackout, but the morning sun flooded through several windows, as startling as the beams of a spotlight on a darkened stage. Ahmad burst into the room only moments after I was seated. He expressed surprise to see a Western reporter with her hair covered and dressed in a *shalwar khameez,* the long tunic and loose pants worn by Pakistani women. He seemed pleased to hear me explain that although I was not a Muslim, wearing a form of Islamic dress in the presence of devout Muslims was, for me, a sign of respect.

Muslims often complain that their religion is not respected in the West; in fact, this is one of the main reasons for what Ahmad described as growing animosity between the two worlds. As Maudoodi wrote in the foreword to Khurshid Ahmad's *Islam and the West,* Muslims "are pained to see the overall attitude of Western people towards Muslim history, religion and culture is not only unsympathetic but positively hostile. They often outstep the limits of academic criticism and in attempt to paint the Muslims black, resort to assertions, which it would be only too mild to call 'intolerant.'"[5]

Ahmad wrote in the same book: "Islam has been misunderstood and misinterpreted in the West. It is one of the most queer facts of history that despite the annihilation of space and time, despite the West's stupendous strides in quest of knowledge and learning, despite the centuries of contact between the world of Islam and the West, Islam is perhaps the least known and the most misunderstood religion in the West."[6]

Ahmad told me that while he had dedicated himself to trying to improve the relationship between the Islamic world and the West, he believed the West must change its attitude of superiority and dominance before there can be hope for any improvement. In an interview in June 1988, Ahmad explained: "If the only practical ground of cooperation is the assimilation of the Western culture and rejection of Islam as we understand it, then there is no ground for any meeting. But if the cooperation is to be achieved on equal footing, then it is most welcomed."

In the second chapter of *Islam and the West*, Khurshid Ahmad listed the following reasons for the hostility toward the West that had developed among Muslims: Western imperialism, economic exploitation by Western interests, forced Western education, cultural dominance, imposition of Christianity, and attacks on Islam.

In a 1993 article he wrote for the *Middle East Affairs Journal*, Ahmad strongly criticized the foreign policies of Western governments, led by the United States: "Muslims, while on their quest for self-assertion, have been amazed by the double standards demonstrated by some Western leaders. If the Iraqi occupation of Kuwait was a crime, then of equal iniquity are the Israeli occupation of Palestine, the Indian annexation of Kashmir and the Serbian 'ethnic cleansing' of Bosnia-Hercegovina."[7]

Ahmad chastised the United States and other Western powers for what he saw as their insensitivity to the desire of Muslims to develop their societies in keeping with their own culture and values. And he criticized the United States for supporting undemocratic secular regimes in the Middle East while castigating Islamic movements that are fighting for democracy:

> The West must take a hard look at itself and realize that economic and cultural imperialism are no less destructive than political imperialism. The United States, in particular, as the sole superpower on the global stage, must become more sensitized to the fears of less developed states that see the U.S. embarking on a new imperial order. In so doing, the U.S. is willing to ignore the suppression of democracy when it seems that the opposition will not bend to its will.[8]

Ahmad believed Islamic societies must be allowed to develop their own systems of governance, in keeping with guidance in the Qur'an and in the recorded writings and deeds of the Prophet Muhammad. This does not rule out plurality and democracy, although the ideal system would not be identical to those in Western countries. He had written of establishing a "theodemocracy" or "a democratic system inseparable from divine guidance":

This definition repudiates the concept of theocracy because such a government is restrictive in its scope, i.e., it confines the leadership to a particular religious class who reserve the right to interpret religious law and wield political power. A theo-democracy, however, establishes the basic rules of law, much like a constitution; and from these essential principles appropriate laws are implemented, similar to the amendments made to the U.S. constitution and the laws Congress ratifies within the framework of that constitution.[9]

Ahmad's Islamic ideal would gradually eliminate nation-states and lead to unions based on Islamic ideology, "thus creating the framework of a commonwealth of Islamic regions." Many Islamic moderates expressed such a dream; they believed that such an ideal cannot be achieved overnight and should not be sought through violence.

Although Ahmad told me that he, like many Islamic leaders, abhorred violence, especially in the name of Islam, he said he understood its motivations, and even sympathized with those who resorted to violence to overthrow tyrannical regimes. He had written:

If Muslims engage in violent acts, it is mostly as a response to the subjugation imposed by secular tyrannies. Violence may occur in any society, particularly where the people's will is not sufficiently addressed. The riots in Los Angeles, unexpected by so many White Americans, was the direct result of ignoring the Black community's plight. When the Conservative party in England introduced the Poll Tax, riots broke out in central London, something virtually alien to that metropolitan city. Race, color, language, lifestyle, ideology, all of these elements lead to different variations of violence and fanaticism.[10]

As we shared strong English tea and cakes, Ahmad said he was struggling to make the concerns of Muslim people easily understandable to the West. To propagate Islam, he believed its leaders would have to be able to communicate with all kinds of people, across a variety of cultures. And for Islam to flourish in the modern world, he said, it would have to convince the West that it should not be blamed for the violence that sometimes was perpetrated in its name. While his arguments were convincing, it could also be argued that leaders such as Khurshid Ahmad have to be convinced to speak out more strongly against violence and not allow any excuses for attacks against innocents, whatever the motivation.

INTERVIEW WITH KHURSHID AHMAD

JANUARY 1994, ISLAMABAD, PAKISTAN

JD: You have a long history of involvement in politics in Pakistan, especially as an Islamist. Why did you opt to join an Islamic party, the Jamaat, instead of working through other parties?

KA: My background is that I come from a very important political family. My father was juror in Delhi and was an active delegate of the Muslim League. So, actually I inherited politics in a sense. During my college days, I realized that Pakistan was established not merely for the sake of independence but also to realize some social, political, economic, moral, ideological goals. And as a student, I was myself involved in the Pakistani movement.

But when I saw in Pakistan people [were] becoming immune to people's real needs . . . the leadership [was], I think . . . neglectful of ideology. The founding fathers died within the first three years, and with the result, the leadership was in the hands of those who were not in the forefront of the original struggle. So vested interests took over. I was faced with the question as a really active student leader . . . what should be our future? So I opted for Islami Jamiat Tulaba [Islami Jamiat-i-Tulaba]. That was a student organization, committed to Islamic idealism. So it was in that context that my future life and course of action was set.

JD: Do you feel that there is a developing problem, tension, in relations [with the West]? And, looking at the Islamic world in general, do you feel that there is a growing problem in relations between the two peoples?

KA: Thank you very much. I think this is the most important question. And I will attempt to answer it. As far as my appreciation is concerned, I feel that the problem is growing, and growing quickly. Both in relation to Pakistan and in relation to the Muslim world in general. However, I differentiate between the American government and the American people and the American system. These three I treat in their own light, differently, although there are some areas of convergence amongst all these three. Now, my feeling is that as far as the American system is concerned, it has many achievements to its credit and it is also faced with many problems, at the moral, cultural and social levels in particular. And criticism and dissatisfaction with those aspects which relate to this critical aspect of the Western civilization and American culture is something which is a common concern of all humanity. It is not a question of decrying a system or condemning a system or revolting, nothing like that; it is common concern of humanity, and well-meaning human beings, men and women in America, in Europe, are equally concerned about social and moral problems. So, when Muslims express concern about those issues, it should not be taken as enmity.

As far as the American people are concerned, by and large, I am very sympathetic with them. I have found them open, frank, prepared to learn, yet the level of knowledge is terribly, terribly poor. And this is not merely in the case of Pakistan and Islam. I found out that somehow, the Monroe Doctrine was not confined to politics. It had its cultural and intellectual overtones. And Americans have been a rather inward-looking people. The bulk of them came from immigrants who were persecuted in their own homelands. So instead of being concerned with the countries from where they came, they were more concerned with the political haven they were trying to build, the freedom they were trying to achieve; [in accommodation with] the multicultural, multilinguistic dimensions which they were able to develop. So I think they were more concerned about their own selves.

It was under Woodrow Wilson that America came into the full glare of world politics and America did play a role. And I would remind you that on the question of the League of Nations trusteeship of Palestine, of Syria, of Lebanon, the people of the region requested [that] America . . . be given the trusteeship, not the British or the

French. Because they had suffered at the hands of British and French imperialism and they had the hope that America stands for democracy, for Bill of Rights. America has given freedom to people of the Philippines and not subjugated them in the manner Western European imperialism had their colonies. So, they thought that Americans would behave differently.

JD: But they were disappointed?

KA: They were disappointed. And that is, I think, the tragedy. And then I come to the third factor, that is, American leadership. Here again it would be unfair to condemn them whole hog. There have always been dissenting voices. But by and large it seems that effective political lobbies have firmly entrenched themselves, with the result that whether Democrats are in power or Republicans are in power, we find that, unfortunately, the American foreign policy is not as principled as it claims to be. It has not even been in the long-term interest of America itself. And that, too, because they do not really go deep into understanding the cultures, the history, the vital interests of other people and how there can be convergence of interests instead of national interests. For example, when it was Cold War phobia and that syndrome, all emphasis was on containing communism and, by hook and crook, raising walls of resistance all around the communist world, whether they were despots, tyrants, democrats, criminals or general politicians, it became irrelevant. So much so that there had been American strategists who openly pleaded if there are pro-left dictatorships emerging in Africa and Asia, we should try to have pro-West dictatorships. This is how the military was used in a number of Muslim countries as well as other African countries.

And we do find this increasing projection of Islam as a threat, as a menace and again in this context, not only ignorance, but I will be frank with you, certain lobbies, who are committed to project Islam and Muslims in the worst colors . . . like the pro-Zionist lobbies. As far as Zionism is concerned, as far as Jews are concerned, as a Muslim, I regard them as my brethren in faith, as we call them *Al Kitab*, that is, believing in revealed books. And throughout Muslim history, when Jews were persecuted and hunted in the Christian world, the Muslim world was their refuge. They were given freedom, they were given protection, they were given every opportunity there. So, we have no quarrel with Jews or Judaism at all. Zionism is a secular, colonialistic philosophy. And their philosophy has been translated into reality. And the Zionist lobby has been one of the lobbies which has been spreading this scare against Islam and the Muslims.

JD: Why do you think they're spreading that scare?

KA: Well, because it's very simple, you see. They have taken our pound of flesh. They want to hold it. They were offered a place in Kenya. They were offered a place in Uganda. They were offered a place in Russia. They didn't take that. They said no, we'll go to Palestine. That is the reason. But anyway at the moment, my concern is that these lobbies are also trying to play it around. And also, unfortunately, some of the American strategists think they always need some enemy to really put forever and forever in their policies. If communism has gone down, then they need someone else. And I must also say that in the making of this [scenario], certain Muslim countries and individuals have also provided them with the opportunity. For example, Iran is a classic case.

JD: For the West, Islam is a scary case.

KA: Yes [LAUGHTER], I agree with you. Iran—we find—that America tried to build Iran as a surrogate. The point I was trying to make was that American policy is based on a very fragile base. And the information base, perception of the Iranian people, their real sources of strength and weakness. Shah, Shah's aspirations, Shah's roots, Shah's support, opposition to him, all these, despite all the American presence in Iran, the level of knowledge of the Iranians was very, very poor. And because of that their policy making was on very fragile grounds.

JD: And what you've just said is still the case?

KA: It's still the case. Yes . . . you see . . . once the revolution took place, Americans were off guard. And they did try to counter the revolution. It was in reaction to that that some of the students took Americans as hostage. In my view that was wrong, but it was a violent, childish reaction on the part of these students. But from then onwards, we find that Islam and Iran have been projected out of all proportion in the American media as well as with American policy makers as the devil incarnate. And I would also express my reservations about the way the Iranian government reacted by calling America a Satan, the great Satan. So that language on the part of both has embittered the relationships. Libya, for example, has again done some similar things. Yet I think the American reaction is out of all proportion, is unrealistic, is having the flavor of anti-Muslim or at least scared of Islam. While my view is that Islam does not pose any threat at all to America or to Europe. We have no territorial quarrel. No territorial dispute, no lingering political dispute with any of these countries. The whole Islamic resurgence, the whole Islamic revival, is simply about one thing and that is that Muslim people also want to order their own houses in accordance with their own values, their own aspirations, their own principles in the same way that Americans are doing, that Europeans are doing. We want the same right, nothing more and nothing less. We have no quarrel with America, we are not going for world leadership. We have no military potential, we have no technical potential to be a real threat. So, as far as Muslim people are concerned, as far as Islamic movements are concerned, if we are critical of the West, it is not in the sense of political rivalry or colonial encounters or clashes. It is at the level of civilization and culture, which is the common concern of mankind.

JD: But you don't think that there is inevitably a clash between Western culture and Islamic culture?

KA: Not at all. I totally disagree with Huntington's thesis and all the debate that has gone with it.*

---

* Ahmad was referring to ideas discussed by Samuel Huntington in "The Clash of Civilizations," published in the September 1993 issue of *Foreign Affairs*. In the article, Huntington argued that in the post–Cold War era, conflicts are likely to emerge between states and groups from different civilizations. Many of the Muslims I interviewed rejected this theory and considered it another attempt to cast Islam as an enemy of Western civilization.

I believe that yes, there are differences of civilizations and competition between civilizations. There can be a lot of learning as well as a widening in this context. But it is totally incorrect that the political struggle, the political hot points, the clash points are conditioned by or motivated by cultural considerations. I see no justification in that. Instead I regard this kind of cultural competition as a very promising area for the entire mankind, to learn from each other's experiences. And it is my thesis that one of the greatest achievements of the twentieth and the twenty-first centuries would be that wars that used to be fought for ideas, for ideologies, or for cultures, their days are over.

Why? Because, number one, military technology has reached a stage where war would mean destruction of all and not survival of any. So fighting for the supremacy of an idea would be self-destruction. Secondly, ideas are now communicable all over the world without any hurdle. Formerly, sometimes, these wars had to take place because the opportunity of contact, of exchange, of dialogue, of discussion, of acceptance and rejection, were not there. The political boundaries were also barriers to that. Today, both because of the new international protocols, because of the movement of populations, because of the free flow of ideas and information, because of the information and technological revolution of our time, because of the close contact and movement of human beings from one place to another, we find that the possibility of dialogue and exchange of ideas is there without the need of any armed person. So with the result, as far as with this clash of civilization is concerned, this has reached a new plane, a new level. And that level is one of dialogue and not of arms.

JD: Except I'm wondering if this increased communication between cultures and this increased propagation of ideas across boundaries, if that isn't part of the cause of the problem. Because the people who have the power to communicate, basically the West, is sending out its messages of its culture and its values into another world. That is causing a backlash in some cases. We went through a period where it affected the youth, and they were copying and wearing jeans and miniskirts. But aren't we now entering the phase of backlash, of rejection of this?

KA: This is a very important point, very important point. And I agree. It is the way it has been done. It is the possibility of who is doing these things . . . the second is the way it is being done . . . the manner in which it is being done, it has cultural, imperialistic overtones. And that is creating disenchantment and disaffection amongst the people. But I'll give you an instance; this is a very superficial approach. What happened with Algeria . . . now, in Algeria, the French tried to impose their culture on the African people to an extent that Arabic language was almost eliminated. And when Algeria became free, the means of communication among the Algerian people was French and not Arabic.

When Abbas, the FLN leader, came to Pakistan, and I was a student leader in the '50s, we arranged a big reception for him, and I took with me an Arabic interpreter to talk with him, and when I talked to him, he said, I can't speak Arabic, I need an French interpreter, so this is the tragedy. But what is it now? You find the same youth who are exposed to French television, an the French television directed toward Algeria, is more sex oriented, more crime oriented than what is shown even in France; and yet the reaction is that now they are growing beards and becoming anti-French, anti this culture. So my view is that the manner in which it is being done is counterproductive. But the point I want to make is that the possibility of reaching each other . . . and there will not be backlog for long, I assure you. With the satellite communication, Muslims, Third World countries, they will also be able to reach the West soon. And also you see we will be able to reach ourselves, our people. So, while CNN is here, we are also trying to see that Pakistan television is seen in other countries.

I regard this to be basically a healthy development and a safety valve against wars for ideas or culture or religions or civilization. And against that the real competition would be in the field of knowledge, in the field of dialogue and discussion, and that is an area where the West is free to preach to us and we should be free to preach to them, and wherever there is a higher moral principle, wherever there are values which will be able to sustain human society, I think that will be a blessing for all. They tell me in Britain, you find in Liverpool, two ten-year-olds killing a two-year-old boy. Forty injuries on the body. Three hours torturing. And what were they getting? Not any physical gain, not any monetary gain. Sheer sadism and sheer self-destruction. So a civilization that is prepared to produce these . . . and they are not isolated events, this is what is becoming, unfortunately, the order of the day. So this means that we are faced with certain common problems of civilization. And if Islamic respect for values, moral sense, commitment to religion, seriousness on moral issues, respect for family, if these things are the example of the experiences before the West, we are sure this will have an enriching contribution and not a negative contribution.

JD: Would you, for example, in your ideas, would you envision an Islamic state that would allow missionaries, Christian missionaries?

KA: Why not? Why not? There are Christian missionaries everywhere. And the first critique of Islam came from John of Syria in the year 90 of *Hejira* [Muhammad's flight from Mecca], which is the first century of *Hejira*. And it was never condemned or censured by Muslims. The first great critique from the Judaized came from Marmanots, and Marmanots was also the medical doctor to the Egyptian monarch. And before publishing his book, he showed it to the Muslim monarch and the Muslim monarch said as long as it is free of abuse, uses decent language, it has arguments, even if it criticizes me, my book, my religion, you have a right to say so.

JD: So that's the true spirit of Islam, to be very tolerant and open?

KA: Exactly. From that viewpoint, we have no problem at all. So what I say is that we do not have any territorial, any such conflict which should put Islam and the Western world enemies to each other. Then what is the issue? The issue is again that the West also has to realize that, consciously or unconsciously, they have a monolithic concept of their power. This is a hangover of the age of imperialism, where they thought that they are the best settlers of the world, they are the teachers of civilization. They are going to others who are barbarians. And now, this new world order, where it is assumed that Russia has disintegrated, there is only one superpower and there should be a Pax Americana, which should set the tone all over the world. That in my view is the real threat to world peace and to America. Because America cannot overstretch itself to this position. America has seen that merely by military muscle and military power, they could not control Vietnam. The Gulf war they were able to win, but mainly because the contest was between America plus 28 other countries. America mobilized 70 percent of its total technical air power and 40 percent of its total military power for fighting a little sparrow . . . Iraq. So they were able to do it. But along with that, they were also counting the coffins. And the strategists were thinking that if the number of dead exceeded that particular bottom line, the people would not be able to take it. Look to Somalia. When 18 people died there, their mood changed. And you may have the best army in the world, but if your people are not prepared to die for a cause, and if you have to provide a fighting army with cultural escape roots as were provided in the Gulf war . . . see I have very strong reservations about a country which could rule over the world with military power.

JD: I think you've hit a very important point. This is what many Westerners fear about this new Islamic revival. We're confronted with a force that is not totally accepting of the West; a different force, with people who are prepared to die.

KA: Fair enough. And this is our strength. This is our arsenal. We may not have the atom bomb, but we have this courage to stand for our honor. And that is what would pave the way for real peace in the world. Because in that case if you can have a vision of a pluralistic world, where America and Europe have a right to live according to their values, their standards, but Muslims should also be given the right to set their own house [in order] according to their own values. And we should not be accepted as deviants, as rebels to civilization. But as a different civilization, a different culture. And there is interaction at the intellectual level, at the cultural level, at the level of movement of capital, movement of human beings. And learning from each other's experiences. And that would make the world a far better place to live in. And this is our vision.

JD: But would I be wrong if I put you in with moderates?

KA: Well, all these are very relative terms. What is moderate from the viewpoint of X may really be revolutionary from the viewpoint of Y . . . and you really cannot draw these lines. But I find myself in very comfortable company with persons like Hassan al-Turabi. I would not hesitate to say that I want to change the world, first of all my own. And I have vision of a new world order. But not one that would be imposed on others by force or violence.

JD: In that regard, you sound to me similar to Rachid al-Ghannouchi, whom I interviewed in London. Though he very much believes that things are not right with Tunisia, he has resisted calling his people to violence.

KA: That's right. I do not believe in violence. And I believe that violence is justified only if you are really put to the wall and you have no other option in self-defense but to react.

JD: Do you think that's the case in places like Algeria?

KA: In Algeria, unfortunately. In Kashmir. But this is something I regret. Because even one single human soul, innocent person killed, is a loss for the entire humanity. I believe in the Qur'an, which says that killing one person, an innocent person, without a justification, legal justification, is like killing the entire human race. And saving one innocent person is like saving the life of the entire humanity. So this is what I believe.

JD: Tell me, how has Pakistan been able . . . I see Pakistan as a model of plurality in the Islamic world, allowing all voices, as long as they are within legal restrictions.

KA: That's right . . .

JD: How has it been able to develop this and yet places like Egypt and Algeria have not?

KA: I think there are a number of reasons. First, I must say that the British rule in the subcontinent had been oppressive, had been colonial, yet they respect the institution of the judiciary, political procedures, and even when they had to commit a crime against the people, they would observe certain formalities. Now that tradition in my view is one factor. Second, I believe in Pakistan, the temperament of the people also counts. Like Malaysia. There are people, you seek, who are are temperamentally pluralistic. There are people who have not those traditions, of pluralism. In Egypt, for example, I find that the traditions of violence on all sides, relatively, have been much more than in the subcontinent. Muslims ruled the subcontinent for over a thousand years. There are no instances of Hindu-Muslim riots. Never. Courts have always been in oppression. Yes, monarchs did transgress, they exceeded limits, Muslim or otherwise. Yet there were some rules which were respected. And this is also, you see, what grieves us. That on one hand, the West has been expressing concern for human rights for human values; on the other hand, the oppression released by Nasser, for example, on Muslim Brotherhood in Egypt was never taken note of. Forty thousand young men rotting in prisons. And prisons becoming torture houses. No law. The result is they are now resorting to violence because they are desperate. They are saying if we have to be annihilated and liquidated, okay, let us then strike back.

So in my view, the use of violence from [the] state is the greatest crime; and use of violence on the side of the people, where they are not forced, is truly unjustifiable.

And finally, I believe that there should be possibility of trade relationship, of flow of resources from one part of the world to the other part. Flow of goods. And I believe that economists—first I am an economist. I believe that mobility of capital, of goods, of human beings would be a blessing.

JD: Yes, but isn't there a basic difference, or a conflict, between the Islamic economic philosophy and the Western economic philosophy?

KA: Of course there is. Of course there is. But what I say is that at least this is common between us. So, merely America's interest to directly control the primary resources, to me this is an imperialistic approach. Instead America is prepared to have an understanding of free flow of resources. You need oil, we can't drink oil. So it's our common need to share it. So it should be shared through normal trade, through agreement, through negotiation, through historically organized economic modes of cooperation. So that would reduce conflict, and the flashpoints that are there presently can be controlled and managed. That's how we look upon it.

JD: Do you consider Pakistan a true Islamic state? Are there any in the world today? And what do you see as some of the biggest challenges facing Islamic leaders?

KA: Well, Pakistan is a Muslim state.

JD: What's the difference?

KA: Yes, I'm coming to that. Pakistan is a Muslim state. Pakistan wants to become an Islamic state. We are in a process of a transition from Muslim to Islamic. The difference is that we become Muslim merely by commiting ourselves to a vision, to an ideology, to a set of values. But you become Islamic when you really translate that vision into reality. And from that viewpoint, we are still far, far, far away from the Islamic model. Why? Again, because we are stepping out of 500 years of colonial rule. We are coming out of our own domestic degeneration and weakness. We don't paper that, we don't hide that. We are coming out of an age of ignorance. We have not been masters of our own situation. The world was made for us. We had no part in that. So it will take time to have that.

But I think Pakistan is unique in the sense that we were the first people almost in the contemporary Muslim world to emphasize that for a political future, ideological identity is important. And it is the ideological identity that will also ensure our future growth as a polity, as a society as an economy. We have also disappointed ourselves, almost 50 years. We have not been able to turn the corner, both for domestic and international reasons. Yet the nation has this aspiration, this commitment. And from that viewpoint I am quite hopeful that, in the future, we will be able to develop that more. And to me most of the Muslim world countries are exactly in the same struggle at different points.

JD: I have assumed throughout our conversation that, because I've read something about you, you have liberal ideas with regard to the place of women in Islamic societies . . . that they should have equal rights . . .

KA: Again, I don't say that it is liberal. I say this is Islam. Because, you see, Islam has treated women and men as equal beings. Islam never said that there was an original sin, that woman was responsible for that. That men and women were sent into the world as a punishment because of that sin. We do not believe in that mythology. In the Qur'an it is very clear that the criteria of success for a Muslim man and a Muslim woman are the same . . . in the moral and the ideological area. Similarly in law, in economical dealings, even in political dealings, but certainly, there are also certain restraints and we are not shy about that. We say that men and women are equal, but equality does not mean that each one must be forced to do the same job, the same work. We ought to see, because of their nature, because of their role in society, where they can contribute best. We believe in an optimal division of labor. Not saying that every woman, if women have not been able to become good soldiers, then they are bad humans. No. If they excel in a particular field, they make their contribution there. If men can excel somewhere else, fair enough.

JD: But what I'm hearing is, you are not saying that, for example, if your daughter wanted to become an engineer, that she shouldn't be able to become it.

KA: Why not? Why not? My daughter is actually studying in London now and she's in the university. And she is doing her course in business administration and psychology. This is what she liked. She is studying law. Islam does not constrain these things. My wife owns property. My daughter owns property. If they want to become entrepreneurs, they are free to do that. There is no problem at all about that.

JD: Well, the last question is, what do you feel is the challenge facing Muslims around the world?

KA: Well, as far as I am concerned in my own mind, the greatest challenge is from within. I believe that the greatest problem that man faces today is neglect of the inner dimension of life. While there is a lot of lip service to the individual and individualism, and individualism is the basis of Western imperialism, my problem is that [the] individual has really lost his moorings, which are moral, which are spiritual, which represent integration of the physical and the spiritual dimensions of life. So from my viewpoint, the greatest challenge is this for all, including Muslims.

But definitely, I would also say that the modern civilization is also universal, a universal civilization. It has reached everywhere. It has brought many blessings and many conveniences and amenities for mankind. Yet unfortunately the dualist standards which are being pursued at all levels . . . relationship between husband and wife . . . between parents and children . . . between the state and the people . . . the whole question of human rights, the whole question of democracy, the whole question of economic justice. So in my view, the real problem is moral clashes of mankind. And I believe that Islam has something to offer. Not merely by preaching but by demonstrating. It's not the word of mouth or the printed word, it's the example. That is the most important. And in my view, the real challenge lies in presenting before the world a living example of a good Muslim individual and a good Muslim society. And I am devoting my life toward the creation of that individual and that society. That is the real challenge.

FOURTEEN

ABIDA HUSSAIN

FORMER AMBASSADOR TO THE UNITED STATES
FROM PAKISTAN

PROFILE

THE RAIN WAS FALLING HARD and it was already dark when Abida Hussain's little red car turned into the driveway of my hotel in Islamabad. I didn't know what she looked like, and vice versa, but when a car with two women stopped in front of me, I got in.

One of Hussain's closest friends, Silvat Sher-Ali Pataudi, a former member of Pakistan's parliament, was in the car with her, and I scooted into the backseat. Hussain gave me a quick hello and maneuvered her car slowly back toward her home. She told me she had only recently left Washington and her position as Pakistan's ambassador to the United States and was getting reacquainted with friends she had not seen for months. We had not gone very far when Hussain slowed for a stop sign next to a raised, grassy median. From my window, I was struck by the sight of a man with shriveled legs running on his hands next to the car. His face was hairy and dirty and he was literally covered in rags. Despite his handicap, he moved very fast and had almost caught up with our car when we were hit with a sudden bang.

The driver behind us had apparently been distracted by the same sight and had crashed into us.

"Are you all right?" Hussain turned to me.

"I think so," I answered, feeling shaken and disoriented, but not in pain. Hussain stayed behind the wheel and Pataudi got out of the car and walked toward the offending vehicle. There were at least six men crammed into the tiny car. Pataudi, a middle-age woman, stood in the drizzle between the two cars and waited for the driver to get out of his car. Other people had apparently heard the accident and were walking toward it as well. Pataudi talked to him in Urdu and then returned to Hussain.

"Just tell them to follow me to my house," Hussain replied with the dispassionate authority of someone used to giving orders and having them obeyed.

The men did as they were told. Hussain's house was only a few blocks away, and the men followed until Hussain turned into the driveway of her courtyard, protected by a tall, stone wall. Her husband, a prominent Pakistani politician, was not home, but several male servants greeted her. She left them to deal with the carload of men that had followed us home.

"They probably don't have insurance," she told me as we walked into her spacious, modern home. "I'll have to pay for repairs on the car. And to make it worse, it isn't my car. I borrowed it from a friend."

After our ordeal, Hussain's living room seemed inviting. A few original paintings hung on the walls, and I got the impression that Hussain was a patron of local artists. She told me she even "dabbled" in painting herself. While clearly an upper-class home by Pakistani standards, with many rooms, it was homey and unpretentious. Two large sofas and well-cushioned chairs encircled a large stone fireplace, which during this pleasant night in January remained unlit. By the time hot tea and cakes appeared, Hussain had thrown off the wool cape that covered her *shalwar khameez,* settled on the sofa next to me and lit a cigarette. She was an attractive, earthy, middle-age woman who had strong opinions and was used to expressing them. Her thick black hair was speckled with gray, and diamond studs sparkled at her ears. As she told me about her life, her accent seemed more British than Pakistani but her opinions reflected the same deep resentment of the

West expressed by so many of the Muslim intellectuals I had interviewed. Abida Hussain said she was a member of Pakistan's minority
Shia community, but she was neither an Islamic activist nor a scholar.
She described herself as a "liberal Muslim" and said her religion was
very much a part of her identity. For Hussain, that seemed to mean she
was a believer and honored the general rules of Islam but did not allow
religious dogma to rule her life. For example, during the evening I
spent in her Islamabad home, Hussain smoked continuously, so much
so that I found myself developing a sore throat. Although I knew of no
specific injunction against smoking, I had never met a devout Muslim
who smoked. And as we prepared to adjourn into her dining room for
dinner where several servants were setting the table, a handsome,
clean-cut young man called on one of Hussain's daughters. Hussain
told me this daughter had just graduated from Harvard University and
was looking forward to a career in business, while another daughter
was still enrolled there. Hussain's son was in high school. Hussain
questioned her daughter's date good-naturedly about where they were
going, and she joked about whether he was spending too much money
on her. Strictly conservative Muslims believe Islam prohibits dating,
but liberal Muslims find such prohibitions outdated and too restrictive
for modern life. Yet Hussain seemed to honor the Islamic prohibition
against alcohol. During dinner, only water was served. And as Hussain's house began to fill with friends stopping by for an evening of
after-dinner conversation, tea was the only beverage served.

   Yet being a liberal Muslim is not the same thing as being a secular
one. Many liberal Muslims, such as Hussain, share with many Islamists a disdain for the concept of separation of religion from politics.
Hussain dismissed such separation as irrelevant for Muslim states,
arguing that it is based on the history of the relationship between the
Christian church and Western states.

   Like many strictly observant Muslims, Hussain seemed defensive
about Western attitudes toward Islam and the developing world. She
related to me a conversation she had with General Colin Powell, then
chairman of the Joint Chiefs of Staff under President George Bush.
Hussain was at a formal dinner as Pakistan's ambassador to the United
States when, she said, Powell asked her why Pakistan was so intent

upon pursuing its nuclear program in light of U.S. objections and its cutoff in financial aid.

"'You know that nukes are unusable,'" she said he told her, "'so why do you want to have nukes?'

"I said, 'General, why do you have nukes?'

"So he said, 'Oh, we're cutting back.'

"So I said, 'From how many to how many, General?'

"He said, 'We're cutting back from 6,000 to 2,000.'

"I said, 'General, you're going to keep 2,000 nukes and you want us to rid ourselves of our few miserable whatever it is buried deep into the ground? You're asking us to commit suicide. We're next to a nuclearized state. Would you surrender your nukes if, for instance, Canada or Mexico still retained nukes? Would you do that?'

"He looked at me and he said, 'Look, I'm not talking morality, Ambassador. I'm just saying to you that we're the United States of America and you're Pakistan.'

"And I said, 'General, I thank you, because you've been honest.'

"So that's it," she concluded. "Might is right. It has always been. That modus doesn't change."

Hussain implied that the United States subjects countries in the developing world to different standards than it applies to itself, especially with regard to the nuclear issue. It is as if the United States believes countries such as Pakistan are peopled by suicidal fanatics who are eager to obliterate themselves in a nuclear holocaust.

"You know, as I would keep saying to friends in America, we love ourselves and our children and our lives as much as you do. We don't wish to immolate ourselves. So why the hell should we be irresponsible with weapons? But the fact of the matter is that India and Pakistan have not been to war since both countries were pursuing nuclear programs and there will not be a war between India and Pakistan, because if the balance of terror works for one part of the world, it works for the other."

"The sad thing is that nobody else has ever launched an atomic device on anybody except the Americans. And your bombers go out regularly every decade to bomb some territory and some humans somewhere in the world. You've never been bombed at."

Hussain's arguments in favor of Pakistan's nuclear program was not uncommon among the country's leadership elite. In fact, in the summer of 1998, Pakistan ignored American warnings of sanctions and reprisals and conducted a series of nuclear tests, in response to India's testing it's own nuclear weapons. Abida Hussain was among those within the government of Nawaz al Sherif who decided to defy the United States and much of the Western world.

Although I often detected muted sarcasm and a biting bluntness in her comments about the influence of the West on developing nations, Hussain rejected the notion that Muslims feel any hostility toward the West. She preferred more subtle words, such as "understanding our own predicament" and "acknowledgment of the forces and factors that have produced this predicament."

It was clear to me that Hussain believed that Western powers have exploited the developing world and are continuing to do so.

She was especially passionate in her defense of Islam and its teachings on women, mindful that people in the West often believed Islam promoted the subjugation of women. Her arguments were identical to those of many devout Muslim women, both young and old, I had interviewed.

"My religion didn't inhibit me at all and nor has it handicapped me," she said. My face must have registered skepticism because she abruptly added, "What I'm saying is the truth as I perceive it. In fact, I would go on to say that Islam, when it was codified as a religion 14 centuries back, it was the first organized religion that spoke specifically of the rights of women. And there is a school of interpretation of modern Muslims that argue that Islam came to liberate women more than men." Hussain blamed colonialism for forcing women in many parts of the world out of public life. Women stayed inside their homes, or covered when they had to leave, to avoid abuse from the Western men who had invaded their lands, she contended. It was a version of history I had heard many times before from Muslim women around the world. But I also had heard many times that the Turks, who conquered a wide swath of the Middle East, were responsible for forcing women to stay at home and to cover when in public.

Hussain insisted that being a woman in this male-dominated Muslim state had been far more of a help to her than a hindrance in her pursuit of a political career. She acknowledged that hers was a special case, as she was the only child of a wealthy landowner who died leaving her financially independent. Yet Hussain initially won a seat in Pakistan's parliament under a law that set aside specific seats for women. "Because there was so few women in public life, I made rapid progress," Hussain said.

The same was true, she said, of Benazir Bhutto, who had twice held the position of prime minister. Referring to Benazir as a "sort of pop queen," Hussain declared, "she's prime minister because she's a woman."

Yet Hussain and Bhutto were clearly upper-class exceptions to the rule in Pakistan, and few women in their country could hope to rise to their levels of power and independence. An estimated 75 percent of the 50 million women in Pakistan live in rural communities, working an average of 16 to 18 hours a day and bearing six to eight children, according to a report published in 1992 by Asia Watch, a division of Human Rights Watch. Its report, "Double Jeopardy: Police Abuse of Women in Pakistan," concluded that some women were better off than others, but it contended that all women in Pakistan suffer from discrimination:

> The situation of women in Pakistan is by no means uniform. Conditions vary depending on geographical location and class, with the situation of women better in urban, middle-class and upper-class sections of society, where there are greater opportunities for higher education and for paid and professional work, and women's social mobility is somewhat less restricted. However, despite the relative advantages of women in some sectors, women from all walks of life in Pakistan remain second-class citizens.[1]

Hussain told me rather casually that she never made women's rights her agenda. And her life seemed to be an exception to what human rights monitors had described as the deplorable state of women of all classes in her country. Hussain said she had never experienced sexual harassment, despite her many years in public life. She even boasted that sexual discrimination in the workplace was virtually unheard of in Pakistan. It was hard for me to believe that was true, especially since I knew that many Pakistani women faced sexual crimes far more serious than harassment.

In fact, Hussain herself had been an outspoken critic of what are called the *Hudood* laws in Pakistan—laws enacted in 1979 that set criminal penalties for adultery, fornication and rape. Upon conviction, punishment includes stoning to death, public flogging and amputation. Hussain said the laws had been used to justify the abuse of thousands of women who were imprisoned under the laws after they reported that they had been raped.

"I mean, if a woman is raped, she has to prove that she's been raped," Hussain said. "If it is proved that she was raped, then there's an ordinance that comes into effect, which means that she is then a partner in adultery, so to speak, as well. It is very unfair." She told me that hundreds of Pakistani women, especially in rural areas, were thrown in prison as adulterers as a result of reporting rapes. They were subject to abuse from police officers, which included rapes and beatings. Such practices are clearly not sanctioned by Islam, she argued.

Asia Watch's report concluded that the *Hudood* laws as well as the police and the courts discriminated against women:

> The courts tend to see women as complicit in sexual offenses, despite a lack of evidence, or evidence to the contrary, and required from female rape victims extraordinarily conclusive proof that the alleged intercourse was forced. Moreover, many women who alleged but were unable to prove rape have themselves been charged with adultery or fornication for consensual sex, although a failure to prove rape does not prove that consensual sex occurred. The courts effectively have set a lesser burden of proof for the prosecution in cases involving female defendants.[2]

Hussain said she had fought during her career to have the *Hudood* laws repealed and she would continue her fight until they were. Her stand against the *Hudood* laws put her at odds with some conservative members of Pakistan's religious establishment. But she had been in such a position before. She told me that in 1988, she defeated a well-known *ulama* from her district for the National Assembly. After the election, she said, he was assassinated.

"This led to a lot of tension in the town," she said, "and because the cleric and I had opposed each other in election, some of his followers extended some amount of harassment," which included threatening her life.

Recently, she revealed, she had been harassed by supporters of another political rival, whom she described as "one of Benazir Bhutto's main henchmen."

Hussain was an opponent of Bhutto and a supporter of the man whom she defeated to regain the office of prime minister, Nawaz Sharif, then head of Pakistan's Muslim League. Sharif appointed Hussain his advisor after he assumed the office of prime minister in 1990; in May 1992 she took over the coveted position of Ambassador to the United States.

Hussain had been involved in politics since 1972, when she was elected a member of the Provincial Assembly, equivalent to the State Legislature, in the Punjab, a position she held for five years. In 1977 she was elected mayor of Jhang, her hometown in the Punjab, a post that she held for eight years. In 1985 she was elected to Pakistan's National Assembly and was reelected in 1988.

When I spoke to her, she was "an out-of-work politician," as she put it. Yet in 1997, she would once again be employed in a Nawaz al Sherif government, this time with several portfolios as Minister of Environment and Urban Affairs, Minister of Population and Welfare, and Minister of Social Welfare and Special Education. She was occupying herself with agriculture, a business that included growing cotton and breeding horses. A self-confident, sociable person, Hussain appeared to enjoy hosting friends in her home and leading them in intellectual repartee. The night I was included in her inner circle, Chandi (as Hussain's friends call her) and her guests shared their opinions on such topics as Western society, Benazir Bhutto's decoration of the prime minister's residence and the proper attire for Muslim women. Among the dozen or so men and women convened in Hussain's living room, I was not the only foreigner. An Iranian woman draped in black sat on the sofa across the room and calmly but authoritatively told the group that the Qur'an clearly stipulated that her attire was the only proper dress for believing women. The other women were dressed in the traditional attire for Pakistani women, the *shalwar khameez,* the long-sleeved tunic and baggy pants. They are generally worn with a sheer scarf that can be draped over the hair. Many of the women there had the scarf draped across their shoulders, not over their heads. The Iranian woman insisted that such dress was not in keeping with the Qur'an's injunctions, which she said, required that women tightly cover their hair as well as their necks and allow only their hands and face to show. She said it was specifically stated in the Qur'an, in the fourth Surah entitled "al Nisah" or "Women," verses 35 and 36. We all believed she must be an authority on the subject, and no one seemed inclined to disagree with her until one of the Pakistani women decided to get the Qur'an and read the verses aloud. But those verses had nothing to do with proper dress. The Iranian woman seemed confused and embarrassed. She offered that perhaps verses in the Iranian Qur'an and the Pakistani Qur'an are numbered differently, wherein a judicious search was undertaken in the index to find any verses that related to modesty and dress. The index referred us to the twenty-fourth Surah, entitled "Light," verses 30-31:

> Tell the believing men to lower their gaze and be modest. That is purer for them. Lo! Allah is aware of what they do.
>
> And tell the believing women to lower their gaze and to be modest, and to display of their adornments only that which is apparent, and to draw their veils over their bosoms, and not to reveal their adornment save to their own husbands or fathers or husbands' fathers, or their sons or their husbands' sons, or their brothers or their brothers' sons or sisters' sons or their women, or their slaves, or male attendants who lack vigor, or children who know naught of women's nakedness. And let them not stamp their feet so as to reveal what they hide of their adornment. And turn unto Allah together, O believers, in order that ye may succeed.

We could find nothing more specific about dress than those two verses. The Pakistani dress seemed to fit clearly within the Qur'an's guidance, as far as I and the other women were concerned, but the Iranian woman held firm to her view that it wasn't.

There was an uneasy silence as she fumbled through the book, then set it aside and vowed to find the reference later and inform us all. For me as a student of Islam and Muslim culture, it was an intensely informative episode. It reinforced my conviction that in all religions, much of what many people believe to be the word of God simply isn't. I wanted to pursue the issue, but Hussain, the diplomat, politely changed the topic of conversation, and everyone seemed relieved. Not long after that, realizing I was exhausted from a combination of jet lag and our accident, Hussain had her driver return me to my hotel. There was every indication that Hussain's salon would continue late into the night. Before I left, I gave the Iranian woman my card and asked her to let me know when she found the missing verses. I do not expect to hear from her, however. I now know those verses do not exist.

Interview with Abida Hussain

January 1994, Islamabad

JD: You've had quite a lot of experience relating to Western leaders and Western people, the Western world in general. I want to talk to you about what you perceive to be the relationship between the Islamic world and the West.

AH: Well, you see, we have to examine the historical perspective when we deal with the situation of the contemporary world and the various regions, and the positions in the contemporary world. The material reality of recent history is that most of the lands where Muslim people live in the Middle East, North Africa, and extending into South Asia, were colonized by the European colonials from the sixteenth to the twentieth century.

Different Muslim peoples and terrain were occupied by different colonial rulers. For instance, the French went to Algeria, the Italians went to Libya, the British came down to Egypt. The British were in much of the oil-bearing regions of the Middle East and right up to South Asia. Then, of course, in what is Malaysia today, or what is Indonesia today, which is also where Muslim people live. The Dutch were in Indonesia, and the Malaysians were part of the British Empire. So Europe colonized the lands where Muslim people live. Now, in these postcolonial periods of history, Muslim people have been gradually becoming autonomous, defining their sovereign independent states. But between World War II and today, roughly the end of the twentieth century in this last 50-year time frame, the nation-states that are dominantly occupied by Muslim people each have [had] a distinct history on how they came to be a nation-state. We've seen some states disappear and some others created in the last 50 years. Palestine disappeared, for instance, and TransJordan disappeared. Jordan was created, then all of these, what were known as the Trucial States, Abu Dhabi and Dubai and so on, became southern states. In what was British India, there was a partition and Pakistan became a homeland for the Muslims of India, and so on. So having come, emerging out of colonial rule—and colonial rule is very invasive, you know. Colonial rule means that people come from a distance, and they come and occupy you. And they occupy you through use of force. There is no such thing as a voluntary attempt by people to allow themselves to be occupied.

So, it was the European use of force that led to colonialism. And most recently, we have seen, for instance, six new Muslim states appear out of the collapse of the Soviet empire. The states of Central Asia from Azerbaijan extending up to Kazakhstan, a vast region of the world where Muslim people lived, who were part of the Soviet state, and have very recently, extremely recently, become sovereign and independent.

Now, as the states where Muslims live have been emerging with their sovereignty and independence, we have also, at the same time, been knocked into a world where there is considerable economic inequity. The Western world, if you like to define it as such—that is, Europe and America—have been in the twentieth century and have emerged as powerful industrialized economies, with the ability to make technological advancements. And, inevitably, this has been at the expense of other parts of the world that produce raw materials. So Muslim lands, now broken up in sovereign independent states, feel the situation where each state, each sovereign state, is handicapped by limitations on its resources. Where we produce raw materials, the raw materials are needed by the industrialized nations. The industrialized nations determine the price of the raw materials and then sell manufactured goods back to us at prices, again, which the industrialized states determine. So there is a handicap of resources.

Now, as Muslim people are becoming more confident, as they are finding more knowledge and more skills, their awareness is increasing about basic injustices and inequities and imbalances that exist in our world. For instance, I farm land in the Punjab, and my family has been located in this particular area for the last three centuries. My family originated in Central Asia. My forbears came down from a town called Bukhara into the lands of northern India, where the family has lived all this time.

JD: This was since when?

AH: Over the last 300 years. And so I inherited a family farm. I farm with modern methods. My farm is well laid out. I crop my land and breed animals there, cows and horses which are of good quality. Now I grow—as my main cash crop, I grow cotton. And I grow good cotton, long staple cotton. It's as good a cotton as anywhere in the world. But the cotton that I grow on my land, fetches me one-twentieth the price that cotton would fetch a farmer growing cotton, let's say, in Alabama.

JD: Why is that?

AH: Because it's Wall Street that controls the prices of raw materials, as I said. Now, I have a piece of land. I farm with the same skills, put in the same effort, use the same chemicals as my counterpart in Alabama, but that guy in Alabama gets 20 times what I get for my product. So when I am at the end of my crop, and I am looking to my savings, and I am seeing how my capital is going to be utilized, or how it's going to grow, and so on, I live on an economy of shortages. And when I say "I," I'm using this as an example. So, countries like mine have an economy of shortages. We are short, basically, of capital. And how are we going to accumulate the capital? We can only accumulate the capital if we work hard but also if we're allowed to accumulate the capital.

Now the world pricing system and global economy works in such a way that the rich actually, in the last 50 years, have been growing richer and the poor have been growing poorer. You know, if you have a look at the global economy, this is roughly what you'll get. Since much of this reality pertains to lands where Muslims live and since Muslim people are beginning now to, as I say, access education and information and knowledge and statistical data and so on, there is a certain amount of regret about this reality.

First of all, with many Muslims and certainly in a country like mine, the negative comment is on ourselves: our own inability to be able to get our act together. But, inevitably, along with the recognition of our own limitations must also come a recognition of the exploitation that we face.

JD: Well, wait. So what I'm hearing in this explanation is that this hostility that many people would assume to be based on a different belief system is actually far deeper than that.

AH: Well, first of all, allow me to say that I wouldn't use the term "hostility." I use the term "understanding," "acknowledgment," an understanding of our own predicament, acknowledgment of the forces and factors that have produced this predicament. Acknowledgment of the reality that, for instance, Pakistan is the ninth largest nation in the world in terms of population. All right?

Pakistan has roughly half the population of the United States of America, but Pakistan would fit—our land area would fit into the state of Texas. And our economy is only as big as the economy of Orange County in the state of California. Now you imagine, in the United States, half of your population living in Texas with the resource base of Orange County, California, and then you would understand what poverty, deprivation, neglect and so on mean. So it's not a question of hostility. It's an acknowledgment and an understanding of reality. Because, in the dialogue of the weak and the strong—as you examine human history or examine human relations, in the dialogue of the weak and the strong, the strong views the situation through his or her own perspective. So will the weak.

So in the dialogue of the strong and the weak, there is always an element of it becoming the dialogue of the deaf, because the strong don't really want to concede that the weak may have a reason for being weak. And the weak don't really want to concede that the strong have become strong because they must have some reason to become strong.

So my point is that as far as the world today is concerned, if Americans perceive that Muslims are hostile—this is from my perspective—this is a misperception. Muslims are not hostile. Muslims are just beginning to understand the predicament we're in. We were colonized for three centuries and currently we're handicapped. We have to fight our way through, struggle our way through, or work our way through our predicament so that we are able to live with our own religion, our own culture, our own forms of expression, without feeling dependent and without feeling that we are pushed around or exploited.

JD: What about on the other side? Do you perceive in your dealings with the West a hostility from the West toward the Islamic world?

AH: No, no quite honestly I don't. I don't perceive hostility, but I do perceive a lack of understanding. You know, I don't think that the United States is hostile to Muslims, but I think there is a lack of understanding of Muslim history, of Muslim thought, of the religion itself, its basic tenets, its cultural expression in different regions where Muslims live. We tend to, in Pakistan for instance, know much more about the United States, about how you guys live, about how you guys think, about how you guys do it, than you do about us.

JD: And when you talk about the misperceptions and misunderstandings that might exist, this might especially be true I think with Shias. I understand that you come from a Shia heritage. Do you have any— do you find that there are myths that Americans hold with regard to your specific beliefs?

AH: Yes. I mean, the whole—I don't think that 30 years ago, or 25 years ago even, the average American even knew what the hell a Shia is or what the hell a Sunni is.

JD: Yes, we learned what a Shia is from Iran, basically.

AH: The Iranian people decided that they wanted to do their own thing, and they didn't want American or Soviet interference in their country. They've had—the British oil companies controlled them for a while, and then all of this became a little more indirect but they threw out foreign influences out of their country. And the Americans didn't like it. So the politicization of Islam became a phenomenon.

And because the Iranians are predominantly Shiites, the average American thinks that these Muslims are aggressive; they're terrorists; they're horrible people. And they're really the worst characters among the Shia. Now, the Iranians were Shia before the revolution also, but the Americans didn't have a problem with them, so long as the Shah of Iran was around. The Americans didn't have a problem with the fact that the Shah of Iran was created by an oil company. The monarchy was created by an oil company; that his grandfather was a foot soldier; that he had a court which was very Frenchified; that he had crowns made for himself and his emperors in Cartier. You know, that was absurd. But when there was an ascension of religious expression, because it was politically inconvenient, it all became very negative.

I'm from a Shiite background. In Pakistan the Shiites are a minority. We are only about 15 to 20 percent of the population. And the difference between being Shia and Sunni is a very simple differ-ence. The Sunnis, broadly speaking, will pay equal respect to the four Caliphs of Islam after the Prophet Mohammed. And the Shiites have— the fourth Caliph is their favorite, because he was the son-in-law and the cousin of the Prophet. So the Shiite symbolically attach themselves to the family of the Prophet, while the Sunnis attach themselves to the Apostles of the Prophet. So it's a dogmatic divide which is actually not even as distinct as the Protestant and the Catholic within the Christian church. But, you know, it's like a divide in a religion—of schools [within a] religion.*

I grew up in a world where, other than the fact that in our family we observed Shia rituals, and I read Shia history [there was no real difference between Shias and Sunnis]. But, you know, one was very conscious of the difference between Shia and Sunni. Half my family are Sunni in India. In recent times with the entire episode of the Iranian revolution, we've had a fallout also in Pakistan. But this is a phase. Because, you know, Shias and Sunnis have been around for 1,400

---

* Sunnis and Shias differ on which descendent of Muhammad was entitled to take over leadership of the community of believers. The two groups sometimes follow different rituals and some of their interpretations of religious laws differ.

years. They are likely to carry on being around, and this low-level conflict from time to time between Shia and Sunni invariably does get contained.[†]

But, for instance, Saddam is Sunni, right?

JD: Yes.

AH: And the United States, in fact, was very concerned about Saddam's repression of Shiite Iraqis. So, you know, that is to say that you could have political differences, and not necessarily based on religion. And the Saudis, for instance, are Muslim. And the Saudis are orthodox Muslim. I don't like the term "fundamentalist," because actually the term "fundamentalist" comes from a historic episode with regard to the Christian church. We haven't had a reform in Islam, so I don't see how this term "fundamentalist" will really attach itself to us. So I see Muslims as orthodox Muslims or liberal Muslims, modern Muslims.

JD: Would you say you're a liberal Muslim or an orthodox Muslim?

AH: No, I'm a liberal Muslim clearly. But Saudi Arabia, you know, is an orthodox Muslim state. But America doesn't have a problem with that. Americans don't have a problem with the Saudis. But you know, if the Algerians have an election where they vote in a particular party or the Iranians throw out foreign influences, then the Americans do have a problem with that. So what I'm saying is that this is a part of the political order of the world. It's got nothing to do with religion.

JD: This is a theme that has come up over and over again, the idea that the U.S. doesn't seem to have a foreign policy based on principle. Do you agree with that?

AH: You know, I think that the interests of states for—for a state, it's own interests are always paramount. And what may be a principled

---

[†] Many Shias say they suffer discrimination by the Sunni majority, and there have sometimes been violent confrontations between Sunnis and Shias in the history of Islam.

position for one state may appear to be an unprincipled position from the perspective of another state. Every state has its own principles. I think that the United States is a great country . . . It's a state which has developed out of an amalgam of many cultures, many places, people originated from different parts of the world, and it's a good nation. It's also economically and strategically, in its ability to exercise the use of bombs, the most powerful nation in the world. And obviously, America would like to retain its power. Now, in that context, if America exercises her own interests and those interests encroach upon the rights of others, that is a part of the dispensation or the brutality, if you like, of power. But I would not indict the United States for being any more unprincipled than the next nation. Perhaps in some ways my nation may also appear to other nations that are smaller than us or weaker than us to be not entirely principled. But that is the liability of the exercise of power.

JD: So basically what you're saying is there are practical considerations with regard to relations between nations. But, if that's the case, what's the hope of there being any type of a better relationship between the United States and the weaker nations, the Third World?

AH: I think that the relationship between the United States and Third World countries is a bad relationship in the sense that the United States has its own way. So the United States shouldn't be complaining. But, you know, I think it's a question of levels of tolerance. It's a question of the development of the human being. If a human being is well developed, a human being is tolerant. If a human being is well developed and tolerant, a human being will not seek to impose his or her persona upon another human being. And so it follows for states as well. As the world community develops, as humans develop, as America develops, as Pakistan and other nations in the Third World develop, one can hope for more and more tolerance, more and more understanding of each other, and more and more acceptance of each other . . .

But I think there is a certain amount of stereotyping that goes on in the world today. And if I may say so, the modern phenomenon of an all-pervasive media that the world is increasingly dominated by, whether it's the electronic media or whether it's the print media. The media, because it's something instant and because it's something based on the good old business of a good sell, the media actually does create a lot of stereotypes. And I think that there's this stereotyping going on about Muslims, and Americans . . . and, from the Muslim point of view, in a rather negative light. Words like "Moslem," "terrorist," "hostile" "aggressive," "intolerant," "oppressive," these sort of words go together, more or less. You see, the point is, there are all over the world some people who are big on religion and others who are not. Now, the United States is a state clearly that was founded for religious freedom. So, the secular notion is very important to the United States.

JD: What's your position on the separation of church and state? Do you agree, do you disagree with that?

AH: Well, you see, again, that's church and state. Christianity has a clergy. Now Islam does not. The clerics are not a fundamental Muslim institution. The clerics have emerged as part of a sociological process, but Islam does not have a church. And this is why, to be a Muslim, it means you live in a certain way. And if all Muslims live in a certain way, the location that they're in becomes a Muslim state. So as for the Islamic notion, there cannot be a separation because there is no church. So you're a Muslim, you live like a Muslim. If you are living in an area which is predominantly Muslim, you're all living like Muslims. You are in the contours of what is described as a state in modern language, then you are a Muslim state.

JD: I wanted to ask you too about the issue of women and Islam. It's still unusual not only in the Islamic world but anywhere in the world for a woman to rise in the political ranks. How has your being a Muslim affected your career?

AH: Well, actually, if I had been born and raised in a Western nation, and if I was the same person but I did not ascribe to the Muslim thing, I don't think my career would have been more distinguished than it has been growing up and living in a Muslim country.

I also feel that if I had been born the opposite gender, if I was the same person, same kind of mind, but I was male and I had the same environment that I was raised in and the same sort of opportunities, I would probably have made less progress.

JD: You would have made less progress?

AH: Yes, that's right. Because my gender status has been an advantage more than a handicap, purely because I was able to access opportunities because I was a woman. Many of the opportunities I accessed was because I was a woman.

When I started out in public life 24 years ago, there were very few women in my country that were in public life and relatively few women that were economically independent. I happened to be economically independent. I inherited from my father who died young, and I happened not to have siblings. So, being economically independent, I was socially independent and able to express myself. And because there were so few women in public life, I made rapid progress. So I have not been handicapped by my gender status.

You take—the other case is that of our prime minister. She's prime minister because she's a woman. Her gender status has been a net advantage to her. The fact that she's a woman, she's good-looking, and glamorous, has made her a sort of pop queen. I mean, she's like a sort of a mixture of Hollywood stardom and some politics, and, you know, with the whole business of legacy and martyrdom behind her. You know, there she is—prime minister twice over in a country that is almost entirely Muslim.

So I don't think that gender status is necessarily a handicap to women today. However, I will say this, that coming through our history of colonization and so on, we have had women confined to their homes. You know, colonialism is very invasive. And to guard the privacy of the family, most Muslim people restricted the family and the movement of the family. So that coming out and emerging out of the shadows of our colonial past, and with women accessing education more and more in our countries where Muslims live, you find that women are joining the workforce and learning to express themselves. It's all a question of economic opportunities and educational opportunities.

JD: So as you see it, your religion in no way prohibited your participation in politics, even though there obviously are some people who would say that women should not be in politics?

AH: No, my religion didn't inhibit me at all and nor has it handicapped me. What I'm saying is the truth as I perceive it. In fact, I would go on to say that Islam, when it was codified as a religion 14 centuries back, it was the first organized religion that spoke specifically of the rights of women. And there is a school of interpretation of modern Muslims that argue that Islam came to liberate women more than men. You know, Islam conferred upon women, 14 centuries back, the right to inherit, the right to participate, the right to earn, the right to their own basic choices. So, you know, we have been—if women in Islam have been left a bit behind, it's been really as a result of our history. It's got nothing to do with the religion . . .

I don't believe that women need to be treated as a quota or as a handicapped group. We're half of the population of the country, and in many ways women in our culture have a very honored position as mothers, as sisters, as daughters, as wives. There is a place of dignity and honor in our cultural dispensation. For instance, let me tell you, when I was in your country, I talked a lot to women and found it very interesting. And one of the things inevitably that would come up would be the issue of sexual harassment. Now, when I was asked how this played in where I was coming from, it would invariably surprise whoever my interlocutor was when I said that sexual harassment is a phenomenon. It's a very nominal business in our culture, because in our culture the male will very seldom, very, very seldom, approach the female unless there is some sign from the female that she's ready and willing. In my working life, which now is a quarter of a century, I regret to confess, I have never had but maybe one or two occasions when a gentleman might have said something somewhat unacceptable. But it has never gone beyond a sentence, because it's all a question of whether the woman is setting out the signals or not, and, if she's not, she's left alone.

I had a young American woman working in my hometown for six months, and she enjoyed it, and when she was leaving I said, "Sarah, what did you appreciate best about this environment?" And she was a very pretty girl, and she said, "You know, it's the first time since I turned 14 that I've had no unwanted male attention and I enjoyed it, it made me feel very free."

JD: If you had some advice to give to Western policy makers, congress-men, those kinds of people, as to what they could do to foster a better relationship with the people of the Islamic world, what would that be?

AH: I think that to build better bridges of understanding, increased communication is always a good idea. And then, you see, I used to say to friends in the United States that if the notion that knowledge is power is a valid notion, then you are handing it to us, because we know so much about you and you know so little about us. You know, projecting into the future, just think, we're watching movies from America, we're watching soap operas from America, we're listening to your music, we're seeing how you drive your cars, how you live, how you speak, and you have no idea about all of this about us.

So we're going to be able to understand America much better than America is understanding us, and that knowledge in itself for us would be a good thing, but you're denying yourselves a body of knowledge which at some point in the future may not be good for you. So, to build bridges of understanding and to communicate more. To create institu-tions where you're seeing on your TV screens or in your cinemas the images that life in this region of the world is based on would be a good idea. There is now more literature which is sort of building under-standing. You have writers from what the British described rather nicely as "The Orient of the East." You know, you have writers that are writing about the past and the present in this part of the world, and writing in English.

So, there is the beginning of that communication. We have in South Asia several writers that have tossed out rather attractive novels in the last few years, you know, which give a context to what our social fabric is about.

JD: Who are they?

AH: Well, yes. There have been—I would like to avoid saying Rushdie, first of all, but the name does come to mind.

JD: But isn't that dangerous?

AH: Well, I'll tell you, I enjoyed his first book, *Midnight's Children,* enormously. I think he was thumbing his nose at us in the book that brought him into trouble, but certainly his early work was very interesting.

JD: I have heard that you've had some death threats against you. Is that so? Are they not serious?

AH: Yes, I got caught in a situation where, way back in 1988, I won election from a cleric, and five months after the election the cleric was assassinated outside his home. And this led to a lot of tension in the town, and because the cleric and I had opposed each other in the election. So his followers extended some amount of harassment. And more recently, my direct political rival is one of Benazir Bhutto's main henchmen. So he's decided to join the gang on making life a little difficult for me.

JD: You've not been attacked or anything, I mean, personally?

AH: Well, I've had the odd potshot taken at my vehicle. But that's one of the hazards of being in public life, and it's not something which unduly bothers me, frankly.

FIFTEEN

MUHAMMAD ASLAM SALEEMI

JAMAAT-I-ISLAMI, PAKISTAN

PROFILE

GETTING TO THE HEADQUARTERS of Pakistan's Jamaat-i-Islami on Multan Road in the village of Mansoorah was an adventure in itself. From Lahore, it was a chaotic half hour or so of near misses with reckless taxis, rickety horse-drawn buggies, sputtering motorcycles and buses painted so many neon colors that they defied description. I was concerned that the Jamaat's headquarters would be hard to find, but it seemed that it was so much a part of the community in and around Lahore, asking for directions was absurd.

When my taxi finally drove into the Jamaat's compound, Muhammad Aslam Saleemi was waiting outside to receive me. A solid, tall man, with an authoritative gray beard and long robe, he looked far too stern for me to offer my hand as a greeting. As in all situations when I knew I'd be meeting devout Muslim men, I had covered my hair and dressed in keeping with their expectations. I was glad I had done so. In fact, initially I found Saleemi so intimidating that I felt compelled to lower my eyes and simply nod a meek hello.

The leaders of Jamaat-i-Islami Pakistan, the strongest and best-organized Islamic movement in the country, were in the middle of soul searching when I arrived at their complex in early 1994. The Pakistan Islamic Front, the political party the Jamaat had formed only a few months ago, was still smarting from a blistering defeat in national elections. The Jamaat's leader, Qazi Hussain Ahmad, had just resigned, assuming personal responsibility for the Jamaat's poor showing in elections that returned Benazir Bhutto to the office of prime minister. And there were reports of serious dissension within the ranks of the Jamaat's leadership.

As one of several deputy *ameers* (a title akin to vice president), it could be assumed that Muhammad Aslam Saleemi was very much embroiled in the Jamaat's internal struggle. His name had not been placed into nomination to replace Qazi Hussain Ahmad. If he had been pushing for a new ameer, he declined to say so. And if he felt that Jamaat should follow a new course, the image he portrayed to me was of a party loyalist, one of those who dutifully presented a unified stand to the outside world. It became evident that Saleemi was the kind of idealistic follower who was the backbone of organizations like the Jamaat, who made it a strong social force in Pakistan and who hoped to one day make it a serious contender for political power.

Saleemi was born in 1933 in the Punjab and was well educated, with degrees in labor law and tax law. He was married with eight children, whom he also described as "well educated" and also happily married. Saleemi spoke excellent English as well as Urdu, Persian and Arabic. He became a full member of the Jamaat in 1962, working his way up through the ranks of the organization until he was appointed a deputy *ameer* in 1987.

Although he was in the hierarchy of the Jamaat's leadership, he did not appear to covet power. In fact, no one inside Jamaat was supposed to seek a leadership post. In the Islamic ideal, officers are elected but those who run for office are nominated by others. They are supposed to accept the burden of leadership if their colleagues believe they are best suited for the job. In elections within the Jamaat, there was supposed to be no campaigning or self-promotion. Leadership was not supposed to be an opportunity for self-aggrandizement but a sacrifice for the community. Leaders become apparent to their colleagues because of their years of service to the propagation of Islam and to bettering society. Despite the organization's formal creed, I found it hard to believe that even in the Jamaat there were not ambitious men who found a way to vie for power without appearing to do so. And if no one really competed for power, I wondered whether the Jamaat might not benefit from some such competition.

Jamaat members believed Islam demanded dedication in all aspects of life. Simply becoming an official member of the Jamaat was a demanding feat, requiring years of study of the Qur'an, the Sunnah (the practices of the Prophet) and the schools of Islamic law as well as community service. It also required years of conformity to the Jamaat's strict rules and regulation. Although the Jamaat said it had more than one million supporters and workers, called *arkan*, Saleemi told me only 8,300 men and women met the qualifications to be called *muttafiq*, the highest category of membership.

One of the main goals of the Jamaat was to cultivate an elite of Islamic scholars who were qualified to provide educated leadership for the creation of an Islamic society. Such leadership required personal piety, extensive knowledge of Islamic law and history, and commitment to social and political activism. That did not mean that all Jamaat members had the same idea of the proper interpretation of Islamic law, nor that they all agreed on the ideal Islamic society. In my conversations with Jamaat members at their offices in Mansoorah, it became evident that there was intense debate on such issues as women's participation in the organization, the future of the Israeli-Arab peace process and relations with the West.

Saleemi and the other Jamaat members I interviewed made clear their views on issues such as the women's role in society. I believe they told me exactly what they thought, since they thought their views were not only logical but supported by God's word. Saleemi believed in segregation of the sexes, but many younger Jamaat members were quietly encouraging more openness. Older Jamaat leaders such as Saleemi insisted that there was a place for women in Jamaat, in the women's wing. It was undeniable that Jamaat was run by men, although he said women were sometimes called to attend meetings and to express their views. When they did attend, women were kept cloistered in a room adjacent to where the men were seated, in which they could hear the meeting but not be seen. Saleemi did not realize how demeaning such a scene might seem to a Western woman.

He told me with pride that women were invited to hold conferences and to attend special events at the Jamaat. I knew this to be true, yet I also knew it was akin to the "separate but equal" theory that once was used to try to keep American blacks from enjoying full equality in the United States. In the offices of the Jamaat, I saw no women, not even as secretaries. In fact, the only place I saw a woman was in the hospital, where she was serving as a nurse.

From its enclave of gray concrete buildings in Mansoorah, Saleemi explained that the Jamaat operated a wide range of social programs, from adult literacy classes to medical care. Its complex was situated on several acres and included housing for staff and Jamaat members, visitors' dormitories and office buildings, meeting and research facilities, a library and a mosque. But Jamaat members seemed especially proud of their hospital, which specialized in plastic surgery for soldiers wounded during the Afghan war. The Jamaat supported the Afghan *mujadeheen* in their *jihad* against communism. And Jamaat members also supported those who called for *jihad* to liberate Kashmir from Indian rule. As several tired-looking men sat on a wooden bench in the narrow hall, apparently waiting for medical care, I examined a bulletin board crammed with before and after pictures of Afghan veterans treated at the hospital. Many of them had amputated limbs and grotesque wounds, burns over much of their bodies or missing eyes and severe facial scars. Many of the pictures showing men after treatment were almost as chilling as those taken before.

Since the war had officially, if not actually, ended, the hospital was offering free medical care to the poor. But the Jamaat had not always been able to provide such services openly in Pakistan. Like most Islamic organizations, it had experienced stormy relationships with the governments that ruled Pakistan, although the country was carved out of India with the specific intent of creating an Islamic state. People like Saleemi joined the Jamaat because they believed Pakistan had betrayed the reason for its founding.

The Jamaat-i-Islami was formally established in August of 1941 in Lahore, under the leadership of Maulana Maudoodi. He remained its leader until his health began to fail in 1972. Maudoodi is considered one of the greatest Islamic leaders of modern history and one who was concerned about the dominance of the West in the developing world. He had been compared to Hassan al-Banna, founder of the Muslim Brotherhood, which profoundly affected the Arab world. The Jamaat-i-Islami was created with the same intention of making Islam a vibrant, activist force in society and of reestablishing the preeminence of Islamic civilization. Members of the Jamaat and the Brotherhood shared the vision of a united Islamic world and of reforming their societies based on guidance from the Qur'an and the Sunnah. They shared a disdain for what they considered to be the immoral influence of Western culture and for people in their world who sought to imitate it. Most of them rejected attempts by "modernists" in the Islamic world to reinterpret the Qur'an and the *Hadith* in light of a new age and believed in strict adherence to traditional interpretations of Islamic law. They resisted modernization for its own sake, but believed Western technology and innovations should be used in keeping with the higher Islamic ideal of nourishing the spiritual as well as the physical aspects of life. In a pamphlet entitled "The Movement of Jamaat-i-Islami," written by Khurshid Ahmad, another deputy *ameer,* the Jamaat was described as "a third force, a movement of the middle, bridging the gap between the so-called modernists who almost uncritically adopted the modernization model of the West and the so-called conservatives who refused to accept any modification or departure from the Muslim status quo." It was described in the pamphlet as "an ideological movement and not merely as a religious or political party." Jamaat tried "to influence almost all dimensions of Muslim life; intellectual, cultural, moral, educational, literary, economic and political." And the pamphlet noted that Jamaat "stood not for partial reform but for total change." It set for itself the following goals:

- Intellectual revolution resulting from a clear exposition of the teachings of Islam.

- Maintaining an inner core of highly dedicated upright men and women as the foundation of an Islamic revival.

- Social change to effect reform in the light of Islamic teachings.

- Change of leadership, including intellectual, social, cultural and ultimately political leadership.[1]

All of these goals, Jamaat founders thought, would contribute to the
establishment of an Islamic society based on moral principles and
purged of greed and corruption.

But problems often arise for such organizations when their
popular support begins to threaten the ruling governments and when
they seek to gain political power, sometimes through civil unrest.

The Jamaat under Maudoodi also had been criticized for being too
dogmatic in its ideology and for fomenting unrest in Pakistan. In the
1950s, Maudoodi was accused of inciting religious riots in his opposition to the Ahmadiyah Islamic sect and its participation in government. Maudoodi believed its members were heretics because of their
belief in a Mahdi ("rightly guided one," who some Muslims believe
will one day rule the world) and their attempts to modernize Islam. He
stirred up protests, demanding they be removed from government and
that Pakistan become a "true" Islamic state. But the issue also raised
the question of whether only a Muslim could serve in Pakistan's
government and who would decide the qualifications for being a
Muslim. In 1953 violence erupted, and Maudoodi was sentenced to
death after martial law was declared. He was charged with writing a
pamphlet the government considered seditious. His sentence later was
commuted to life in prison.

Under the regime of Zia al-Haq, who seized power in 1977, the
Jamaat and other Islamists found new support as Zia tried to gain
legitimacy through religion. The Jamaat's attempts to seek its goals
through existing political parties ended in 1994 when its members
decided to vie for political power in their own right. It did not do well
it in its first elections, however, falling behind both Benazir Bhutto's
Pakistan People's Party and Nawaz al-Sharif's Muslim League. But by
then the Jamaat was firmly entrenched in Pakistani life. It was widely
respected among the poor, yet many in Pakistani politics still eyed it
with suspicion. They believed the Jamaat's strict and apparently
uncompromising version of Islam would hurt the country's attempts
to join the modern world and that it would inevitably divide society.

"Ask them what is the definition of a Muslim," one official suggested as he reminded me of the religious riots of the 1950s. After those riots, a national conference was called to answer the question, he said, and it was decided that the simplest definition should be used. Anyone who considered himself a Muslim should be considered a Muslim, he said, insisting that the Jamaat didn't believe that. I put the question to Saleemi, however, and he said there were two qualifications: that you believe in one God and that you believe Muhammad was a prophet. When I told him that, although I consider myself a Christian, I believed in both those statements, Saleemi's stony face softened and his eyes glowed with apparent surprise and joy. "You are welcome," he said, beaming. But I knew that simple statement was really not enough to make anyone a Muslim. The truth is, a profession of those beliefs is only the first step into Islam. Much more is required of believers, especially among the Jamaat's *arkan,* or loyal workers.

Most Pakistanis were clearly not ready for the all-encompassing Islam that the Jamaat proposes. As one well-connected Pakistani put it, the average man on the street accepted the guidance of the *ulama* inside the mosque, but that's as far as it went. While it may be true that Pakistanis were not sure what the Jamaat's Islamic state would bring, it would be a mistake to count the movement out of political power in Pakistan. Not long after my meeting with Saleemi, I dined with an affluent attorney in a swank Karachi hotel. He berated the two main parties for their incompetence in dealing with Pakistan's economic problems, and he bitterly castigated them both as corrupt. Just that morning, he told me, he went to the airport to receive a package that had been sent to him from abroad and had to bribe customs agents before they would release it. It's like that anytime you do business in Pakistan, he said. It's like that in all aspects of government. People were getting fed up with both Benazir Bhutto and Nawaz Sharif, he warned. Unless both parties woke up, he promised, voters would soon realize there was now a third option, one that he said had already proved its commitment to the lowest ranks of Pakistani society. It was only a matter of time, the lawyer told me, before Pakistanis turned to religion out of disgust with rampant corruption.

It was impossible to know if the lawyer was right. That year's elections certainly did not support that forecast, and Saleemi admitted that Jamaat's leaders were confused and chastened by their defeat. One thing was clear, however. One of the world's best-known Islamic movements had learned a valuable lesson. In Muslim countries where there is a semblance of political pluralism, people do not necessarily turn to Islamists to change the status quo. That is not to say that the Jamaat will not one day hold power in Pakistan, but its leaders need to convince the people that they can do more than simply debate Islamic law. They have to convince them they can indeed govern. Pakistan's experience with the Jamaat revealed an interesting fact: Islam as a political platform is not a sure step to political power, not even in a country that touts itself an Islamic democracy.

INTERVIEW WITH MUHAMMAD ASLAM SALEEMI

JANUARY 1994, LAHORE, PAKISTAN

JD: Would you tell me a little bit about the Jamaat here and what its role here is in helping to shape an Islamic society in Pakistan?

MS: Yes. Actually Jamaat Islami was founded in 1941 in Lahore and after the partition of subcontinent, the Jamaat was also divided into two, the Jamaat-i-Islami Hind and the Jamaat-i-Islami Pakistan. Before partition, we were governed by other cultures and they were ruling us under the Government of India Act of 1935. The Jamaat Islami Pakistan stands for establishing an Islamic order in Pakistan—that is, an Islamic society wherein educational system, the economic system, the judicial system, the political system, all the systems of life in Pakistan should be transformed into Islamic systems. Islam is a complete code of life. It encompasses the private life as well as the public life of the individual as well as society as a whole. So, unlike the West, we think that divine guidance is required to lead a good, orderly, collective life.

JD: I see. So in your estimation now, Pakistan is not an Islamic state?

MS: Not, not as yet. Unfortunately, no other country in the Islamic world is Islamic as yet. Some have some portions of their society

Islamic, but the other portions of the society are not according to the principles of Islam.

JD: We were talking a little before I started recording about the tension, the developing hostility between the West and people such as yourself, who are striving to bring about Islamic principles into all aspects of your life. Can you talk a little bit about that and tell me how you perceive the relationship?

MS: It is very unfortunate that this notion, or this perception, is only hatched and being propagated in West. And this is perhaps just Islam phobia, which I think is not only incorrect but perhaps misdirected also. We as Muslims do not have any bad designs, any ill will against any human being. Because we think that Islam is a religion for humanity, and Islam is a religion of peace. The literal meaning of the word "Islam" means peace. And the desire for peace, the struggle of peace, the message of peace [is encompassed in] Islam. So how can a religion like Islam, a religion of peace, be hostile to any part of humanity? The West is a part of humanity. So we don't have any grudge, any ill will against the people living in the West. Rather, we have a desire to disseminate this message of peace to them, so they can also come within the fold of this message so they have a happy life, they enjoy a prosperous life, they enjoy a good life. Unfortunately, it is the West that has established or that is nurturing some grudge . . . They are trying to demolish the Muslims and Muslim society.

JD: Do you have a concept of why this phobia may be developing in the West? I mean, when you look at it, do you understand the motivation?

MS: This is perhaps due to some political leaders in the West. They want to rule the whole universe, and there are some other societies or some other communities, you can call them, which are in the hands of some political leaders who are propagating against Islam: "The Islamic ghost will devour you, will finish you," whereas that ghost never existed. We urge the people, we don't have any grudge against people living in West . . . East or West. We think both are creatures of the same God. And any religion is neither Eastern nor Western. So any civilization can be Islamic civilization. So it's not particular that the Middle East is Islam and Far East is not Islam and West is not Islam, no. We don't stand for that. We think we stand that Islam is for the whole humanity, for the whole mankind.

JD: Talk to me a little if you can about the structure of the Jamaat. Is there a women's wing? Are women involved in the whole process?

MS: Yes. We have a women's wing. The women's wing is headed by a woman secretary general. She is Kamar Jameel living in Karachi. Then we have women's organizations at the provincial level, at the district level and at local levels. You can see them in charge of [the] women's wing at [the] local level at Lahore also. So we have the central-level women's organization headed by the secretary general. Then we have provincial organizers, and then we have district organizers and then we have local organizers. They have their own meetings. They have their own programs.

JD: How important are they to Jamaat as a whole?

MS: They are very important. They are part and parcel of the Jamaat. The women members of the Jamaat have a right to vote for the central *ameer*. And these days we are going to elect our *ameer* at the national level. The women voters are also eligible to vote for whether they want to elect Qazi Hussain Ahmad or if they want to elect someone else. Every woman member has a right to vote for the *ameer* also.

JD: Does she have a right to run for the *ameer*?

MS: No.

JD: No? That's reserved only for men?

MS: Yes.

JD: Why is that?

MS: No, no. We have no disqualification also. We have not disqualified any woman to be *ameer.* But up till now, no woman has . . . Not only not speaking of woman, a male member cannot be a candidate for himself. In our constitution, the party constitution of Jamaat Islami, no member can desire of being elected to such an office. For the election of *ameer* it is the central council which proposes three names. And they call it, we think these three persons are suitable for being elected to the office of the *ameer.* So this time also, the central council, during its meeting we occasionally call certain women members, they sit in separate compartment. They can hear, they can participate by writing down their views and sometimes we call them.

JD: I see. Well, let me talk a little bit about the general idea of the Jamaat and its participation in the political life right now. How strong is your organization in politics? How popular is it? And how do you plan to even better your presence in society?

MS: We are running for elections, but, unfortunately, our performance in elections is not very good. Because we don't have a large voter bank. We have such a vote bank but that is not very large.

JD: How do you plan to get a larger voting bank?

MS: We try to work with the masses to acquaint them with our program. We have a very good program. We have a good party and a disciplined party of sincere and committed workers, but in the general public, they don't have full acquaintance with our program. So we are organizing it in the farmers, in the laborers, in the women, in the youngsters.

JD: I have heard that you're very well organized. Where do your members come from?

MS: The Jamaat-i-Islami is a party of loyal middle-class people. We have a good appeal for intelligentsia. We have attracted quite a good number of people in the intelligentsia, teachers, medical doctors, engineers. And we have organized them on their professional level organizations also. We have a teachers' organization. We have a Pakistani Islamic Medical Association, an engineers' forum and a peasants' organization. In labor, our colleagues work in the name of National Labor Federation.

JD: How many members are in the Jamaat? Is it a large organization?

MS: Actually members in the Jamaat are the persons who have committed for life. They have devoted their lives for the advancement of the cause of the Jamaat. Their number is 8,300.

JD: Now, this is a difficult question for me, but one of the things in looking at the Islamic parties, those people who really have a commitment to religion, is there any attempt to unite the various groups? I understand there are three main organizations . . . the Jamaat-i-Islami, the Jamaat Ulama and there's one other one. Why are there three? Is there any way to unite these groups so that you have a stronger base of support?

MS: We try to forge a united platform, and we were successful in forging unity among a few groups, but another few groups remained outside that platform. So, the main factor behind this disunity, you can say, is that different organizations have different ways of working. So the difference in their way of working is a hindrance in the cause of unity.

JD: But are there things that you all share? Is there anything, a common thing that you can look at, yes, we all agree on this?

MS: Yes, there are many common things. And sometimes we forge unity on that common thing. But that unity is a fragile type of unity, which remains intact for some time and then it shatters after some time. So, in the present elections, after 1993, we tried to forge a platform of all the religious parties, but we couldn't attract all of them.

JD: If the Jamaat, your group, were to come to power in Pakistan, what would be the first three things that you would set your mind to do concretely? Have you all talked about that?

MS: Yes, yes. I think we'll have an Islamic education system introduced first. And we'll try to introduce the economic system of Islam. And the judicial system . . . and the political system also. The top priority, according to our party, is education.

JD: Would there also be an educational system to educate the masses? One thing I notice is that so many Muslims are good Muslims but they don't really know anything about the religion.

MS: This is very unfortunate in our religion. We believe that the first revelation on the holy Prophet Muhammad, peace be upon him, was *read . . .* read in the name of thy Lord. He said, I am not literate. And the angel Gabriel caught hold of him and tried to attract his attention and said, *"Read in the name of thy Lord."* Twice he repeated so and he started reading. So we think that the Muslim is bound to read, read and read. And our Prophet has said, Read from the lap of your mother to the grave, up to the grave. That means, when you start appreciating things, start reading then and then go on reading up to the last breath of your life. So unfortunately, when we were ruled by alien powers, they smashed our educational system and introduced an educational system which is alien to our way of living. So, we remained backward in the field of education. Time and again Muslim scholars and Muslim thinkers have tried to remind the Muslim community that you must have more educational institution, you must have more education, higher education, advanced education, but they have not been properly heeded upon by the community. But Jamaat Islami will not only will set up more institutions for youngsters, but we will also arrange some system for the adults who are illiterate. They must have something, some coaching through TV, through radio, through teachers in their fields, so that they may become at least literate.

JD: What's the literacy rate now in Pakistan?

MS: About 37 . . . 30 percent.

JD: Thirty percent? Now, the economic system, I understand, would prohibit interest rates, any profit being made, that kind of thing, on loaning money. But is there anything else, substantively, that would be different from the capitalistic system?

MS: Yes, it would be different from the capitalistic system. Different from the communistic. Both. We are against the socialist and against the capitalist. That is perhaps the fear of the West, that the West is grudging some fear and nourishing some fear that we are against their system of economy. But we can't help it .

JD: But what is it? A Western business could still come and operate. I could still come and bring cotton, or something, and sell it here?

MS: Yes, yes.

JD: Or import cotton and bring it here from the U.S.?

MS: Yes, yes.

JD: There is nothing that would prohibit that?

MS: But we will not deal and allow to deal anybody the liquor. We will not allow to establish Western banks, or perhaps the Citibank of America. They will have to either close down or they will have to shape their banking system according to Islamic system.

JD: I couldn't use my VISA card, for example?

MS: [LAUGHTER] Yes. Unfortunately, our banks have started the VISA cards also. They are following West. But we want to change all of them. But not that a visitor from the outside would feel some difficulty in buying something or in selling something, of course, no. In the medieval Islamic period, a trader could start from Morocco and could go to China in dealing things and buying from this country and selling in that country. That is possible. We are not against the barter system. No. We want to make a healthy change in the system. In fact, the phenomenon of usury, the phenomenon of high rate interest, which is a peculiarity of capitalistic system, we are against that.

. . . We are against, against exploitation of one man, or one community or one society against another man, or another community or another society. Any exploitation. It may be exploitation of the poor against the rich. Or exploitation of the rich against the poor. Both. We are against both types of exploitation. We are against setting up huge organizations on the system of loans and usury. Then exploiting the poor people who don't have, who are have-nots. So the Islamic economic system is against both socialism, and Maulana Maudoodi, the founder of Jamaat-i-Islami, has written a book on it. The name of the book is *The Interest.* He has written in that book that, in fact, communism and capitalism are part of, are branches of the same tree. One branch is said to be against the other branch. But both the branches are bad because the tree is bad. We want to plant another tree which may benefit the whole humanity without exploitation of any group or any community.

JD: The big question. If you could advise those people who, sincerely in the West, want to try to better relations with the Islamic world, what would you tell them to do?

MS: We would welcome them. We are ourselves trying and we are asking, beseeching, rather, the intelligentsia in the West to come and study Islam as it is. And not study Islam through Orientalists who have a biased view of history, a biased view of the sociology of Islam. I welcome you in our headquarters because you are interested in knowing. And I think that through you I will be able to express myself to some portion of American people. We are not against American people at large. We want to address them. We want to tell them what Islam is. What is the pure Islam, without any prejudice, without any grudge. Please study, come here and study what Islam says. I have some books for you. I think you should read this also, and try to tell people in the West what Islam stands for.

JD: Does it also tell me what is a Muslim? You know, I mean, I get so many definitions. Am I correct that the only thing it really takes to join the community of Muslims is that you profess a belief in one God and that Muhammad was a prophet?

MS: Yes. yes.

JD: So basically, you think that dialogue and having people come and see Islam at its source would certainly help dispel some of the myths?

MS: Yes. We will rather encourage the mutual dialogue and seeing each other. We don't have anything to conceal. Rather, we are so open, we want everybody to come in Pakistan and see for herself, for himself, what we stand for.

JD: And where does your money come from? People pay dues to participate? Is there a tax levied on the members so you can function?

MS: No. It's not called tax. It's voluntary. This is called help, voluntary help of the community. One is asked to promise how much voluntary help he will have to give to the institution. Ten rupees, 100 rupees, 300 rupees.

JD: I see, so it all depends on what you can afford. Now, if there were an Islamic state here, could Christians live here?

MS: Of course. The Christians lived in early Medina. The first Muslim state was established in Medina and Christians and Jews, Jews were there. The Christians met the Prophet. And when the Prophet, the Holy Prophet was living in Mecca, and the infidels were teasing the believers and they were torturing the believers, he asked some of his believers to go to Abyssinia. He said that was ruled by a kind and just Christian king. And they went there, and they lived a prosperous life there. They lived a happy life there. The infidels of Mecca followed them. They said, "Oh, give our men back to us." He said, "No. I'm a just king, I will not give you these men. I'll ask them why you have come to me." And they recited the Surah of the Holy Qur'an, a chapter of the Qur'an called Mariam. There is a chapter in Holy Qur'an by the

name Mariam, the Holy Mother. And when they recited the verses of
Qur'an of that Surah, the king, the Christian king, he picked up a straw
and said, my God, Holy Christ is neither less nor more than what you
have described.

split over how best to tackle the country's deteriorating economy. Mahathir wanted to control strictly Malaysia's currency and financial markets and isolate them from the economic turmoil engulfing Asia, while Anwar insisted on a more western, free-market approach. Their differences, and suspicions that Anwar was quietly working to oust Mahathir, led the prime minister to fire his finance mister: An act that provoked even more instability in the country, and that freed Mahathir's main political rival to work against him from the outside.

When I first met Anwar, he was just rushing from a meeting at the annual conference of the World Bank when I met him at the Washington Sheraton. The hotel was bustling with businessmen and government officials from all over the world. Anwar and his staff had created an office out of a small, two-room suite. Two secretaries answered telephones and greeted visitors in the outer room, while guards at each end of the hallway prevented any uninvited guests from wandering in. I had seen pictures of Anwar Ibrahim in traditional Malay attire, his lanky frame swallowed by a long tunic and trousers and his angular face sharpened by the pillbox-style Malay hat perched on his forehead. Here, in Washington's international business crowd, Anwar cut a lean and tan figure in a well-cut business suit, highly-polished shoes and a silk tie. He exuded the kind of self-confidence and refined charisma that is a characteristic of those accustomed to leadership and power.

Anwar was born on August 10, 1947, into a middle-class family in the Bukit Bertajam, an area in the northern part of the country. Since his days as a university student in Kuala Lumpur, he had been destined for leadership in his country and in the Islamic movement. In 1971 Anwar helped found ABIM, the initials for Angkatan Belia Islam Malaysia, or Malaysian Islamic Youth Movement. Under Anwar, ABIM grew to be a powerful force among Malay students in and outside of the country, but it now no longer enjoys the absolute power that it had had when Anwar was its leader and few dared challenge its platform of Islamic activism. When it was formed, ABIM had 153 members. By 1980 it had grown to more than 35,000 in the region, with most of its members between the ages of 15 and 40. But it also had grown more radical as it strengthened, and gradually that religious radicalism began to erode its support on college campuses. In fact, since the late 1980s ABIM has had to make room for the emergence of other student organizations with differing agendas. One of the strongest, the Students United Front, advocated a multiracial platform with a more liberal approach to campus life than ABIM's religious discipline.

But during its heyday, Anwar rose to national prominence as ABIM's president, encouraging students to study the Qur'an and criticizing the government for not promoting Islamic values in society. Anwar actually had a secular education and did not consider himself an Islamic scholar. In fact, he and other members had been criticized by traditional Islamic scholars for their lack of formal study of Islamic law and history. Like many modern-day Islamic activists, Anwar and his young colleagues were (and perhaps still are) idealists, part of a generation of youths who thought they could change the world.

"I was of the generation of the '60s," Anwar told me. "You know, concern for the injustice of society . . . poverty. We followed people liked Malcolm X and Mao."

Yet Communism had no appeal for Anwar, while the activism of the Islamic movements then surfacing around the world did. The Muslim Brotherhood in Egypt and the Jamaat-i-Islami in Pakistan were calling for social and political reform and for morality in government. And Iran had been able to overthrow what many Muslims considered to be a thoroughly corrupt regime and to institute an Islamic state. Anwar, as president of ABIM, was one of the first foreign visitors to Iran's new Islamic republic, although he took pains to point out to me that the Islamic movement in Malaysia started well before Iran's revolution and that Malays did not look to it as a model. But Malaysian youth clearly saw the embryonic Iranian revolution as a example of the potential power of Islamic activism. And they looked to leaders of Islamic movements, such as Pakistan's Maulana Maudoodi and (among women) the Jewish American convert Maryam Jameelah (who now lives in Pakistan), for inspiration and guidance.

"We have seen the hypocrisy of the so-called modern political elites," Anwar explained. "What we felt was the rampant corruption and moral decadence. So we moved to see the relevance of Islam in a societal context." Anwar saw in Islam an ideology for bettering government and society and a way for youths to develop an identity that was not imitative of the West. At the same time ABIM was founded, many Malaysian students were studying in the West, and they needed an ideology that would help build their self-esteem and connect them to their homeland. Much of the group's support came not only from Malay students inside the country, but from those who were studying in Europe and the United States. In fact, in 1976 Anwar traveled to Jefferson City, Missouri, to establish the Malaysian Islamic Study Group to unite the various Malay student groups in the United States.

But unlike youth movements in other parts of the Islamic world, ABIM did not demand establishment of an Islamic state. Its activities were mostly peaceful, and its brand of Islam was progressive and moderate. Yet, moderate did not necessarily indicate a lack of passion and activism. In fact, between 1974 and 1975, Anwar was held in detention for his part in peasant demonstrations against what they considered an unjust government marketing policy for their products.

ABIM's main goal was to educate Muslim students about their religion and to use Islam as a platform for social protest and reform. "It is important to remember the movement's ideals concentrate more pronouncedly on issues like poverty and corruption," Anwar said. "Those were also really important contemporary issues."

He said the movement tried to maintain a moderate stance on incorporating Islamic values into Malaysian society, perhaps wary that although 90 percent of ethnic Malays are Muslim, Malays make up little more than 50 percent of the country's population. An estimated 35 percent of Malaysians are Chinese, who traditionally have been the most affluent group in the country. The remainder are largely Indian. Relations among the groups have been stormy in modern history. Malays resented the economic dominance of the Chinese, and, in 1969, tensions between them erupted into riots following elections in which Chinese opposition parties more than doubled their seats in parliament. Malays went on a rampage against the Chinese and, as Margaret Scott described in a November 17, 1991, article in the *New York Times Magazine*:

> By nightfall a crowd moved from Kampong Bahru to the nearby Chinese enclave around Jalan Chow Kit. Anything or anyone identified as Chinese was attacked: rows of Chinese shops went up in flames; passengers were dragged from cars, buses and motor scooters and killed. Bands of Chinese, too, were on the streets hunting down

Malays. Chinese secret society hoods barged in to attack Malay patrons. By one count, 184 people were burned or stabbed or beaten to death that night. By another count, 248 people died.[2]

The ethnic violence led to changes in Malaysia's constitution and the creation of the New Economic Policy, an affirmative action program designed to redress the grievances of the Malay majority. The so-called Bumiputra (indigenous Malaysians) policy, which offered preferential treatment to Malays in business, employment and education, had been controversial, but Anwar believed it had worked to diffuse racial tensions. That may be true as far as the Malays were concerned. While the New Economic Policy to improve the economic status of Malays had reduced their anger and resentment toward the Chinese, it had brought other problems. As Scott observed:

> In the years since 1970, the lot of Malays has dramatically improved. The N.E.P. has created a Malay urban middle class. Poverty in peninsular Malaysia has been reduced from 49.3 percent of the population in 1970 to 15 percent at the end of 1990. And Malaysian's preferential policies have not ruined the economy . . . Malaysia, though, is a fragmented nation. The price of social engineering has been high; it has polarized the races. There is resentment and anger among non-Malays who are discriminated against by the N.E.P. Many sons of the soil have developed a crippling dependency on the state. Some Malays find the N.E.P. humiliating, hating the stigma it attaches to their achievements.[3]

Anwar staunchly supported the affirmative action policy, however, although he had gone on record as adamantly opposing racism and as promoting mutual respect among Malaysia's ethnic groups. He believed there was no other way to improve the economic and political power of Malaysia's most disadvantaged people. This was the only way, he said, to ensure racial harmony.

Malaysia's diverse population had tended to moderate ABIM's Islamic program and to encourage moderate leaders like Anwar. ABIM had always been committed to tolerance of other religions and respect for other ethnic groups. "This does not mean that you need to abdicate or relinquish whatever ideals and beliefs you have in religion," Anwar said. "The whole approach is certainly different from what I see or is perceived by Muslims in the Middle East or the Arab world."

In his youth, Anwar admitted, he frankly had a disdain for politics and a disgust with politicians. He had criticized the ruling United Malays National Organization (UMNO) as "un-Islamic" and for not doing enough to encourage Islamic values in society. But by the time he was in his mid-40s, Anwar had decided that the best way to change the system was to join it. His decision to join UMNO, the country's dominant political party, disappointed many of his youthful followers, who thought he was betraying his ideals. Yet Anwar argued that politics and Islam were inextricable and that his entry into the political arena was a natural outcome of his Islamic commitment. His decision to associate himself with UMNO was based on a vow from the government to begin addressing issues that were the reason for ABIM's founding.

One of ABIM's main projects was the establishment of several independent secondary schools in urban areas. The curriculum combined secular and religious studies, and teachers were members of ABIM, who were paid a minimal salary. ABIM had also strongly criticized the government for not providing schools in rural areas, but Anwar said the government took the criticism to heart and started a program to address it.

"It's a new governmental effort," he said. "The one thing that's positive about the Malaysian government, although I am a strong critic of the government, is that they were very responsive. . . . They adjusted very fast to the demands of society." Anwar believed the government was working to right some of the wrongs that inspired the youth movement, and part of his reason for entering politics had been to help speed up the process.

In 1982 Anwar began his new career by winning a seat in parliament and withdrawing as leader of ABIM. Later the same year Mahathir appointed him a deputy minister. As a member of UMNO, he quickly rose through the ranks. In 1983 he was appointed minister of culture, youth and sports, and between 1984 and 1986, he served as minister of agriculture. From 1986 to 1991, he was minister of education. And in 1991, he was named minister of finance, although he had no expertise in the subject before assuming office. Critics doubted that Anwar was competent for the post, and some suggested it was merely a stepping-stone to his ultimate ambition of succeeding Mahathir as prime minister. Yet one year later Anwar was roundly praised for delivering a budget with a plan to fight inflation, curb government spending and cut personal and corporate taxes. In analyzing Anwar's budgetary success, the *Far Eastern Economic Review* observed in an article on November 12, 1992:

> His performance at the Finance Ministry will enhance or undermine his credibility as a potential successor to Prime Minister Datuk Seri Mahathir Mohamad. Anwar, who dismisses speculation of this sort, was given an uncomfortable first 12 months by critics who viewed his economic management as too expansionary. Most analysts now believe that the finance minister has made good on promises of a "restrained" inflation-fighting budget.[4]

It is interesting to note that Anwar had not used his post as finance minister as a bully pulpit to try to institute Islamic law in the economy. There already were some Islamic banks in Malaysia before Anwar became finance minister, so he could not be credited, or criticized, on that front. He had pushed programs to redistribute income to Malaysia's poorest sectors, in keeping with Islam's economic theme of economic justice, but he had been able to do so without alienating the wealthy. "We have done remarkably well in terms of improving the Gini Coefficient [of income distribution]," Anwar told the *Far Eastern Economic Review* in June 1991. "I don't think that we should be concerned that in the process of growth the rich get richer."[5]

Anwar also had not objected to dealing with banks that charge interest rates, which some Islamists consider contrary to the teachings of Islam. And he advocated a gradual social "Islamization" of Malaysia, while respecting freedom of religion and exempting non-Muslims from *Sharia* law. And although Anwar took pride in what he considered to be his moderate approach to Islam, he was unwavering in exacting the harshest penalties for crimes he believed can only lead to the destruction of society. "Drug addiction must be dealt with strongly," he said. "I fully support the death penalty for drug pushing." He reminded me that Malaysia was severely criticized in some Western circles for its tough stand on drug possession. Yet this had come to be a badge of honor for many Malays. I remember talking to an official in the Malaysian embassy before I traveled to his country in 1992. "We don't care what anybody else thinks," he told me. "This is our law. Visitors to Malaysia are warned three times that the penalty is death for possession of drugs, once in the plane as it descends, the second time with a big sign as you enter the airport, and the third time as you leave the airport."

But devout Muslims were forced to compromise on other issues because of their multiethnic society. Although the government did not allow some risqué movies to be shown in Malaysia, and many young women dressed in Islamic attire, Kuala Lumpur was certainly not the Islamic ideal. Rock music blared from nightclubs and alcoholic beverages were easily available. While Anwar was supposed to be moving Malaysia toward an Islamic system, he took a relaxed attitude toward issues that other Islamists consider sacred.

"Personally, I don't drink," Anwar told me. "A Muslim should not drink, but we know that many Muslims do drink. I don't think we should pass laws to make it illegal. I prefer to see societal pressures against drinking."

He also prefered to see societal pressure for modest attire for women, although he had been quoted as saying that Islamic attire is not necessarily Arab attire. And he told me there is no prohibition in Islam against women working outside the home. But as with most Islamists, a woman's first calling is as a wife and mother. Anwar's own wife was a medical doctor who confined her practice to women, and Anwar also had been quoted as saying that he preferred segregation of the sexes in schools.

Under Malay *Radat* (custom), which was not always compatible with the teaching of Islam, young women traditionally enjoyed little status in society, especially if they were unmarried and without children. But in recent history, since the country's struggle for independence from Great Britain, women's social and political organizations had flourished and women had moved into all aspects of Malaysian society. Women helped establish UMNO, which helped secure Malaysia's creation as an independent state in 1948.

When I visited Malaysia in 1992 while researching the series on Muslim women that aired on affiliates of National Public Radio, it was clear that women were very much a part of the economic, social and political life of the country. Government statistics say they make up 40 percent of the workforce and that number is growing. I interviewed women who were serving in parliament and were members of the women's branch of UMNO, and I interviewed businesswomen, teachers and students. Dr. Hussein Al Atas, a Malaysian sociologist and Islamic scholar, told me that although some roles were still off-limits to women, they had made great progress in eliminating cultural taboos that would restrict their public role. "In Malaysia you see women practically everywhere," he told me. "They are in the courts; they are magistrates; they are cabinet members. At the moment, a high percentage of the student population in the campuses are women. There is not a problem as far as employment is concerned. Women stand for elections and become members of the top leadership hierarchy." Women accounted for about 11 percent of ABIM's members during Anwar's presidency, and the organization officially promoted both education for women and their right to work.

Anwar had been described as an astute politician who adeptly tailored his rhetoric to suit his listeners. In our conversation, as he talked about why Muslims reject some aspects of Western society because of its injustice, he talked about inner-city poverty, about Malcolm X and the Los Angeles riots of 1993. He spoke of leaving the luxurious calm of northwest Washington and driving into the city's southeast section, where he was shocked at the daily suffering of America's dispossessed. Anwar said he spent his youth railing against that kind of suffering. And, he said, that is the kind of suffering that erodes the moral authority of the United States in the developing world. Whether he would give the same speech to an American banker or senator, I can't say. But Anwar clearly can play different roles at different times; as Mahathir was soon to see. Because as economic and political stbility threatened Malaysia in the fall of 1998, Anwar seemed poised to play a pivotal, if not decisive, role in shaping its future.

JD: I understand you come from the youth movement ABIM, which is the Malaysian youth movement?

AI: When I was young, yes.

JD: Well, you still look young. But what I wanted to find out was a little bit about ABIM and about how you and others developed that idea.

AI: I was a young man. I was of the generation of the '60s, you know, concern for the injustices of society . . . poverty. So in our generation, we followed people like Malcolm X . . . and Mao.

JD: ABIM came out of a desire from young people like yourself during the '60s to try to better your society. But how did you have an Islamic awakening? From what I have read, you didn't begin [in the Islamic movement] and you didn't have a lot of religious study early on.

AI: We were practicing Muslims. Early on we understood that we would practice Islam. [Initially] we did not have an administration [in ABIM] that was religious. Because our religion was a separate issue. But we were not with the leftist movement then either. Yet we had seen the hypocrisy of the so-called modern political elites. We felt the rampant corruption and moral decadence. So we moved to see the relevance of Islam in a societal context.

JD: Do you think your organization has improved Malaysian society? Has it had any effect at all?

AI: It is important to remember the movement's ideals concentrate more pronouncedly on issues like poverty and corruption, although my generation was not used to participating in [protest] activities. Those were also really important contemporary issues.

JD: But, for example, in our generation here, people became Communists or Socialists. Why didn't you become Communist or Socialist? If you were concerned about those issues, what led you to the Islamic rather than to communism or Marxism even?

AI: I feel I cannot reconcile how a Muslim can be a Communist. I think a Muslim should be moderate as well as good. You know Malaysia is bit unique because it is a multiracial, multireligious society. And a lot of our personal friends at college universities are either non-Muslim or non-Malays. And I think that has helped us to moderate our stance a lot. In my student days, for example, a lot of interreligious forums, interracial seminars and discussions took place. This does not mean that you need to abdicate or relinquish whatever ideas and beliefs you have in the religion. The whole approach is certainly different from what I see or is perceived by Muslims in the Middle East or the Arab world.

JD: But I understand there is a certain camaraderie between ABIM and Iran, for example.

AI: We began our movement before the Iranian revolution. I'm not underestimating or downplaying their role . . . this is different context altogether. But the Shah was never seen to any educated youth in that period as exemplary of a great, modern, dynamic, progressive leader. He symbolizes a very corrupt regime and decadent. And whether it is Iran or it happens to be apartheid in South Africa, it is still the same attitude that we have.

JD: You have very much been a proponent of equality among races and among people. Can you tell me a little about that and how it related to your Islamic philosophy?

AI: This relates even here in the context of discussions in my address to the World Bank. I believe in affirmative action. If you have an obsession about growth and market-driven economics, and you neglect the importance of the minorities and the downtrodden, it is certainly to my mind not rational. Is development for a few and pass over the rest? This is not an excuse to allow people to be lazy. We don't need to wait for riots in L.A. to realize that something is wrong. This has a lot of relevance because leaders tend to ignore basic fundamentals in terms of cohesive forces in society. They need to relate to all, the urban, the rural, the rich and the poor; the educated, the less educated. That is why I think that if you want Malaysia to progress, then all must feel confident, comfortable, well protected. We have the Malays in the rural areas. In the '60s, there were hardly any good schools nor medical facilities and we could not accept that. We ask what is development for? For whom?

JD: And ABIM and your movement was able to bring some schools to the rural areas and to the poor people there? Do I understand that correctly?

AI: Yes. It's a new governmental effort, you see. The one thing that's positive about the Malaysian government, although I am a strong critic of the government, is that they were very responsive. They adjust very fast. Not necessarily to the entire credit of ABIM, but this was a growing trend. They adjusted very fast to the demands of society.

JD: And now as minister of finance, how do you see your role in Malaysian society, especially as you also are a devout Muslim? How do you mesh the two when you deal with the financial problems that Malaysia has?

AI: A practicing Muslim needs to be modern, moving toward progress and to ensure that there is justice for everybody. All [of which] are normal modern ideals.

JD: But yet I understand you didn't want to get into politics initially. That two governments had to beg you to join. Why was that?

AI: Well, not really. It was true that certainly I was very cynical of politics. We used to joke about it in the mid-'70s. I thought of politics and politicians as an uncharismatic, low moral profession. But a few years later, here I was in politics.

JD: Do you consider yourself a politician?

AI: Well, I am in politics. I think that's somehow related to the cause, you know, of political Islam.

JD: Do you think that politics and power are corrupting?

AI: I mean, you do make compromises, yes. You are dealing with millions of people. But why do you do it? You want to progress; you want to make sure that you move. I will do everything to make sure that Malaysia succeeds, progresses economically. I want Muslims, non-Muslims to feel that they are comfortable, that they [can] work, that they will benefit. But I am also a firm believer in affirmative action.

JD: Now in the Malay context, affirmative action means promoting the interests of the Malay people, who have been deprived of their economic rights for a long time.

AI: And the poor. There are poor Indians. There are those pockets that have been dominated by the Chinese, that need to be assisted.

JD: One of the purposes of the interviews that I'm doing is to talk about the relationships between the Western world and the Islamic world. Do you think there is a gap? Do you think there is a problem?

AI: Yes, if you look at [Samuel P.] Huntington's "Clash of Civilizations."* But I can think of no better rebuke of this Western conception other than people like Edward Said, Ali Mazrui. I think that suffices to express my views on their [the West] preaching to the world and they're not listening. They assume they know. Give us a break. The psyches are different, the cultures are different. Many things about America I like to emulate. But I don't need to be an American. I don't need to forget myself in American culture. Similarly, why can't they accept the fact that Malaysians must be different. Africans must be different. We should be modern; we should be democratic. We should not condone corruption or oppression in any form, or deny basic rights . . . fair enough. But don't tell me that democracy and freedom can only be preached by some countries and political leaders in the West.

---

* Samuel P. Huntington wrote an article in the Summer 1993 issue of *Foreign Affairs* entitled "The Clash of Civilizations." The article provoked much discussion in the West as well as in the Islamic world because it suggested that in the post–Cold War world, conflict could center around differences in civilizations.

JD: Do you see that the West and Western leaders want to have a monopoly on the development, especially the development of ideas and on the development of democracy?

AI: Again, they choose to believe they are really superior intellectually and in practice. But look at Washington and the places around Washington.

JD: What about them?

AI: I took a drive.

JD: You took a drive?

AI: Every time I get to the World Bank, I don't only stay at [the] Sheraton or Marriott. I look around, in the [out of the] way, backward areas. And the crime rate. What human dignity are you talking about? It is not that we are anti-American. I mean it's always that when you speak up, you are seen to be either for or against. And it's not true. I learn so much from the American experience. In many aspects of the culture I rejoice, the arts, the novels. I enjoy American novels more than some of [those of] my country, you know. That shows that we are open to different views.

JD: And you say, when you look at American society, you don't see all good, you see injustice. When you talk about the West preaching and not listening, what should we be listening to?

AI: We should promote civilization and dialogue. I am quoting Malik Ben Nabi, the Algerian thinker. We should not be talking about clash of civilization, or cultural clash.[†]

[†] Many Muslims I interviewed were especially sensitive to Huntington's article because they feared it reinforced fears about Islam being an enemy of Western civilization.

JD: Did that article disturb you? You read the article, obviously; did it disturb you?

AI: No, it did not disturb me; it was just confirming some of the views and attitudes of scholars here.

JD: You don't think things are getting any better? You don't see that the Western world is becoming a little more open? Do you see any progress at all?

AI: Some areas, yes. Congressmen, political leaders I have met, some of them take a different view. I don't think you can lump Western thought or Western political leaders in one school. It is so complex and so complicated. All we ask is that we develop our own system and our own cultures. For example, drug addiction must be dealt with strongly. I fully support the death penalty for drug pushing. Yet we were severely criticized for that in the West. This is our right to make our own laws. And this right must be respected. The only solution to this problem with the West is to promote mutual respect and dialogue.

SEVENTEEN

M. HABIB CHIRZIN

THE MUHAMMADIYAH, INDONESIA

PROFILE

M. HABIB CHIRZIN was one of the few Islamists I had ever met who was comfortable with religion being separate from government. Islam as practiced in Indonesia can be considerably different from Islam in the Middle East. In Southeast Asia, Islam was imported in the fourteenth century and heavily influenced by the region's ancient, indigenous cultures. Islam coexists with powerful Eastern religions such as Hinduism and Buddhism. Thus, Muslim leaders such as Chirzin had unique ideas about the proper role of Islam in society, ideas that sometimes were at odds with the traditions of Islam in the Middle East.

As chairman of international relations and cooperation of the Muhammadiyah, one of Indonesia's most respected Islamic organizations, Chirzin was one of its most influential members. He was an Islamic scholar devoted to using the moral teachings of his religion to promote world peace and cooperation. But for Chirzin, creating an Islamic state in Indonesia was not an immediate priority. In fact, he brushed off my question about whether Indonesia should implement Islamic law with a chuckle.

"There is no such obligation," he said, laughing. His laughter seemed designed to temper the surprise that had to be evident on my face, for I had never heard an Islamist advocate a position even remotely similar to the American idea of separation of church and state. Yet Chirzin had all the qualifications for being included in the ranks of Islamists. He had formally studied Islam in Indonesia's preeminent religious schools and was considered knowledgeable in religious matters. "I was supposed to be an *ulama* [religious authority]" he told me, again with a chuckle. Born in 1949 in Yogyakarta, Indonesia, Chirzin grew up under the influence of the Muhammadiyah and had worked in the organization all of his life.

Much of Chirzin's education had been in Islamic schools. His undergraduate work was done in philosophy at the Gadjah Mada University, and, in 1984, he graduated from the Indonesian Islamic University's school of law, where he was chairman of the university's student senate. As a leader of the Muhammadiyah movement today, Chirzin was an observant Muslim who was devoted to making Islam a progressive force in the modern world. Yet unlike the vast majority of people who live an Islamic lifestyle and are devoted to their religion, Chirzin was not calling for an Islamic state in Indonesia.

Muslims are the overwhelming majority in Indonesia. In fact, Indonesia is the world's largest Muslim nation, with more than 90 percent of its 180 million people professing belief in one God and the Prophet Muhammad. In many ways, Islam has helped to unite the hundreds of ethnic groups in Indonesia, although Buddhism, Hinduism and Christianity are all represented. Because it is estimated that there are more than 300 ethnic groups in Indonesia, tolerance has been officially promoted through slogans such as Indonesia's national motto *"Bhinneka Tunggal Ika,"* which means, "They are many, they are one." Yet in Indonesia as in much of Southeast Asia, there has been simmering resentment of the success of the Chinese business community, and Chinese living there complain that they are subject to cultural, religious and political discrimination.

During the near chaos in the spring of 1998, when Indonesians faced the collapse of their economy and the impotence of Suharto to manage the crisis, the resentment of the small, but economically dominant Chinese community turned violent. Indonesia's ethnic

Chinese became the scapegoats of a society wracked by economic and political turmoil. Chinese businesses were burned during riots, Chinese people attacked, and many fled the country, taking with them much of the wealth needed to try to revitalize the economy.

Before the riots of 1998, Suharto's strong military had ensured that law and order prevailed and that extremists (or opponents) of any stripe were firmly kept in check. All of that changed with Suharto's resignation, however. Yet, even though the Muhammadiya's president, Amien Rais, was at the forefront of efforts to oust Suharto and his family, he did not call for the establishment of an Islamic state in their place.

Although the Muslim faith is dominant in Indonesia, when the country declared its independence from the Dutch in 1945, it did not do so with the intention of declaring an Islamic state, Chirzin told me. He cited that as the strongest example of the tolerant nature of Indonesian Muslims. He said the government was not based on *Sharia*, or Islamic law, but on what Indonesians referred to as the Pancasila, or Five Principles: belief in God, humanity, nationalism, representative government and social justice. Chirzin believed these principles were enough to ensure a just, moral society in Indonesia, which is in keeping with Islam's teachings. Any society based on one religion would alienate segments of the population, he said.

While some Indonesian Muslims did call for an Islamic state, Chirzin believed that most Muslims in his country agreed with the status quo. Yet in a country such as Indonesia, where political opposition was stifled, democracy was a sham, and an aging leader refused to relinquish power or anoint a successor, the ground was well tilled for Islamic groups to try to mount an opposition to the government.

Chirzin wanted no part of that, however. He had other work to accomplish. He said he was dedicated to trying to improve relations between Indonesia's various religious and ethnic groups. In addition to his work with the Muhammadiyah, he was founder and director of the Forum on Peace and Development Ethnic Studies, which is devoted to that end. He worked with international peace organizations as well as with the United Nations to promote interreligious dialogue and to further education efforts in the Third World.

I did not interview Chirzin in Indonesia. We talked (in English) in a wood paneled, book-lined meeting room at the United States

Institute of Peace in Washington. But I told him I had recently visited his country and had interviewed Nani Yamine, a woman of international renown who had worked in several UN programs dedicated to improving the situation of women in developing countries. Yamine traveled widely, attending conferences and speaking about the plight of the world's poorest women. She even founded a legal clinic in Jakarta dedicated to family law and to protecting the rights of women in the country's *Sharia* courts, which handle family and civil matters for Indonesia's Muslim population. It turned out that Chirzin knew Yamine well. He told me she had died only weeks earlier of a sudden heart attack. When I met her, she seemed a healthy and vivacious woman, just entering her 60s. People who knew her were shocked because she seemed the essence of vitality, with her smart business suits, high heels and well-coiffed hair. Yamine's staff of lawyers included many women who volunteered their time and talents. Much of their work was on behalf of women, educating them about Islam's teachings with regard to the status of women in society, especially with regard to issues of divorce and polygamy. Yamine was a virulent opponent of polygamy. As typewriters clicked and phones rang in her Jakarta clinic, she insisted that men had misinterpreted the Qur'an. The Muslim holy book actually requires a man to treat all wives with absolute equality, she said, which the Qur'an also says is impossible. But Yamine's strongest argument was in the simple statement, "Don't ever hurt the one you love."

Chirzin said most Muslims in Indonesia agreed with such arguments, which was why the government made it extremely difficult for a man to marry more than once. In addition to securing the approval of the first wife, the man must prove a need for another wife, such as the inability of the first wife to bear children or her physical or mental incapacitation. Even then the man must prove he can support another wife financially, Chirzin said.

Of course, in some parts of Indonesia, the rights of women have never been an issue, even after Islam swept the area. In Sumatra, for example, where a matriarchal system predates Islam, women there have long been dominant in business and trade. Chirzin said he and other Muhammadiyah members encouraged Yamine's work in that it was fully in keeping with their mission to reform the practice of Islam in Indonesia. Chirzin's approval of Yamine's work was a clear indication of his liberal, progressive attitude within the Islamic spectrum, but at the end of our conversation, I came to understand just how liberal many of his ideas were about religion, the state and society.

Chirzin was visiting the United States under a tour sponsored by the U.S. Information Agency, which in itself seemed surprising. Considering the suspicions government policy makers harbor about Islamists, and the hostility that so often exists on the part of Islamists toward the U.S. government, I wondered how such a visit had been arranged, and why. I knew that there had been a great flurry of controversy only a week before over a request by Tunisian exile Rachid al-Ghannouchi for a visa to visit the United States for an Islamic conference. The Washington Institute for Near East Policy, considered a pro-Israeli think tank, had issued a statement opposing the visa request because al-Ghannouchi, leader of the opposition EnNahda (Renaissance) Party, opposed the Arab-Israeli peace process. The institute's analyst, Martin Kramer, wrote that al-Ghannouchi maintained links with Islamists in Iran and Sudan. Yet Muslims in the United States and abroad were concerned that if al-Ghannouchi, widely considered a moderate Islamist who eschews violence, were denied a visa, he would be humiliated in the eyes of Islamists and extremists' claims that there is no hope for dialogue between the West and the Islamic world would be more credible. If an Islamic leader such as al-Ghannouchi could stir such controversy by simply requesting a visa, I wondered, why would the U.S. Information Agency host a Muslim leader from Indonesia?

As I talked to Chirzin, I came to understand that his idea of Islamic activism was far less threatening from a Western perspective than that of many devout Muslims, especially those in the Middle East. And the Muhammadiyah had no quarrel with its government, even though the reins of political power rested firmly in the hands of one man, President Suharto, backed by the country's powerful military. Suharto came to power in 1965, after helping to put down a Communist coup. He had ruled ever since, although he and his party had subjected themselves to national elections. Unlike Islamic groups operating under one-party, or one-person, rule in countries of the Middle East, the Muhammadiyah, Chirzin told me, was not calling for

more democracy or for an Islamic state. The organization also promoted its country's economic and political ties with the West.

Most Islamic activists I had met believed that Islam should govern
all aspects of life, from the privacy of family life to the working of the
state, especially in countries where Muslims are the majority. While
there were indeed Islamic political parties in Indonesia, they did not
enjoy the solid popular support of the Muhammadiyah, which tried to
stay out of politics. The Muhammadiyah opted instead for widespread
involvement in social services programs, including education, health
and social welfare. Individual members were free to run for office and
join any political party, Chirzin said, but the Muhammadiyah took no
political stand, except that its members had criticized the government
for its actions in East Timor, a former Portuguese colony on the island
of Timor, annexed by Indonesia in 1976.

The estimated 600,000 residents of Timor are Roman Catholics,
and more than 100,000 were reported to have died after the annexation due to the ensuing fighting and famine. Chirzin said the
Muhammadiyah had worked with international human rights organizations to investigate reports of abuses committed by Indonesian
troops against Christians in East Timor. He acknowledged that there
was evidence his government had acted with extreme disregard for
human rights. In one incident in 1991, government troops killed
dozens of students protesting Indonesian rule.

Despite its criticism of the government in East Timor, until the
spring of 1998 the Muhammadiyah has steered clear of any confrontation with the government that could lead to its being banned. And
until 1998, the Muhammadiyah had enjoyed cordial relations with
Suharto. Chirzen even told me with obvious pride that the first
president of Indonesia, Sukarno, had been a member of the Muhammadiyah. Yet in May 1998, it was Muhammadiyah president Amien
Rais who organized "people's power" marches against the government
and called for Suharto's resignation. Many lauded Rais as a hero, and
others wondered if the Muhammadiyah's future role in Indonesian
politics might be more provacative than its past.

The Muhammadiyah was founded in 1912 by Ahmad Dahlan on
a platform of Islamic reform in Indonesia. The first major conver-
sions to Islam in the country were recorded in the fourteenth century

and were credited mainly to the influence of Sufis, Islamic mystics. Their tolerant, pacifist approach to Islam blended well with the Hindu and Buddhist culture in Indonesia, allowing a gradual, peaceful conversion. But the Muhammadiyah believed it also allowed some teachings of Islam to be distorted, which was why the group advocated a close examination of the Qur'an and the *Hadith,* the recorded words and deeds of the Prophet, to purify Islam in Indonesia, to free it from cultural shackles. For example, in parts of Java, there were people known as the *abangan* who mixed Islam with pre-Islamic traditions that included recognition of spirits and meditation. The *abangan* also disregarded two of Islam's main pillars, fasting and making the pilgrimage to Mecca.

Traditionalists in Indonesia were dedicated to Islamic scholarship, but their practices were a mixture of Indonesian culture and mainstream Islamic teachings. The Muhammadiyah was part of yet another group that sought to modernize Islam and to make its teachings compatible with the necessities of living in today's world. They seemed to advocate *ijtihad,* encouraging a personal study of the sources of Islamic law and a new interpretation of those sources.

The Muhammadiyah took great inspiration from the teachings of Muhammad Abduh, the Egyptian sheikh who preached that Islam should be reformed to make it more relevant to modern life. Many Indonesians studied with him at Al Azhar University and returned to their country energized by his ideas about Islam's activist role in the modern world. Such Islamic modernists were convinced they could benefit from the best of the modern world, including scientific and technological advances, and still remain true to the teachings of their religion.

Dahlan, the Muhammadiyah's founder, believed Muslims should be self-sufficient and independent. He started programs to improve health care and education for Indonesians, needs that the Dutch addressed poorly during their 350-year colonization of the islands.

The Muhammadiyah ran an estimated 4,600 primary and secondary schools as well as 74 universities throughout the country. The group also sponsored Boy Scout and Girl Scout programs to provide religious and moral guidance for youth. In their concern for the welfare of Indonesian children, Chirzin said, the Muhammadiyah had undertaken programs to encourage foster parenting for orphans.

Although he contended that Islam prohibits adoption as known in the West, it encourages people to accept orphans into their families. While Islamic teachings forbid attempts to change the family names of children or to deny their bloodline, Islam does not prohibit loving and caring for orphans while honestly acknowledging they were born into another family, he said.

Despite their social work and religious study, Islamic modernists were often criticized as being Islamic apologists by those wary of Western influence. In their attempt to fit into the modern world and to help develop their countries, they were castigated as imitators of the colonizers, covetous of the affluence of the West. The Muhammadiyah had copied the tactics of Christian missionaries in spreading their faith, tactics that had been undeniably successful in winning supporters. And the group saw nothing in Islam that prohibits Muslims from enjoying prosperity and even wealth, as long as it is gained through honest, hard work. Chirzin seemed less concerned about righting the injustices of the past than with building a better future. He seemed far less hostile to the West than many Islamists I interviewed. Even while describing the pain of three centuries of abuse from Europeans, including the Dutch, Portuguese and British, Chirzin spoke not of revenge but of cooperation. His attitude was pragmatic and seems rooted in a strong survival instinct. He saw no point in nourishing hate and wasting the intellectual and spiritual energy needed to build his country.

Chirzin offered a model of Islam that was nonthreatening, that advocated religious and ideological tolerance and that was open to communication with the West. Although most of the Islamic leaders I interviewed would lambaste the Muhammadiyah's leaders for not advocating an Islamic state in Indonesia and not promoting a more open political system, Chirzin said he maintained strong ties to the larger world of Islam. Men such as Chirzin may be able to play a vital role in beginning the difficult dialogue between Islam and the West. And Muslims such as Chirzin may help dispel fears of an ultimate and inevitable collision between the tenets of Islam and the values of Western civilization.

JD: How does the Muhammadiyah compare with other Islamic organizations around the world? Is it mostly a social service organization, or is it also involved in politics?

MC: More in the reform, especially in the theological reform, ethical reform. But more through the actual work.

So, we engage in more activities, based on our understanding of the *Sharia* and the Qur'an. From our understanding, we try to apply it to develop a more humane society, a more peaceful society, a better understanding of the Qur'an, but at the same time better life, better relationship with other groups of people.

JD: Now, Indonesia has a majority, an overwhelming majority, of Muslims. And it has the largest population of Muslims anywhere in the world, right?

MC: Yes, 180 million. And in size, Indonesia has 13,000 islands, with more than 250 dialects and more than 250 ethnic groups.

Indonesia is based on Pancasila, the five pillars of our national state. It was a gentlemen's agreement of our founding fathers. Our state is not based on Islam or any religion. One of the main aspects of Pancasila is belief in God first; second is humanity; third is nationalism; fourth is democracy and fifth is social justice. This is our basic idea and the basic philosophy of our country.

JD: And so this is actually what the West would call a separation of religion and state?

MC: Yes.

JD: What is the percentage of Muslims in Indonesia?

MC: Ninety percent.

JD: Why did the Muslims opt to have a secular government rather than one based on Islamic law?

MC: It was agreed among all of the leaders in 1945, one day before independence. It was declared one day after independence.

JD: But what was the motivation behind that?

MC: Because we are multiethnic. We are multiracial. We are multireligious. So [we need to] to unify the country because we are a large population from many ethnic groups.

JD: How do you respond to criticism that must come from some Islamic groups that there should be Islamic law in Indonesia?

MC: No, there is no such obligation. [LAUGHTER].

JD: So what is Muhammadiyah trying to reform, exactly?

MC: You know Islam came to Indonesia several hundred years after the Prophet. And there has been some deterioration in understanding. We know that since the fourteenth century, there was stagnation in the Islamic world due to the colonialization and also the backwardness of Muslim society after the falling down of the Abbasiyad and Ummayad in Spain. And then also, the thinkers, they only review and make commentary of the *Sharia* and books written by the so-called grand muftis, or grand writers of *Sharia*, and then there is no such development. Let's say there is a kind of decline in the Islamic thought, so the founder of Muhammadiyah, Ahmad Dahlan, he thought that we should do something because there is something wrong in our understanding of Islam, in our faith, in our tradition, in our practice of Islam.

JD: Did he think that it was not strict enough, or did he think that it was misguided?

MC: Misguided. The first thing he taught was that we should read the Qur'an but we should look at our society. We should learn about history and the social life and even economic life. We should understand Islam within context, social, historical and even political context. We were colonized by the Dutch almost 350 years. The only way of reforming society is by reforming our understanding of our spiritual resource of life, spiritual resource of development.

JD: So you're after purifying society and preventing some of the distortion of religion. Can you give me an example of some of the distortions? Would the treatment of women in some parts of the Middle East be an example?

MC: Yes, the first thing Ahmad Dahlan did was to organize the women. When I talk about the purification [of society] it is not an abstract thing. It's done by organizing people in the Boy Scouts, Girl Scouts and in organizing women, organizing the school, orphanages . . . organizing it and managing it in a modern way. When we say reform, we mean reform of social structures, of way of living. So we adopt the modern values, the modern way of organizing, the modern way of management. That's why from the very beginning the people called Muhammadiyah "the Modernists." But modernity in terms of management, in terms of methodology, in terms of what is the appropriate thing for modern science.

JD: You're trying to find a balance between religion and the modern world?

MC: Yes, religion is modern. I mean, religion is from God to meet the needs of modern society and even to give guidance for the future. That's why Muhammadiyah stressed education and health. At that time, health was managed by the Dutch, but he [Dahlan] thought we should have an Indonesian-managed hospital, an Indonesian health system. We should have schools run by Indonesians. And we should also have a place where the orphan gets care. Because at that time, orphans were left without any care. That's why the Muhammadiyah has taken care of the orphans because it's one of our religious duties.

JD: I understand adoption is prohibited. That most Muslims believe adoption is prohibited. Is that something you're changing?

MC: No, adoption, strict adoption, yeah. Because we encourage the so-called foster parenting.

JD: Which means that the child keeps his family name but he can be cared for by another family?

MC: Yes, yes. If you become a foster parent, the Prophet said you would be like this [holding up two fingers close together] with him in heaven. So foster parenting is quite encouraged by the Prophet and even in society. But we modernize it and teach how to manage it. So [we concentrate on] three things, education, health and foster parenting. But also widening and diversifying the services. But by education, we uplift the social condition of life and also, most of the Muhammad-iyah members are intellectuals, in the government, civil service, or are traders. Most of them are traders, actually. My grandfather, my father, my mother, were in that situation. It's by birth that I am a Muhammad-iyah. My father, my mother, all of my family come from Muhammad-iyah. I was born in Muhammadiyah hospital. I grew up in the primary school and secondary school of Muhammadiyah. I went to the Muhammadiyah library. I went to the Muhammadiyah hospital.

JD: Now, Muhammadiyah is supported by the government? Not supported financially, but there is a certain cooperation, isn't there?

MC: Yes, yes. Oh sure, sure . . . You know the first president [of Indonesia], Sukarno, was a member of Muhammadiyah. He asked to be buried with the Muhammadiyah flag. And the present president was teacher at a Muhammadiyah school. He said, I am a Muhammad-iyah, I was a teacher in Muhammadiyah schools, and I grew up in a Muhammadiyah family.

JD: Unlike, for example, the Muslim Brotherhood in places like Egypt or Jordan, where there is some tension with government, Muhammad-iyah has a very good relationship with its government.

MC: Yes, very good.

JD: What's the difference?

MC: It's the way of looking at the so-called power, the so-called government, the so-called political interest. Because, according to our understanding, Islam is to humanize the people and to safeguard the human being, but also the earth, because we are sent by God to be His first children. And there is a trusteeship to develop a humane society, but also to sustain this earth, to nurture this earth.

JD: So there's an environmental aspect to the Muhammadiyah. But you're not trying to change the government in any way. You're not trying to implement *Sharia* law?

MC: That's a more technical matter. *Sharia* is something to deal with social affairs.

JD: But not with government affairs?

MC: Not with government affairs.

JD: Are there organizations in Indonesia that are trying to do this?

MC: Yes, we have a party which is one of the strongest and largest in Indonesia before the 1960s, when our state was still trying to find the most proper basis in terms of law, in terms of philosophical underpinnings. So there were some Socialist parties, Communist parties and there was one Islamic party.

JD: What's the name of it?

MC: Mashoomie. It's was a big, big party.

JD: Still?

MC: No, it was banned in 1960 with the Socialist party.

JD: So it's still banned. Does it cause trouble underground?

MC: No, because they are intellectuals.

JD: They were never violent?

MC: No, never, never. Because they were constitutional. What I respect about them is that they were constitutional, democratic and intelligent. Both of the leaders of Mashoomie and socialists party were respected people.

JD: So why were they banned?

MC: Because, you know, the trend in the early '60s, the former president tended to the left. There was this Pyongyang-Moscow link. And even the Pyongyang-Beijing link. And there was tension nationally. And there were big, big differences between the former president and his critics. Also, constitutionally, the president cannot be president for life. But he decreed himself president for life. And they objected to that.

JD: The Muhammadiyah didn't object to that?

MC: Yeah, we objected to that. But not in a political way; in a cultural way.

JD: You really try to stay out of politics and concentrate on social building?

MC: Yes, but personally, we could be a member of any party. Golkar party, for example, the assisting government party. We could also be a member of the PPP [Muslim United Development Party]. It's the development and unity party, the Islamic party. And then PDI [Indonesia Democratic Party] belongs to the democratic party. So then, we could belong to all of those parties. In all of the parties, Muhammadiyah people are there.

JD: What kind of relationship does Muhammadiyah have with other Islamic groups around the world?

MC: We have been invited by other groups to their congresses and we invite them to our congress. We have a congress every five years to renew some of our objectives and program.

JD: Do you have close ties or similar philosophies with any other groups in the Middle East?

MC: We don't know exactly, because according to some studies, there is no such close ideas. But ideally, maybe we are close to one of the reformers, like Muhammad Abduh. Because he's engaged also in reforming universities.

JD: Do most Indonesians share your idea that Islam should be moderate, should be progressive, that it should be reaching out to other religions, to other countries?

MC: Yes, it's growing, since the last 20 years. Since we are now in the developing effort, to develop our country economically, politically, socially and culturally, we should observe this way of thinking because we are a big nation. We have the same goal to develop our country, so we share a lot. Even we share the faith. We share the concern. We share our ethical values for the future. We share an understanding of human rights, an understanding of the children.

JD: And yet Indonesia has been criticized for its actions in East Timor and for its treatment there of minorities. What's going on there?

MC: That's due to the decolonization of East Timor. But then, the Portuguese, during the process of decolonization, they wanted to recolonize. But there is a problem with human rights. Certainly we are concerned about those violations there. This is part of our concern.

JD: Have you expressed your concern to the government?

MC: Not only to the government but to human rights groups internationally.

JD: As far as the relationship between the Islamic world and the West, do you see hostility?

MC: Actually, after the colonial period, yes. There are still some groups of people who were really affected by the colonial period, or at least, they still have sentiments. They don't see [the need] for the better future relations. For Muhammadiyah, because since the colonial times, some Muhammadiyah people send their children to school in the West. Some of our family went to school in Holland, in France, aside from Egypt. One of my family went to Egypt but then he flew to France and studied economics there.

JD: Indonesians have a reputation for excelling in the recitation of the Qur'an. They take top prizes every year in Saudi Arabia. Is that true?

MC: Yes. I would share with you my experience. In 1985 I attended the annual Qur'anic recitation festival in Mecca. I was there. And I was excited that one of the champions was from Indonesia. He won. It's not only recitation but learning the whole Qur'an by heart. And even to make commentary, in Arabic. And you know he was a shirt maker and he earns only $2 a day but he won that competition. He recited and memorized the whole Qur'an. Whatever you point in the Qur'an, he will recite the whole verse for you. Because everybody in Indonesia, from very early childhood, learn Arabic. They learn the Qur'an. Even my kid, he's in the fourth grade; he knows how to read the Qur'an. Because in the neighborhood it is taught. Some people may be unlearned in the Latin alphabet, but they learns Arabic. So they are literate in the Qur'an, in Arabic. From early childhood, especially among career women, among professionals, they want their children to be good Muslims.

JD: Now, I understand in some parts of Indonesia there is a matriarchy.

MC: Yes. In the west. In Sumatra. And other parts.

JD: Is that any conflict with Islam, as you see it?

MC: No. Some of the most pious people come from that society. Some of the most productive people. They do business all over Indonesia and they open shops, just like the Chinese. In fact, we call them the Indonesian Chinese because they are very active, especially the women.

JD: Now, is polygamy allowed in Indonesia?

MC: Under very, very strict conditions. Very, very strict conditions.

JD: Whenever I speak to Americans about Islam, sometimes people say, but look at Muslims how they treat minorities. Do you see Indonesia as an example of tolerance?

MC: I think so. I think so. You should talk with people in Bali, with some of the prominent [Hindu] thinkers. I am chairman of the interfaith dialogue. We are organizing a national seminar, which will be opened by the president, in the coming August. We will be inviting all of the associations of intellectuals within Christian, Catholic, Buddhist and Hindu community. We have formed the preparatory committee. So every week we have joint meetings, once in a Christian university, once in Muhammadiyah university, once in a Hindu university.

JD: So this is an example of working together to protect the rights of minorities?

MC: Yes. yes. That's what we understand of Islam. Islam is *salaam, shalom,* peace. Our understanding of Islam is that it teaches how to live in peace, with faith in God.

NOTES

CHAPTER 1

1. Amnesty International, *Sudan, The Ravages of War: Political Killings and Humanitarian Disaster.* (New York: Amnesty International, 1993), p. 1.
2. Ibid., p. 4.

CHAPTER 3

1. Mahmood Monshipouri and Christopher G. Kukla, "Islam, Democracy and Human Rights: The Continuing Debate in the West," *Middle East Policy* 3 (1994): 37.
2. Remy Leveau, *"Algeria: Adversaries in Search of Uncertain Compromises,"* Chaillot Paper 4, Institute for Security Studies of Western European Union 1992, p. 7.
3. Ibid., p. 4.

CHAPTER 5

1. Rachid al Ghannouchi, "The Battle Against Islam," *Middle East Affairs Journal* 1, no. 2 (winter 1993): 39.
2. Michael Collins Dunn, *Islamism and Secularism in North Africa,* (Center for Contemporary Arab Studies, Georgetown University, 1994), p. 157.
3. Abdelwahab El-Effendi, "The Long March Forward," *The Renaissance Party in Tunisia* (Washington, D.C.: American Muslim Council, 1991), p. 105.
4. Rachid al-Ghannouchi, "The Battle Against Islam," *Middle East Affairs Journal* 1, no. 2 (winter 1993): 34-42.

CHAPTER 6

1. Michael Collins Dunn, "Fundamentalism in Egypt," *Middle East Policy* 2 (1993): 70.
2. Mamoun Fandy, "The Tensions Behind the Violence in Egypt," *Middle East Policy* 2 (1993): 27.
3. Ibid, pp. 27-28.
4. Ibid, p. 27.

5. "The Khilafah System is a Distinguished System," *The Khilafah: Hizb ut-Tahrir* (Hizb ut-Tahrir, 1997) pp. 21-23.

CHAPTER 7

1. Kamel al-Sharief, "Coordination System of The International Islamic Council for Da'wa and Relief General Directorate," Office of the General Islamic Congress for Jerusalem, Amman, 1993, p. 3.
2. Ibid., p. 5.
3. Ibid., p. 6.
4. Ibid.

CHAPTER 8

1. Mamoun Fandy, "The Tensions Behind the Violence in Egypt," *Middle East Policy* 2 (1993): 28.
2. Said al-Ashmawy, *Al Islam al Siyasi* [Political Islam], (Cairo: Sina Publishers, 1987).
3. Fandy, "Tensions Behind the Violence in Egypt," p. 27.
4. David Sagiv, "Judge Ashmawi and Militant Islam in Egypt," *Middle Eastern Studies* 28 (July 1992): 542.
5. Ibid., p. 532.
6. Ibid., p. 533.
7. Farag Foda, "A Murdered Writer's Prophesy," trans. by Mamoun Fandy, *New York Times,* 19 November 1993.
8. Said al-Ashmawy, *Middle East Times,* December 20-26, 1993.

CHAPTER 9

1. "Modern Egyptian Woman" (Arab Republic of Egypt, Ministry of Information, State Information Service Press).
2. Leila Ahmed, *Women and Gender in Islam,* (New Haven, CT: Yale University Press, 1992), p. 190.
3. C. Kooij, "Bint Al-Shati: A Suitable Case for Biography," *The Challenge of the Middle East* (University of Amsterdam, 1982), p. 67
4. Syed Jalal-Ud-Din Omri, *Woman and Islam* (Lahore: Islamic Publications Limited, August 1990), p. 10.
5. Ibid., pp. 14-15.
6. Ibid., p. 39.

CHAPTER 11

1. Charter of the Islamic Resistance Movement, Article 8. Translated by Muhammad Maqdsi for the Islamic Association for Palestine.
2. Robert Satloff, "Islam in the Palestinian Uprising," (Washington Institute for Near East Policy, October 1988), p. 8.
3. Ahmad Rashad, *HAMAS: Palestinian Politics with an Islamic Hue.* The United Association for Studies and Research, December 1993, p. 18.

CHAPTER 12

1. Yusef al-Qaradawi, *The Lawful and the Prohibited in Islam* (Indianapolis: American Trust Publications, 1980), p. 95.
2. Ibid., p. 248
3. Ibid., p. 201.
4. Ibid., p. 202.
5. Ibid.
6. Ibid., p. 194.
7. Yusef al-Qaradawi, *Islamic Awakening Between Rejection and Extremism,* 2nd edition (Indianapolis: American Trust Publication and the International Institute of Islamic Thought, 1990), p. 33.
8. Ibid., p. 38-39
9. Qaradawi, *The Lawful and the Prohibited,* p. 324.

CHAPTER 13

1. Khurshid Ahmad, *Islam and the West:* (Lahore: Islamic Publications Ltd., 1979), p. v.
2. Khurshid Ahmad, "Economic Development in an Islamic Framework" (Leicester: The Islamic Foundation, 1979), pp. 8, 9.
3. Ibid., p. 14.
4. Ibid., p. 15.
5. Ahmad, *Islam and the West,* p. vi.
6. Ibid., p. 3.
7. Khurshid Ahmad, "Islam and the New World Order," *Middle East Affairs Journal* 1, no. 3 (spring/summer 1993), p. 6.
8. Ibid., p. 7.
9. Ibid., p. 8.
10. Ibid., p. 6.

CHAPTER 14

1. Human Rights Watch, "Double Jeopardy: Police Abuse of Women in Pakistan," (Asia Watch and the Women's Rights Project, Human Rights Watch, 1992), p. 17.
2. Ibid., p. 3.

CHAPTER 15

1. Khurshid Ahmad, "The Movement of Jama'at-e-Islami, Pakistan: An Introduction" (Publicity Section: Jama'at-e-Islami, Mansoorah, Lahore, 1989), pp. 5-7.

CHAPTER 16

1. Judith Nagata, *The Reflowering of Malaysian Islam: Modern Religious Radicals and Their Roots* (Vancouver: University of British Columbia Press, 1984), p. 103.
2. Margaret Scott, "Where The Quota Is King," *The New York Times Magazine,* 17 November 1991, 66.
3. Ibid., p. 64
4. *Far Eastern Economic Review,* Nov. 12, 1992, p. 64.
5. *Far Eastern Economic Review,* June 6, 1991, p. 55.

INDEX